HARLEM MOON
BROADWAY

D0557457

BEATS
RHYMES
& LIFE

at We **Love** and **Hate** About **Hip-Hop**

ITED BY KENJI JASPER AND YTASHA L. WOMACK

OTOS BY ROBERT JOHNSON III

PORTING-AT-LARGE BY MARK ALLWOOD

PUBLISHED BY HARLEM MOON

Copyright © 2007 by Kenji Jasper and Ytasha L. Womack

Published in the United States by Harlem Moon, an imprint of The Doubleday
Broadway Publishing Group, a division of Random House, Inc., New York.
www.harlemmoon.com

HARLEM MOON, BROADWAY BOOKS, and the HARLEM MOON logo,
depicting a moon and a woman, are trademarks of Random House, Inc. The figure
in the Harlem Moon logo is inspired by a graphic design by Aaron Douglas
(1899–1979).

Permissions appear on pages 301–2.

Book design by Michael Collica

Library of Congress Cataloging-in-Publication Data

    Beats, rhymes and life : what we love and hate about hip-hop / edited by Kenji
Jasper and Ytasha L. Womack ; photos by Robert Johnson III ; reporting-at-large
by Mark Allwood.—1st ed.
      p.   cm.
    Includes bibliographical references and index.
    1. Hip-hop.   2. Rap (Music)   3. African American youth—Intellectual life.
4. African Americans—Intellectual life.   5. African American youth—Social
conditions.   6. African Americans—Social conditions.   7. Rap musicians—
United States—Interviews.   8. Interviews—United States.   9. United States
Intellectual life.   10. United States—Social conditions—1980–   I. Jasper, Kenji.
II. Womack, Ytasha L.   III. Johnson, Robert, III.   IV. Allwood, Mark.   V. Title.

E185.86.B3775 2007
306'.1—dc22   2006025892

ISBN 978-0-7679-1977-7

PRINTED IN THE UNITED STATES OF AMERICA

10 9 8 7 6 5 4 3 2 1

First Edition

Kenji: For my father, Melvin Jasper, Jr., the man who taught me.

Ytasha: To my mom, Dr. Yvonne Womack, who dedicated her life to teaching urban kids and never lost faith in their future. To my dad, Lloyd Womack, whose years of service and work in civil rights continue.

CONTENTS

CONTENTS

**BEATS
RHYMES
&
LIFE**

EDITORS' NOTES

I, Kenji Nathaniel Jasper, did not break-dance. I did not bomb graffiti, and aside from an eighth-grade gig as a third-tier hype man for a playground trio, I had no desire to rhyme either. What I wanted was to be cool, to infiltrate the often impermeable barrier of what the Joneses were up to when I was not. I was the kid who always did his homework, the last to go out and the first to come in, the only product of a two-parent home that had recently split in two.

But one day, during a block party in a friend's cousin's neighborhood, I found myself in a stranger's bedroom, one of the many crowded around a portable turntable as N.W.A.'s "Boys in the Hood" spun at thirty-three revolutions per second, releasing more expletives into the air than Eddie, Richard, and Red combined. It was so *bad,* so unlike the ivory-clean singles I'd bought after hearing them on the radio. This music, this deeper, darker thing, was rough, rugged, and raw—everything Kenji "the good kid" was not despite an upbringing in the toughest quarter of Washington, D.C. So as long as the record played, as long as I listened, Kenji Jasper, the then big-headed, big-lipped, socially awkward, and infinitely dreaming young adolescent, was just the same as everyone else in that room. He was the same as everyone else who loved the song, and the many songs that had come before it. He was part of something, finally having pierced that oh-so-important barrier. And it felt good.

So many years have passed since that first head nod. Beat makers and men with mics have taken their stories and pushed them into the multiplatinum stratosphere. More money, more cash, and more hos hungry for the excitement it all brings. Million-dollar videos and the MCs' race to discover the next expensive thing to claim while the tape is still recording. Take it from the studio to the big screen, to the clothing racks and beyond. It's only a matter of time before somebody has a nightly stage show in Vegas.

But like most before me, I'm far from bitter about hip-hop's rise to riches, or the cultural cyclone it's become on the world stage. In that way, it's everything I hoped for, a universal reminder that things born in the hood still matter far beyond it. What I'm mad at is that the art is gone, and very few know how to find it again.

I often liken hip-hop to the Egyptian god Osiris, his body sliced into countless parts and spread across the world, only to be reassembled by those magic folks with the proper tools. But such technicians are so very hard to come by. Out-Kast's Andre 3000 recorded his most recent album with only a handful of verses, substituting his signature flow with singing and spoken word. Producers Timbaland and Ahmir "?uestlove" Thompson have begun to make their bread producing projects outside of the genre. And LL Cool J is going out of his way to be known as James Todd Smith on the silver screen.

I often imagine the music I knew being blown to bits by corporate Death Stars, its defiance suffocated by the material trappings its creators couldn't obtain any other way. It's no longer about being hot. It's about whether your hotness can get you enough material things to qualify for an episode of MTV's *Cribs*.

Walking down my street the other day, I happened to pass four boys freestyling to an instrumental tape, something I hadn't seen in longer than I wanted to remember. I gave them a glance as they stood there in the circle, bodies swaying to the synth congas and rolling 808 drums. I was excited for them, happy to see the next generation getting back to the source.

Then they spoke. Empty threats of "kill, kill, kill" and how they had more money than God. No clever quips, no complex rhymes. Just the same clichés being spit in front of the brownstone with the chipping paint their parents most likely rented instead of owned. What was once a counter-movement against the violence of the city streets has now been absorbed by the black hole–like beast known as commerce. And there's nothing I can do about it.

I, Ytasha L. Womack, woke my parents up bright and early one Saturday morning to show them the Stop the Violence Movement's video for "Self Destruction." A shy eighth-grader fascinated with the edicts of black history, I pointed to the scrolling statistics flashed on the screen and proudly broke down the slang of the day, because that song, unlike the millions of others that had been banned and chastised by my parents' generation, was continuing the tradition of the civil rights movement they spoke of so fondly. But it wasn't that song alone, or its socially conscious message, that transformed me into a hip-hop head.

I was enamored with the moves, the way people danced to this new music that rivaled Chicago's house craze in its abundance of seductive energy—high-energy acrobatics with staccato breaks and freestyle frenetics. The motions in hip-hop were big, powerful, often defying logic. And it boggled me that the same body memory I used to master steps in ballet, modern dance, and tap classes did not help when I tried to master the aerodynamics of doing the helicopter, a move in which your legs in the air served as the propellers that seemingly rotated you at warp speed, your shoulders and chest whirling like a top, as they alternately stabilized you on the floor. There were no hip-hop classes. Seekers had to learn that stuff on the playground between rounds of double Dutch, or watch music videos a thousand times over. You practiced in front of the mirrors in your living room, hoping to one day debut your moves before the throngs of preteen critics at the occasional school dance or the roller rink. During high school, my girlfriends on Whitney Young's pom squad and I tried to sneak new steps we learned at parties and from music videos into our drill-oriented routines. We were a little too elated when our coach approved.

I was a quiet, studious girl adorned with thick octagon-shaped glasses and Payless Pro-Wing sneakers, and my only saving grace from complete nerddom was my pop-lock proficiency. With a Salt-N-Pepa poster plastered in my locker and an African medallion swinging from my neck, I was going to figure out this alternate dance world if it meant spending the better hours of my free time doing it. But I felt like a third cousin thrice removed when it came to relating to most of the lyrics in this new phenomenon.

I didn't understand how Big Daddy Kane could have "Children R the Future" and "Pimpin' Ain't Easy" on the same album any more than I could explain how painting the White House black would resolve the nation's race matters. But by the time I was a freshman at Clark Atlanta University, Ytasha'd become a bona fide, plaid shirt–wearing, wild-haired hip-hop dancer, one who grooved to everything from Snoop Dogg to Biggie Smalls, redirecting pimp idolatry into my own private heroine fantasy, with the legion of adoring guys at the club as my wide-nosed video hos.

I was never comfortable with the hypocrisy in hip-hop: how an artist could advocate to, say, stop the violence in one breath and tout pimp culture the next, love Mom in the first verse but screw those hos in the next, all while the listeners at large kept the time with Timb taps, oblivious to the overreaching dichotomy. Tagged as one of the Hip-Hop Generation, I felt cornered into explaining a phenomenon the artists themselves didn't always understand. My only resolve was that our MCs were there to express the irony in our lives, our inflated fantasies versus humdrum reality, all filtered through the minds of young men (and some women) who'd watched *Scarface* a million times over. They'd witnessed the lure of the streets for better or worse and wanted their share of America's big-money promise, too.

As I grew into adulthood, I explained away violent metaphors and an overreaching disdain for lovers and all things female as a reflection of their torn souls and a mirror to our society's dark side. The artists, I maintained, were doing what artists do: making us think.

"Don't fault the rappers and the industry of hip-hop," I argued. "Fault the consumers who embrace their glamorized turmoil, living in the fantasies of their fictitious street life for their own private pleasures. They're businessmen. The rappers, the producers, the execs, are just giving us what we want and getting paid in the process. Jay-Z got paid millions to mention that product, Busta Rhymes and P. Diddy's 'Pass the Courvoisier' raised the cognac's sales by twenty percent nationwide."

Then I realized that I wasn't talking about art at all. I was discussing new trends in marketing. When I found myself explaining drug-laden lyrics, sexist idolatry, and conscious rap as strategic marketing ploys to satisfy white America's desire to experience its mythical vision of urban street life, I realized something had gone wrong.

An art form birthed in realism, hip-hop has been hijacked by its determination to tell a monolithic street saga, a story that worships a fictitious Cuban drug lord murdered in a coked-out, get-rich-or-die-trying fantasy of unattainable power. And as the movie it mimics was, it's underwritten by corporate America.

At the height of his success, former Bad Boy rapper Shyne told me in an interview that he felt "destined to do something great." This he said before his tragic jail stint. He had no idea what this "great" thing was, or how it was to take form. But this greatness, he foretold, was shadowed by a dark cloud.

Although months later he was locked away in a New York prison, convicted in a now infamous Club New York shooting, his words stayed with me. Hip-hop lovers, too, once believed that the music had the power to do the unimaginable, to somehow level the playing field between the hood and Wall Street, to wield respect for the black people, black culture, and black dollars, women, the poor, and people of color across the globe. But those dreams, like many childhood wishes, have been locked away.

After twenty years of aspiring to live the videos we watched, of blasting hip-hop's melodies in our rented convertibles on Ocean Drive, and drinking Cristal to its hypnotizing beats, we are finding that hip-hop's true calling is more elusive today than ever.

It's funny—my younger brother is a hip-hop artist now. Christened in rap battles as Supacell, he's walking the path of the hip-hop entrepreneur. A black man with a FAMU (a.k.a. Florida A&M) MBA, he launched an indie label with his college friend Dave-Ro. With hip-hop's cookie-cutter formula now the benchmark for all to come, I figure it must be hard to be a new hip-hop artist these days. But he fervently believes in the power of the genre.

"I want to have a real impactful change on our people, and hip-hop has the ears of the youth all over the world," he says. "It crosses political and religious boundaries. The sense of urgency that rap music has is stronger than any other music. People respond immediately. The problem is that the message isn't always the best. But once someone can really get their ears, like a Jay-Z or a 50, and hit them with a serious message, that person can make an impact. [Despite it all] hip-hop can do things that even presidents can't do."

Maybe it's this pursuit of unrealized potential that's led the mogul Russell Simmons to morph his power in music into a political empire. Maybe it's this quest to achieve something bigger with the music that's inspired Diddy to raise millions for young children and pursue the thespian life. Whatever the case, it's a discussion silenced by the corporate billions it rakes in, the millionaires it's made, the global businesses it's spawned, and the new markets it's touched. Once the voice of the underclass, hip-hop is now corporate America's cherished plaything.

US

Our generation made hip-hop. But hip-hop also made us. The symbiosis is always there. From the dancer and her movements, to the MC and his rhymes, to the trendsetter and the self-conscious sheep who follow him, the art and its audience have made and remade and will continue to make and remake each other until the end of time, for better or for worse.

This is not a look back or forward. These are the words

of writers in the here and now, a team of scribes charged with sketching and framing American culture as it is cross-referenced with our own lives. As hip-hop writers who made names for ourselves in the world of newspapers and magazines, we have offered our opinions on which records to buy and which movies to see, noting who wore what to which awards show. We have analyzed the effect that a certain song or composition had on a populace. We saw when change was a-coming. And yet, for reasons often beyond our control, before this book our work has rarely gotten to the meat of the matter.

We have seen hip-hop music grow from a bouncing baby, to a rebellious adolescent, to a not-so-focused adult uncertain of its future, all the while sharing its baby steps and growth spurts with billions, infecting ears and cerebellums with rhymes and beats born in the hearts of hopelessness and disenfranchisement. And now it is everywhere, yet another piece in the ever-enlarging crop of cultural exports on which the rest of the world so depends.

But when culture becomes a business, when the telling of stories becomes a commercial venture, what does that mean for its creators and architects? Are lyrical webs being spun for self-expression or for a diamond-encrusted Rolex? Are shell casings on a playground the sign of continued unrest in the inner city, or are they refuse from the last music video crew that shot there?

What happens when the listeners of a music believe more in the commercial ideal, a world that teeters on complete masochistic fantasy, than the values they are taught in their own homes? Why are suburban kids referring to their subdivision as "the block"? Why has the pimp become a figure of true male power? Why has dodging the feds, a cliché inspired by too many white crime flicks, become an act of honor long after one has made millions as a legitimate artist? What happens when fantasy does more harm than reality does?

We are here to attempt to answer these questions, through eyes that have seen and heard much about what is to be discussed. We have combed through our memory banks for photographs that stand out, artifacts and sound bites that provide irrefutable evidence. And thus we have identified the strongest images in this cultural juggernaut known as hip-hop. Each poses very poignant questions from both internal and external points of view:

THE FAN

We've come such a long way from the golden age of the music, when beats and rhymes were a reflection of lives, a diverse tale made available to the masses through the closest set of headphones. But as the music found success, it also, in turn, found formula. And as it found formula, it found itself the victim of many who saw the music only as a cow filled with cash. And once that happened, the metaphor of the woman we used to love gradually became that of a streetwalker soliciting our patronage. For far too many, that love turned to hate. The voice of our dreams became our own voices telling those behind us to turn it down. What can you do with hip-hop when the thrill is gone?

THE BUZZ

There are a million ways and means to get one. But what are the true reasons behind why we get high? Whether it's affection for marijuana and ecstasy or a swig from the almighty bottle, the hip-hop nation loves to escape itself by chemical means. But what is hip-hop escaping? What issues, concerns, and fears lie dormant underneath the never-ending buzz? What does the lionized role of the drug dealer, often the hero and protagonist in many hip-hop songs, say about the need to be spellbound in the midst of despair?

THE LOVE

What happened to romance? In hip-hop, you can love the power and variety of having multiple sex partners and the thrill of the conquest, but still have no love for L-O-V-E. In some strange turn of events, hip-hop has become alienated from its own love life, not knowing how to comfortably communicate affection without risking its precious vulnerability. Why can hip-hop fuck all day but never truly fall in love?

THE CANE

Pimps are the masters of manipulation, absurdly flashy dressers who use wordplay and the threat of violence to usher women into a deadly life of sex for sale. The image of the pimp in hip-hop culture has become a mainstay in the last decade. Pimping is not just a way of getting a woman to sell herself on the streets. It has become something larger, a symbol of capitalism at its best, embraced by both male and female MCs. It's a Machiavellian approach to self-preservation. It is the art of rhetoric, the power of the pen, the "get mine, get yours, and you won't even know it," ethics be damned. Think corner hustler, think Enron. But is that a good philosophy? Is that a true means of effective survival or just a shady-rhetoric, slime-soaked underbelly of misogyny, ignorance, and exploitation?

THE CROSS

Even the hardest gangster rapper pays homage to God. Rappers relate themselves to biblical figures almost as frequently as gospel singers do. They name themselves after Egyptian gods, personifying themselves as Jesus, thanking God at award ceremonies, and wearing diamond-studded crosses. But while many artists share that their talents and opportunities are God-given, there's an obvious inner turmoil about the responsibilities that come with them. It's the cross that hip-hop doesn't want to bear. What role does spirituality play in hip-hop's evolution? Why have so many artists compared their struggles with the Crucifixion? Why can't the naysayers see God in the music of the streets?

THE COFFIN

Death. Both Tupac Shakur and The Notorious B.I.G. were obsessed with its lure; each predicting his own demise with an arrogance that struck awe in countless hearts across the world. But hip-hop's romanticizing of death often follows inescapable violence. Fans dance around its dark cauldron with lyrics and beats, evoking spirits and situations that should have remained at rest. Funerals and murder are as recurring in hip-hop imagery as the decadent excess that can bring life to its end. Countless songs honor "dead homies," young men and women who died violent deaths long before their time. Rappers speak about death as if it's lurking in the shadows, just beyond their last line of defense. Why has the casket become such a seminal image in hip-hop culture? Why does hip-hop idolize its comrades only in death? And why isn't life a cool thing to rhyme about?

THE WHIP

A lowrider, with hydraulics, spinning rims, and a booming system. Sometimes the rims alone cost more than the car itself. If you can't afford that Bentley, hook up your '79 Chevy. What's hip-hop if it doesn't reverberate in your trunk? But vehicle flash for fun is now an art. Even kids in the 'burbs want a pimped-out ride. A fly whip lets folks know you're coming. A symbol of power as American as a Cadillac, a car screams status in hip-hop and beyond. It fosters jealousy, too. How many men get stopped for driving while black, driving while brown? Be it a red Porsche or a silver Eldorado, a fly ride can make you a wary target of everyone from itchy cops to gold diggers, jackers to car booties. Be easy as this ode to the ever-loving auto takes you for a spin.

THE ICE

Diamonds, the means by which the Dutch came to oppress black South Africa, have always been a symbol of status in American culture. They are tokens of power, lavish wealth embodied in gleaming transparent flash. In the hip-hop community they are the personification of having money to burn. The dominance of ice imagery in the music ushered in a new level of materialism in hip-hop. Yet Bill Gates doesn't need them to exemplify his wealth. Neither does Donald Trump, or Osama bin Laden, for that matter. Why does the hip-hop nation need to show instead of prove when it comes to wealth, status, and achievement? And is that materialism crushing the spirit of the music? What impact does the need for external flash have on the youth of urban America and beyond?

THE STILETTOS

They are standard attire for women in practically every music video. The signature footwear of both models and party girls, elite women, prostitutes and strippers. It's the ultimate power tool for the woman who wants to be sexy and seen. Impractical yet alluring. Painful but pretty. One false move and you fall flat on your face. Leave the Tims and sneaks to the ones with the testosterone, the ones who marvel at thick ladies perched like stilt walkers on pencil-thin heels. A man-made shoe for his ultimate female fantasy, it's a concocted sexual image the women of hip-hop are forced to fit. But why is womanhood confined to male fetishes? And why do so many women embrace someone else's version of themselves as their own?

THE TAG

Tagging is original hip-hop. It predates MCing, breaking, and b-girl fashion, and came long before that first DJ itched to scratch. Spray paint was the brush for the street artist, and dark subways and buses their Louvre. But many of today's hip-hop heads know little about it. Your chances of spotting a spray-painted mural in a rap video, concert, or party are nil to none. Tagging once drew the scorn of politicians everywhere, and now it's risen to the ranks of fine art. But where's the love for the art form? Is a tag truly a tag if it's not etched in a tunnel?

THE TURNTABLE

Turntables were just supposed to play records. But DJs made them tools in a new art form. Turntablism is making something out of nothing, a credo in African American culture and poor or oppressed cultures worldwide. At a time when school music programs were crippled, the turntable became an outlet for musical genius. It is also symbolic of the incredible creativity that lies at the roots of hip-hop music. It's the power of merging youthful rebellion and old-school debauchery. It's happiness, sorrow, power, suppression, displacement, and liberation, each ground into the essence of a single scratch. Art made with antiquated tools that still continue to get the party live. This is a tribute to DJing, and to the crowds that need it to move, to learn, and to overcome.

THE SHELL CASING

It is a reminder of murder, the evidence of a violent act, a time-honored document of aggression and split-second decision making. And we see them everywhere, permeating the silver and small screens as something cool, something riveting, a high-octane ride on the road to a cinematic death. What is it about guns and bullets? Hip-hop's violent metaphors are supposed to be symbolic of the underbelly of street life, but the imagery is more reflective of a *Scarface* action flick than the harrowing conflicts of real-life living in the inner city. Why are so many rappers named after real and fictitious Mafia icons? Why does hip-hop have a fascination with violence when it was founded to counter it?

THE BLOCK

The art of conversation, male one-upmanship, hood-reared aggression by both women and men, for better or worse, all came from the block. The block is both loved and feared, clung to and run from. It defines the borders of inner-city existence, and for some it's the brick-and-mortar gates around their mind. It can be a place for praise or ridicule. It's family love and ire, too comfortable a zone for some, not comfortable enough for others. And more often than not, it's all some people have. Why does hip-hop cling to the block when there's a whole world of them? Why is the block both a cumbersome crutch and hip-hop's greatest strength all at once?

THE FLOOR

A hearty head nod is not a substitute for a good sweat on the dance floor. However, a rapper who also dances is "playing himself" by hip-hop standards. Strippers are preferred to trained dancers in videos, and a rapper who dances is sealing his fate. You see more hip-hop dancing in one Madonna video then you did in all of G-Unit's combined. Yet breaking, crunk, footwork, and snapping are alive and well. Hip-hop is today's dance music. As members of the hip-hop nation turn to the music for release, are they limiting their creative expression for the sake of being cool? What becomes of a culture that no longer values dance?

THE SUIT

Hip-hop is everywhere. But that's because corporate America is behind it now. It holds all the keys and owns all the artists. Hip-hop has been twisted to satisfy mainstream America's interest in all things urban. While corporate support gives the world global access, it also dictates the trends and values of hip-hop. Can a music be of the people and corporately sponsored at the same time? Are hip-hop's current values reflective of corporate interest or of the artists who represent it? Many artists admit that they water down lyrics to make them acceptable to the masses. How much do rappers compromise artistically to be commercially successful? Is there any true way that the people can get their music back?

We have handed these images to the writers who know them best. In turn, these writers have come back with stories not only of themselves but of their communities, their "peoples," and all else that has made hip-hop what it is. These images and the questions that rose from them were the springboard for what follows. We also included the musings of hip-hop innovators, who in timeless commentary shine light behind the velvet rope of stardom to reveal the underworld of artistic frustration, inspiration, and beyond.

At the start of this project, the writers in the pages ahead were given nothing but one of these paragraphs and a word count, nothing but a focal point and a deadline. What follows is a work years in the making—a work that chronicles our creative journeys from girls and boys to women and men, from fans to critics to social analysts, from the inside looking out to just the reverse. We speak without apology, without restraint, without the need to explain ourselves to those who dismissed this culture, our culture, as a fad that wouldn't make it past next week. If they were right, then at twenty-five years and running, this is the longest fad in musical history.

FOREWORD
BY DR. MICHAEL ERIC DYSON

I've been able to connect with the hip-hop generation because I've taken an interest in it. Growing up poor and black in Detroit has a huge influence on why I identify with hip-hop. I don't speak from an Ivy League ivory-tower space only. Those elements that are peculiar to hip-hop's fascination with what some would call "the glorification of rudimentary ghetto experience" were my experience growing up. I listen to the propulsive energies that hip-hop artists have put on record as well as the political, social, economic, and personal concerns they have kept away from the limelight.

Sometimes people demand too much of hip-hop. They say, What are you doing here, what are you doing in terms of politics and society in this culture? Well, we never demanded that R&B do that. No one asks, What has R&B done for this culture? No one asks, What has Luther Vandross or Anita Baker done for black people? Or Jamiriqui or Joe? What has R. Kelly done for us? (Well, that's another subject.)

Part of it is the success of hip-hop. It's such a juggernaut. It's created expectations because the opportunity is so huge and people don't want it to be squandered. People are right to demand that criticism, to demand that responsibility, but not to be unfairly critical.

I think that it's very important that older people listen to younger people. Not just lecture them, not preach down to them or condescendingly remonstrate against them morally, but engage them, hear them, listen to what they are talking about. I don't think older people should make criticisms of hip-hop without listening to it. They should know that MC Ren is not Mos Def, that Talib Kweli is different from Dr. Dre, that Bahamadia is different from Lil' Kim or Foxy Brown. And that all of them have their values, all of them have their virtues, all of them have their visions. What are those visions? How do we parse those out and how do we take advantage of some of the incredibly insightful things that they offer and some of the powerful observations they put forth in their music?

When I go to churches, lecture halls, or political conventions and speak about hip-hop and tell older people to slow down and listen, they're always amazed at the acute relevance of those lyrics to the lifestyles they may lead or the issues they may have. So I say, if you listen to hip-hop, if you listen to some of the rappers, if you listen to the culture in general, you're going to hear some of the most prophetic and articulate expressions, the anger and outrage that bourgeois Negroes should and do still possess, but often fail to manufacture or marshal.

So, for a variety of reasons, I've been able to connect with that generation because I love its music. And I consider myself to be an old head, literally, and a person who appreciates the diversity of hip-hop. I'm what they call a Tweener. I was too late to be a part of the civil rights generation and too early to be part of the hip-hop generation. I think people define hip-hop as being born in 1965; I was born in '58. But being born in '58, I wasn't able to get off a bus and march with Martin Luther King, Jr., or Rosa Parks, or be involved directly in the mass movements led by people like Malcolm X and Fannie Lou Hamer and Ella Baker. And at the same time, when hip-hop was in its infancy, I'm there on the ground. I remember being a college student. I went to college late; I was a teen father on welfare and went to college at twenty-one. But in '79 I was listening to 8th Wonder of the World and the Sugar Hill Gang and dancing to them in the school cafeteria at Knoxville College. So that was an exciting moment. I remember thinking, *This is some interesting music,* and I liked the rhetorical skill expressed by Wonder Mike and all the other fellas on the microphone, and like most people I thought this was an interesting fad or trend in black music.

But as hip-hop began to take, as people began to talk about its value, debate its specific manifestation of a black aesthetic and its relevance, I remember seeing the generational divide and the class divide. As a musical genre it was associated with working-class or working-poor or underclass people, and as a result of that, it created enormous tension in those who would subsequently find themselves either opposed to it or at least ignorant of its basic thrust and claims. I can't claim to have thought initially that it would be a revolutionary musical art form, but as it took form and developed, I became deeply interested in that culture and curious about both its musical and political elements.

Hip-hop, like the blues, is about the articulation of a tragicomic vision in the midst of hostility. Like the spirituals, it's about the aesthetics of redemption: how do we overcome, in the midst of hostility, in order to express ourselves? And like bebop, hip-hop is a response against the commodification and co-optation of its own musical form.

When you think about hip-hop's relationship to the genres and trends in black music, there are certainly some similarities. You think about the blues, where there is a preoccupation with the secular expression of trying to deal with the realities of life. The survival impulse is expressed brilliantly and tragicomically in the blues form. The blues form is an aesthetic articulation of the black will to survive, and survival itself is an extraordinarily important art form that black people have long reflected on through humor and music.

Gospel music, like the spirituals that came before it, is about the same impulse of wanting to articulate a will to survive and to overcome. The redemptive character of gospel and the spirituals is about upholding black people's belief that they have what Martin Luther King, Jr., called "cosmic companionship." This is the belief that spiritual truth is on the side of degraded and oppressed people, and that they can call upon the spirit by virtue of their songs. Music became a way to facilitate the presence of that spirit, and an expression of the desire to reaffirm their humanity in a culture that said they were nothing.

Jazz improvisation is about democracy. It's about forms that were generated while improvising in the face of odds. That music was created to express fundamental black humanity as the basis for redefining American society.

Jazz is not only an argument for the humanity of the black artist; it's also about the beautiful subjectivity of black people en masse. Black people, like jazz musicians, are improvising in the face of hostility in order to assert themselves and to say, Hey, we are not what you say we are. We are more than that, we are deeper than that, and we are connected to the global community. And this is why jazz became a global phenomenon. What's interesting is that jazz became commodified almost immediately. The first jazz creation was by Paul Whiteman; how ironic is that? So from the first recordings of jazz, although the music itself had been deeply entrenched in black communities, it was understood that both commodification and commercialization were standard.

Black music's relationship to the mainstream is a symbi-otic relationship. Black musical expression, black aesthetic articulation, depends to a certain degree on white forms of legacy to the degree that music is recorded by white people first and put out on the open market by white people; there-fore money is being made by white people. So jazz music changes up as white people and other dominant forces com-modify it. When swing music became au courant among the larger white community, bebop came as a resistance to that.

Bebop is a street aesthetic articulated against how swing music had been appropriated by the dominant culture. So it's the street's response, within the genre of jazz, against the commercialization of swing music. We know that Duke Ellington is the apex of the swing aesthetic, and Louis Arm-strong epitomizes the individual improviser within that par-ticular genre of jazz music. Armstrong was at odds with bebop because, I think, he didn't understand the aesthetic, the political dimensions, and the racial expression of a dif-ferent generation against some of the old presuppositions and principles that informed swing and other forms of jazz.

Early hip-hop was commodified, in part, because it was a basic meter. The cadence of early hip-hop had a basic beat that even a cat like me could throw down. But when it be-came commercialized by Vanilla Ice, and by other main-stream forces, look how people started rapping behind the beat. People sleep on Will Smith, but Will Smith was one of the first cats to rap behind the beat. So now the cadences are more complex. You have cats coming in on the beat and maybe falling behind the beat. Take Biggie, who Mos Def calls "the mathematician of flow":

> Who the fuck is this
> pagin' me at 5:46 in the mornin' crack a dawnin' . . .
> —The Notorious B.I.G., "Warning," from *Ready to Die*

So the cadence is like swing music in jazz, but it also changes, as with Jay-Z or Nas. So when you see the different cadences and rhythms, as in bebop, it's a challenge to the authenticity and authority of the simple meter that was articulated in early hip-hop, and now the streets take over and the polyrhythmic, very complex rhythms that these hip-hoppers are putting out are akin to those other forms of music.

There's no question that many white people appropriate black culture. They appropriate the music, the style, and the sensibility. But they don't appropriate the misery, the hardship. Justin Timberlake and Nipplegate, à la Janet Jackson, is the perfect example of this. He wanted to be black until it cost him something. White people want to be black until there is a price to be paid. Until there is an agonizing defeat of their attempted blackness and they can revert back.

White people can do rhetorical and cultural drive-bys. They drive by with our music and look at our communities and keep stepping. They use the N word now. If there's anything white folks learn hanging out with black folks, it's that white folks can't say *nigga*. But one complaint of older blacks is that hip-hop unleashed this word on a global scale and now you have Asian cats with dreads yelling, "What's up, my nigga!" This is an issue because the global context doesn't allow for political insight into that word and why it is deeply problematic, and why black people can circulate that word as a term of endearment and as a political badge of identification whereas white people should find it off-limits. The appropriation of blackness by whiteness is an ancient project, but it does reinforce the complicated state of blackness and black people in this postmodern, post-racial era, which has been heralded by the multicultural fusion of disparate voices in hip-hop.

The reality is that, yes, there's an intermingling and cooperation among many ethnicities in hip-hop that bring them together in ways other cultures and musical movements didn't. But at the same time, let's not forget that this does not substitute for substantive political engagement. It doesn't replace interrogation of identity and it doesn't force the surrender of white privilege.

It's a complex argument as to why the materialism and narcissism in present forms of hip-hop are here. Are they the legacy of the failure of a civil rights generation to transmit its values? Here immediately we begin to see the danger of assigning any label to any group. Take "the civil rights generation," which implies that most of those folks were involved in the civil rights movement. Most of the folks in the civil rights generation weren't involved in the civil rights movement directly. There might be a larger percentage of people involved in the hip-hop generation, in hip-hop culture, than folks in the civil rights movement.

But people will say, yeah, but the civil rights movement was about a political affirmation and an identity, whereas hip-hop is about a musical art form as the basis, and already we're at a deficit. Well, not necessarily. Politics is more than voting, although that's critical, and so is mobilizing social passion. Politics is also about the distribution of resources and how one gets ahold of those. When I think about the hip-hop generation's obsession with materialism, it is true that this is an index of some of the failures of the civil rights generation to transmit its values. It's not necessarily the responsibility of the hip-hop generation to learn them. But it is the responsibility of this generation to develop an astute political impulse that allows it to understand that the pursuit of wealth itself is not necessarily the sign of success.

There were arguments in the civil rights generation as to the best move in the aftermath of the extraordinary climax of a few revolutionary outbursts, in which Malcolm and Martin and Ella and Fannie Lou Hamer, and many others, most of them nameless and faceless, were able to mobilize political passion to forge a larger passion for social revolution and political transformation. But in America that only lasts a minute. Why? Because of the white supremacy backlash, the social injustice backlash, the economic backlash against the have-nots. All that accounts for the narrowing of the opportunity for young black and brown people to express themselves and to get a foothold in the economy.

However, even as arguments about economic justice were put into place by the civil rights movement, the anti-affirmative-action assault allowed only the best and the brightest, so to speak, to be created by affirmative action—to get people into college and into the pipeline and then produce the expansion of the black middle class. The permanently poor or the so-called ghetto poor are the ones who were left behind in the process. So part of the argument about hip-hop is that the wrong niggas got the microphone. Hey, how did Snoop get it? We were aiming for Spelman and Morehouse and Talladega and Harvard and Princeton grads. How did a little nigga from Compton, an Ice Cube or Eazy-E, get the microphone? How did the urban urchin, the citizens and denizens of the ghetto poor, manage to seize authority onstage and on the microphone to articulate their vision? That is a tremendous complication, and then you add the fact that hip-hop has gone through many stages: the political stage, the black consciousness stage, the black revolutionary stage, and some of these things were already internalized.

Now we have the bling-bling stage, where it's about the romance of the diamond. The diamond is the artifact in the archive of black upward mobility, and the rims and cars and luxury items are the manifestations of the American dream. Well, that's an American phenomenon. That's not something that's indigenous to hip-hop. Hip-hop has given in to genuflecting before the altar of American capitalism, and reproduces some of the most interesting—and some would say disturbing—elements of American capitalism in its own lyrics. And I think problematically so.

We should resist the notion that real authentic identity is just about the gadgets and baubles and the accoutrements you can accumulate. It's about self-esteem. People like Mos Def, Talib Kweli, Common, Bahamadia, and Lauryn Hill represent that. But even the bling-bling rappers have political consciousness. When you look at a guy like Jay-Z who says, "I'm overchargin' niggaz for what they did to the Cold Crush," there's a political acumen there. He's saying, *Given the commodification of rap in which you underpaid these cats, this is reparations and I'm here to collect.* Political.

I think that hip-hop needs to expand and become more global about its political-economic analysis, even about the way its own music is made. Why is the bling-bling the only thing that gets on the radio? Why does the bosom- and booty-shaking get on the radio? Mos Def's "Ms. Phat Booty" gets on there, but not "Mr. Nigga":

> If white boys doing it, well, it's success
> When I start doing, well, it's suspect.
> —Mos Def, "Mr. Nigga," from *Black on Both Sides*

Now, that ain't gonna get on the radio to the same degree that "Ms. Phat Booty" will, but it's coming from the same rapper. That's the kind of complex analysis we need to understand so that we can put the culture of narcissism in its own context and realize that even those artists have some political moments that we have to evoke and listen to.

Hip-hop is rife with nostalgia. You have young kids talking about "back in the day," referring to something that took place five years ago. This happens when historical memory is erased and amnesia becomes a substitute for a vital diet of critical, dangerous memories about politics, programs, and people who were prophets, who told the truth and got wiped out because of that. Nostalgia fills the blanks where politics should be occurring.

What's interesting to me is that the people who are down on bling-bling and gangsta rap aren't advocating for political rap either. When political rap was popular, it's not like they were supporting it. It's not like when Chuck D was out saying, "Elvis was a hero to most, but he never meant shit to me" (Public Enemy, "Fight the Power," from the *Do the Right Thing* soundtrack and *Fear of a Black Planet*), C. Deloris Tucker came out and called that a prophetic expression of the racial progressivism we need to air globally. They said, *Turn it down, that's crazy music,* and so on. So now in the aftermath we define the golden era. We see that we did have a great thing: politically motivated rappers who told the truth about the social conditions and the misery they saw, and that some of them personally endured.

I think that Kanye West does represent some of the best of that tradition while joined self-consciously with some of the materialistic impulses. People who are politically conscious might want some diamonds, and people who wear diamonds might deal in politics. It's not like never the two shall meet. What I like about Kanye West is that his hands are dirty even as he indicts the system that made his hands dirty, a system that seduces people into cooperating with its own oppressive mechanisms. The beautiful thing about Kanye West is that he's conscious of that. Here's a guy who can have a one-minute, eight-second version of "I'll Fly Away." That's as gut-bucket gospel as you're going to get. But at the same time he says, when thinking about what he would do if he's aggravated by a manager one more time: "After I fuck the manager up, then I'm gonna shorten the register up" ("Spaceship," *The College Dropout*).

Wow, so we got "I'll Fly Away" joined with that sensibility in the same song. When you think about the range of thematic concerns that occupy Kanye West, you see an example of an interesting trend in hip-hop, which is the self-conscious rapper who tells the truth about his own troubles and about his capitulation to some of the things he's trying to argue against.

I wrote a book on Tupac Shakur. I loved him, loved him as a human being, loved him as a brother who wore his complexities on his sleeve. Here was a guy who was the son of a Black Panther, so that revolutionary impulse—old-style black national politics and that movement—was right there. His political unconscious was part of his very fiber, of his blood. He knew the lingo, the discourse, and the rites of passage that were part of that community. But he also was a poor guy, disenfranchised, and as a result had an affinity for other disenfranchised people who didn't have his intelligence or at least his ability to display his intelligence, to display it in the art form he chose. He always identified with these people: the pusher, the dope dealer, the Mac, etc. He started off revolutionary in terms of his identification with the Black Panthers and then he shifted into the political thuggery of hard-core rap. He was twenty-five years old when he died. He was exploring all the strands of his identity, and he did it in public. People do this in private all the time. He became a larger-than-life figure because he told the truth about the transformations that he endured, even as the contradictions became apparent.

He says, "A shout out to my sisters on welfare, Tupac cares if don't nobody else care" ("Keep Ya Head Up," *Strictly 4 My N.I.G.G.A.Z.*). On the same album you have "All respect to those who break their necks to keep their hoes in check" ("I Get Around"). But on the same album he could also have "I got lynched by some crooked cops, and to this day, them same motherfuckers on the beat gettin major paid" ("Point the Finga").

That's Black Panther sensibility, joined with political thuggery, joined with black romantic ambition, and the hoochization of the black female populace. All of that together, at the same time, simultaneously converges on the same palette he used to paint his vision of black urban life. I was attracted to him because the contradictions were in him. They were both spectacular and effectively destructive. Tupac represented the best and the brightest on the one hand, and the worst on the other, at the same time, which is why he continues to be such a powerful lightning rod and a luminary figure among hip-hop greats.

Nas has superior political awareness, too. He has incredibly acute sensibilities about these issues, saying he's on both sides. Well, he's a human being. I think one of the best is Lauryn Hill. She's slept, but she's one of the top of all time, just in terms of flow and metaphor and the manipulation of voice and articulation of vision.

All of these cats deserve to be heard, and are on the level among people who write at their best, Shakespeare or some other great poets: Tennyson, Yeats, Gwendolyn Brooks, Rita Hughes.

I hope hip-hop just continues to expand on its political trajectory and to understand that one day it's going to be the establishment. It already is, in many ways. Hip-hop is a billion-dollar industry. There is no more powerful symbol of what hip-hop has done than a figure like Russell Simmons, who built an empire, first upon the music, then the culture, and the expansion of that culture into enterprises like *Def Poetry Jam*, *Def Comedy Jam*, and Phat Farm.

People sleep on how this culture has created tremendous

economic opportunity through entrepreneurship in ways that are not often credited. The people who are the naysayers of hip-hop can't point to the same kind of significantly positive results in a subculture in African American society. They'll say the civil rights generation, the civil rights movement, changed political laws because it was a political movement. But the politics of hip-hop are different.

Hip-hop is such a powerful form to express some of the most interesting and uplifting viewpoints about young black people, and indeed all people who struggle against oppression in the world. I'd like hip-hop to challenge society on all fronts, not only economically, but also in terms of gender. The misogyny, the sexism, the patriarchy, and the term I coined in my book on Tupac, the *femmaphobia*, the fear of women—it's still pervasive in hip-hop. I want to see men more consciously engage their own misogyny and be forced to come to terms with that. Of course, we have to force bourgeois Negro culture to become more affluent in the language of feminism, 'cause we know that's not happening at the level it should either.

We also have to develop an appreciation for the complex nuanced identities in hip-hop. Whether hip-hop likes it or not, there are gay people in the culture, both rappers and fans. Hip-hop is both the most homophobic and the most homoerotic genre one can imagine. "Money over bitches." "My niggas over my hos." What's that mean? So now male bonding becomes an extension of patriarchy, but it's also a deeply homoerotic moment, like sports guys patting one another on the behind. I'd like to see the questions of homosexuality, homophobia, and homoeroticism taken up in a productive fashion.

Finally, I'd like hip-hop to open up some more lucid discussions on the class warfare that they so brilliantly represent on wax.

I think it's important that Russell Simmons in his political efforts is organizing those who are not seen as organized or organizable, or are not thought about at all. You have to begin to consciencize your generation and force it to see that you don't want to just make records, you want to record your existence in a political form that makes a difference for the money makers and power shakers in America. To that degree, it's a very powerful message for young people to understand that you are, inevitably, political animals. The fact that you're in a culture that's been dissed so pervasively places you unavoidably in a political trajectory. There could be splinter movements from this.

NELLY

A St. Louis–born rapper whose sing-along hooks
etched his name in the annals of pop rap fame, Nelly
carved room for midwestern hip-hop on the airwaves.
Known for his drawl and lighthearted raps, Nelly
steadily dominated in early 2000, shocking an industry that saw profitable hip-hop as purely coastal. He
even risked all cool points by doing a country-and-
western duet with Tim McGraw, and still came out on
top. With four albums in nearly the same number of
years, he is the spokesperson for hip-hop as is.

The biggest change [that comes with success] is how people perceive you, 'cause you still do the same things
you've been doing, but obviously your life is gonna be different. Your life changes from grade school to middle school,
from middle school to high school. It's [especially] different
for me 'cause I moved around a lot, and in moving around
so much the only person that moves around with you is
your damn self. I switched like eight schools, so it was like
every school I went to I was the only one. Every new house-

hold I went to stay in, no matter which side of the family or friends, I was the only one. [So all I know how to do is] treat people how I wanna be treated.

But a lot of people already got you picked when they see you. People are like, "This nigga sold 8.9 million albums, he gotta be a dickhead," just flat out. Then after they meet a motherfucker they be like, "Oh word, you straight." But you can't please everybody. That's the hardest thing to do. Just to let everybody know you can't please everybody.

If it's ten autographs out there I sign eight. Two people are gonna say, "Nelly's a dickhead" or he's big-headed or something. Or if it's thirty girls out there and I give twenty-eight of 'em hugs, the other two are pissed. You can't please everybody. You just gotta do what you gotta do. If I'm late for somewhere because of time, that's my fault. If I'm signing autographs for two hours and I was supposed to be at MTV an hour ago, that's my fault. Sometimes you get in predicaments where you can't win, and that's those times where you gotta make judgments for yourself, and I think that's the hardest part about it.

The Grammy nominations, the Super Bowl, that shit there was bananas. Just my whole career, because I think when you get into it, you just wanna sell records. You just wanna be able to make another record. A lot of people don't get a chance to make a second record, especially with some new and different shit. Just be able to do another record. That's all we really wanted. But to be able to knock it out and sell so many and have so many people really appreciate what you're doing . . .

Everything has been a big moment for us: getting covers of magazines, having your moms flip out because she saw you on the cover of *Ebony*. Just anything. Just to see their faces, 'cause St. Louis is small but it's a big city, so everybody knows everybody. [So people are] like, "Damn, that's little Nell from down the way. This nigga is on the cover of every magazine." It's a beautiful thing, man.

[When it comes to my music] I don't wanna remind people that they're having a hard time right now, but I do feel there's a need to touch on that. So I do have songs that touch on it. But for the most part I wanna keep you vibrant. I wanna keep you upbeat like, "Yeah, I wanna have a good time tonight. Let's go call some girls. Let's go kick it. Pop that Nelly in and let's get it cracking." We don't diss nobody. We didn't come out poking at nobody, saying, "We the best, fuck them!" We just put it out there like, "Yo, here it is. Like it or leave it." And fortunately we still here.

THE FAN

How does the sweet sound of rhymes and beats go sour in the ears of an aging fan? What happens when we become sick of the imagery, when we tire of clichéd lines and metaphors, when the image defines the music and not the other way around? Generation X is getting older, becoming set in its ways, embracing the day-to-day chores of survival. Has the music of our youth let us down? Or have the beginnings of maturity brought us a better and sometimes painful understanding of the songs we fell in love with?

THE DISGRUNTLED FAN

BY FARAJI WHALEN

Black people would be better off without hip-hop.

That thundering clap you just heard was millions of chew sticks hitting the ground as every b-boy wannabe in America's jaw dropped. Yet the stunned silence that follows will last about as long as Vanilla Ice's street cred. And when it ends, there will be a deafening boom of disagreement from every last backpacker, throwbacker, gold-toothed crunk king, and aspiring Damon Dash that will be loud enough to rattle windows like four fifteen-inch subwoofers in the trunk of a '77 Chevy.

But before the insults and accusations and outrage get started, I have to let you know that I am not Bill O'Reilly. I'm not even Bill Cosby. I'm just through with hip-hop.

I have listened to hip-hop for the vast majority of my life, and for most of that time, I have loved H.E.R. ("Hip-hop in its Essence and Real," as Common put it). In fact, I still do. But much like your wayward cousin who gets high on embalming fluid and jacks 7-Elevens, my favorite music has gotten out of control. Maybe irreparably so. And while every critic worth his twenty-five cents a word has lamented the figurative death of originality and creativity in hip-hop, it's the real-life deaths of people in the street that should be worrying pundits. Just as you sometimes secretly wish your cousin would get locked up so he won't be a danger to the community, I'm really hoping hip-hop goes away for a while to get some rehab before it's too late.

Much as you still see some good in that cousin of yours, there's still a lot of good in the music. But somewhere in the past few years, we've hit that point at which hip-hop has become so degenerate (while at the same time so hardwired into African American culture) that it is doing irreversible and concrete harm to black people. The ridiculous and overblown black buffoons that major labels are selling to you as real-life Negro heroes to be emulated and worshipped are leading a people astray that barely has one foot on the right path.

The stars of today tell kids that they should be drug dealers, thugs, and womanizers. Because of the unique connection that hip-hop has historically held to realities in the urban streets, the music has the credibility to make these dangerous suggestions extremely influential.

However, we don't have to accept the idea that these depictions of us are accurate. They are not. Most black people don't live in poverty. Most of us have access to some kind of decent education. Most of us don't have to do anything illegal just to get by. The children who listen to and absorb these messages have choices. But because hip-hop has become such a powerful force, it affects the choices these kids make. And far too frequently, these choices are bad ones.

From watching *Rap City* on any given weekday afternoon, it's hard to believe the civil rights movement ever existed. The show is a seemingly never-ending parade of escaped slaves who have somehow found their way to a Bentley dealer and a gun shop. These almost coonish depictions do not represent real life for almost any African Americans, and yet the music's creators continue to insist how "real" they are.

Believe me, if you told me when I was sixteen that shit like that would have ever left my mouth, I would have slapped you for lying to me, and then slapped myself in hopes of changing the future. But roughly ten years later, that's where I stand. How I came to change my opinion is still something I'm not even certain about. Maybe it's the way H.E.R. has degenerated in the time that has passed. Maybe it's the laundry list of rappers who have found themselves in body bags or the fact that there are enough rappers in jail to film a celebrity edition of *Oz* on location. How many more bottles do we have to pour out onto the street for the likes of Biggie, Pac, Souljah Slim, Jam Master Jay, and Freaky Tah? And how many more rappers have to end up like Shyne, C-Murder, Cassidy, Young Turk, Freaky Zeeky, and Lil' Kim?

Maybe I just got old and square; got a little money and got conservative (which is what black folks do when we get some money). Whatever the road that got me here, the destination remains the same. Hip-hop has become a problem for black America.

Do the drum patterns, the DJ scratching, or the rapper's delivery have anything to do with bringing down the race? Of course not. The problem is the culture itself. But before all you stoic defenders of beatboxing, graffiti, and break dancing hop out of your b-boy stance to jump down my throat, understand what I mean by "the culture."

Hip-hop in 2004 has little to nothing to do with what began in the late 1970s and exploded in the early to mid-1980s. The origins of hip-hop were a boiling stew of different socioeconomic, racial, cultural, and artistic factors that conspired to big-bang a host of new musical possibilities. Hip-hop was not just the music played in the parks and the housing projects in the Bronx and Queensbridge. It was an entire new way of life. I'll spare the gentle reader the almost requisite journalistic fellating of hip-hop's pioneers. If you don't know who Afrika Bambaataa, Kool G Rap, Eric B, and Melle Mel are by now, no amount of ass-kissing on my part is going to make them particularly relevant to the topic of this discussion.

What would black youth be like had hip-hop never come about, or if it had been the flash in the pan that so many thought it would be? As it happened, it was the style, the swagger, and the beat of hip-hop music that triumphed as the reigning cultural force. With staccato verses over breaks and loops came the fashion sense that has evolved from nut-hugging Lees and shell-toe Adidas to Technicolor cross-colors, to jerseys for teams that no longer exist and $300 jeans. There were also the embarrassing synchronized dances of the mideighties: the Reebok, the prep, the cabbage patch, and so on, followed closely by the stoic head nod, the crip walk, and most recently the famed brushing of dirt off the shoulders.

Hip-hop became to this generation what rock and roll once was: a legitimate change in popular culture. Hip-hop once eclipsed country music as the largest-selling single musical genre. Hip-hop-inspired beats and tired amateur rappers have replaced Muzak and celebrity pitchmen to sell TV audiences soggy breakfast cereal and artery-clogging McHeartAttacks. We should be proud. Shouldn't we?

Along with societal recognition and corporate profits so fat that Lyor Cohen can doggie-paddle through a swimming pool of gold coins like a latter-day Scrooge McDuck has come something much worse: the idea that black youth should conform to and emulate the worst possible racial stereotypes.

The entertainment business machine is marketing these over-the-top ghetto fantasies to white youth as entertainment. The end result: black people, who have been systematically degraded, oppressed, and destroyed, have now willingly picked up the banner of self-destruction and are marching with it like that topless lady in those French revolution portraits. Meanwhile, white people, who make up the vast majority of hip-hop's listeners (come on, do you really think 5 million black people bought Ja Rule's albums?), are bombarded with the ideas and images of black buffoonery, amorality, sexuality, and violence as a kind of ghetto fantasy. Now, I'm not one of those conspiracy-believing brothers who think the illuminati and heads of major corporations are holed up in some secret underground lair, plotting to inundate America with the idea that blacks are inferior. If they were, however, they'd be hard pressed to do better than today's hip-hop.

Let's take a look at a couple of the major characters in this sad drama. Amos and Andy ain't got nothing on these boys. We'll see who the originators are. (The originator title may go to the individual who first popularized the character, as opposed to the one who invented it. After all, Baby may have been the first on the scene with diamonds in his teeth, but it was Paul Wall who really made the shit pop.) And we'll look at which other rappers have advanced the stereotype. We'll judge them on a scale of 1 to 10 on the Keep It Real factor, a subscientific indicator of how closely their words match up with their reality, as well as the Damage to the Race factor, which measures exactly what negative effects these depictions have.

1. THE DRUG KINGPIN

Originator: Notorious B.I.G.
Notable follow-ups: Jay-Z, the Clipse, Cam'ron, Kool G Rap, T.I., many others

Raison d'être: The Drug Kingpin's sole
purpose, it seems, is to stack mad
loot by selling as much illicit sub-
stances as he can to blacks. His excuse is that his poor ghetto
upbringing affords him no other
opportunities to make a living
than slangin' rock, since he does
not possess a "wicked jump shot."

The Kingpin enjoys bragging
about taking over small towns, usually killing and/or evicting the exist-
ing Kingpin, and "setting up shop" to sell crack to the local
townspeople. The Kingpin is notable for his paranoia
about being "watched by the feds," and frequently enjoys
setting up meetings with Colombians, Dominicans, Peru-
vians, and other Hispanic nationals to secure wholesale
deals. These meetings typically go sour quickly, resulting
in some manner of shootout, in which the Kingpin is never
shot or suspected in the shooting of said Hispanic nationals, and he usually leaves the meeting with both the money
and the dope. While the Kingpin is always under threat of
arrest, his large stack of dope money buys him the finest
lawyers, and his street connections allow him to intimidate
witnesses and juries alike. He is typically a ladies' man due
to his wealth and often employs his "bitch" to smuggle
drugs for him. When he is forced to defend himself from
those who would stick him for his paper, he usually resorts
to his trusty Tec-9, and in extreme cases will break out the
AK-47.

Preferred mode of transportation: Range Rover, Mercedes
S-Class

Keep It Real factor: 2. While nearly every rapper in business these days seems to have a great series of stories about his days selling rocks, the fact is that most of these accounts are simply rehabbed stories from older brothers or cousins who had some exposure to the crack trade in the eighties. The idea that Juelz Santana represents a clear and present danger to some drug dealer in Nebraska is about as far-fetched as Saddam Hussein's having had nuclear weapons that could be delivered to their targets by genetically engineered invisible bats. A few Kingpin rappers may have sold small-time quantities at one point or other, but the over-the-top tales of doing deals with foreigners and taking over blocks would have been more appropriate in 1987 than in 2005.

Damage to the Race factor: 7. While utterly unrealistic and overblown, the fast money, high-priced women, and luxury cars depicted by the Kingpin are extremely seductive to many people who see little hope of making a living in a square job. For teenagers unused to the discipline and dedication a real job entails, and who don't have an iota of hope of attending college or being able to secure work that can support the standard of living of a major city, the Kingpin lifestyle seems all the more attractive. When coupled with the attraction of being an alpha male boss type, this is one of the most dangerous characters the rap game has to offer black youth as a model to emulate.

2. THE SUPERTHUG/GANGSTA

Originator: Tupac
Notable follow-ups: Mobb Deep, N.W.A., 50 Cent, Ja Rule, MC Eiht, O-Dog, DMX
Raison d'être: Unlike the Drug Kingpin, whose major motive

is profit, the Superthug/
Gangsta is primarily interested
in committing violence against
haters while showing love to
his homies. Possessed of neither the mental fortitude nor
business savvy required to
deal drugs full-time, he typically makes ends meet committing petty crimes, including
robberies, chain-snatching, and
shakedowns. Frequently shirtless, the Superthug/Gangsta

can also usually be identified by a multitude of tattoos
and his hairstyle, usually a baldy, cornrows, or a Jheri
curl, coupled with a scowl and often accompanied by
some sports paraphernalia from his hometown.

The Superthug's existence on wax usually revolves around
his hard-knock upbringing, which forced him to become extra aggressive in order to survive. Now that he is a grown
man, he deals with the rampant issues of his childhood by
smoking marijuana and drinking away the pain, usually with
Hennessy. He is extremely tribal and spends a great deal of
his time representing his hood while simultaneously berating
and threatening "bitch niggas." His semisuicidal lifestyle is
marked by wild mood swings and psychopathic actions sure
to get him killed, an outcome for which he is fully prepared.
He enjoys the camaraderie of prison, and spends a good deal
of time there. Occasionally, he shows his sensitive side with
an ode to the woman in his life or his mother.

Preferred mode of transportation: Lowrider, '96 Chevy Impala
on twenties

Keep It Real factor: 5. On any given album, the Superthug may be responsible for the murder of more than six hundred black men, countless robberies, and several kidnappings, tortures, or various other atrocities. Unfortunately, the Superthug/Gangsta far too often believes his own hype and finds himself behind bars or dead (see Shyne, Young Turk, DMX, C-Murder, Pimp C, T.I., Tupac, Beanie Sigel). While the incarceration of these notables suggests there is some truth to the lifestyle depictions, far more often the defiant pose is adopted to provide an image for fans so weaned on hard-core thuggery that any deviation from status quo is considered an unacceptable business risk by the record company. Witness Lil' Flip's very public outing by T.I. on his Gangsta Grillz mixtape, Dr. Dre's early days with the World Class Wreckin' Cru, and early femgangsta rapper (and college graduate) Boss appearing on her album cover with a Mossberg and some locs.

Damage to the Race factor: 8. The Superthug represents an attractive combination of antiestablishment rebellion and the ability to be feared or respected. For poor people, and even more well-to-do blacks, the combination of freedom from societal restrictions and the attainment of a sense of respect or attention from others can be impossible to resist.

This character taps into every male's desire to be tougher than the next man, and in this enduring quest to be "harder than the next nigga," thousands of black men die every year and thousands more are sent to prison for murder, assault, and other crimes. On an even more prevalent note, the ideals of thuggery that are emulated by so many black teens (lack of respect for authority, lack of self-control and discipline, violent tendencies, inability to compromise) make them woefully unprepared to progress in society.

High school students who adopt the Superthug/Gangsta persona are unlikely to graduate from high school, let alone go to college. Their inability to be supervised makes them next to unemployable, and their lack of discipline ensures that even if they get an opportunity, they are that much more likely to blow it by disrespecting a superior, quitting in a huff, or doing something inappropriate. At least the Drug Kingpin can theoretically transfer his people skills and entrepreneurial spirit to selling used cars or starting a record label.

3. THE BALLER

Originator: Puff Daddy (P. Diddy, Diddy, or whatever the fuck he's going by at the time you read this)

Notable follow-ups: Baby (Birdman), Fabolous, Ma$e, Lil' Flip

Raison d'être: The Baller is more a part of a personality than an entire character in and of him- or herself (with the exception of Cash Money's Baby, a.k.a. #1 Stunna). The Baller's major motivation is to raise his rock-bottom self-esteem and inspire jealousy and hatred in others due to a sustained campaign of gaudy and tasteless materialism. Unlike real rich people, the Baller is all too eager to let others know the price tag  for his conspicuous consumption. He favors clothing with the most visible logos possible, and enjoys nothing more than to "leave the sticker on the window of his Bentley to show its price, and an arm out the driver-side window just to show off his ice."

One of the Baller's major reasons for showing all his wealth is to attract women who will be willing to have sex with him in exchange for the privilege of riding in his Bentley. While it is unclear where the Baller comes upon all of his money, he usually refers to offhand drug deals and his record contract as the sources of his income. Of primary importance to the Baller is not only having more expensive items than his competitors, but having newer and/or different ways of showing the amount of balling he can do (e.g., upholstering his rims with Fendi-printed monkey fur).

Preferred mode of transportation: G4 private jet, Maybach 62, Bentley

Keep It Real factor: 2. With the exception of a handful of successful rappers and those who maintain a percentage of ownership in their record label, most rappers don't know where their next check is coming from. Given the dynamics of the music business, it is entirely conceivable that a platinum-selling rapper can end the fiscal year owing his label money for expenses alone, aside from the cost of fronting him cash to support his entry into an ever-escalating competition of who can be more frivolous. However, because rappers typically spend their advances on diamond jewelry and leasing high-end Range Rovers, they can maintain the image for years before the façade begins to tarnish.

Damage to the Race factor: 5. The emulation of the Baller character is perhaps one reason blacks tend to have such hapless finances. Even blacks with higher incomes save and invest less money on average, spend more on cars and luxury items, and have lower net worths than whites in the same income category. When black people making close to minimum wage carry Louis Vuitton purses and drive Escalades on 24s to keep up with the Jenkinses (who similarly make between squat and dick per hour), it's no wonder the dollars leave the black community faster than the outer lip of a spinning rim.

In hip-hop's ironic school of thought, the less money you keep, the more social status you achieve. Since money management is a subject that goes largely untaught in schools, churches, or other community settings, most children establish their financial habits by copying their parents. So if Daddy's not paying child support so he can make payments on his Jacob the Jeweler (Daddy knows the time in four other places he'll never visit), and Moms is buying Manolo Blahniks so she can look fly working at Target, it's highly unlikely Junior will ever be able to stack any bread. The end result is that black people do not control their financial destiny and black families will forever be dependent upon the goodwill of white people, as opposed to relying on their own assets, investments, and companies to create income.

4. THE PIMP

Originator: Too $hort
Notable follow-ups: Luke, Ice-T, Snoop Dogg, Pimp C, 8 Ball, and MJG
Raison d'être: The Pimp is a classic character in hip-hop whose attributes are woven through almost all of the other stereotypes. The Pimp's primary ideal is to have sex

with as many women as humanly possible with the least possible monetary outlay. He (or even she) uses the accoutrements of his ballerdom, thuggery, or other personality quirks to attract hordes of naive and impressionable members of the opposite sex. Once he's acquired these subjects, he then persuades them to repeatedly perform sexual favors for him and his posse.

The male pimp is most proud of his lack of attachment to and even outright disdain for women. Come 6:15 A.M. (after she has just arrived at 6:00), he fully expects her to leave his house and hotfoot it home. The Pimp measures the rank of his abilities by the number of conquests attained, and rewards himself with extra pimp points for receiving gifts and money from women who have received such from a baller or lesser pimp. The Pimp also enjoys wearing ridiculous and colorful outfits to show his general pimpness to the community at large.

Preferred mode of transportation: Cadillac

Keep It Real factor: 4. The Pimp character is usually just a mishmash of movie characters the rapper saw as a child or teenager. A generous helping of Goldie from *The Mack*, a little *Willie Dynamite,* and a sprinkle of *Dolemite* for comedic flavoring add up to a recipe for playerhood. Most Pimp rappers speak at length about their inability to attract women before they achieved whatever level of fame and money they enjoy now ("Back then they didn't want me, now I'm hot, they all on me"). These admissions cast serious doubt on their natural game. Additionally, a hard look into many a pimp's personal life will often find him walking hand in hand on the beach with an R&B singer or buying flowers for his wife.

Damage to the Race factor: 7. The Pimp's debased and ugly lack of respect for women delivers yet another dart to the heart of male-female relationships in the African American community. Additionally, his promiscuity assures the spread of STDs and the birth of yet more fatherless children. The Pimp character destroys one of the principal tenets of manhood, responsibility to one's family, because he feels a responsibility only to his libido. This is an extremely attractive image for young men who seek to establish confidence and respect by virtue of their ability to exploit women. The character also distorts the values of young boys as well, who in seeking to emulate the Pimp neglect work and study to spend their time chasing multiple girls.

5. THE SHE-MAN

Originator: Lil' Kim
Notable follow-ups: Jacki-O, Trina, Foxy Brown, Remy Ma
Raison d'être: The She-Man is an odd combination of Baller, Drug Kingpin, and Superthug, with a hint of high-priced call girl thrown in for good measure, adopting many of the hard-core characteristics of her testicle-endowed counterparts while throwing in some feminine wiles to ensure the consumer does not mistake her for a transvestite. Her

finances are much more transparent than most, however, as she derives her income from sleeping with rich men. Her primary focus is to show off how lucrative this profession can be and to build up her self-esteem through shoe acquisitions and confirmations of the quality of her pussy. She takes little shit from men, as she has had her heart broken in the past.

Preferred mode of transportation: Leaves the party in somebody's Ferrari (can't afford her own)

Keep It Real factor: 7. The She-Man has far more credibility than most of the characters in the rap game. While she does frequently engage in overblown self-flattery and ridiculous stories of thuggery, drug dealing, and balling, for the most part her stories are rooted in some manner of reality, particularly if she has managed to lure a Baller or Drug Kingpin who has too little Pimp in him. Many of our She-Men admit to being abused or having worked in exploitative situations pre-rap (Eve was a stripper, Lil' Kim served as girlfriend to several drug dealers), lending an air of authenticity to the proceedings. Even nonrapping semicelebrities such as Superhead and Karmen (Get it, more in Karmen) have published tell-alls about their gold diggery. However, the details of her exploits are usually vastly overblown, as she usually receives precious little in the form of hard assets, real estate, or other sellable property. Frequently, this kind of character receives little more than an allowance and dinner at a moderately expensive chain restaurant. She can even be bilked of her few hard-earned dollars from a Baller by another iconic hip-hop character: the Pimp.

Damage to the Race factor: 6. The She-Man is something of a totem to women fed up with men who have emulated the other four major characters. Thus she lashes out by attaching a value to her most prized asset: her pussy. Unfortunately, emulation of this stereotype has left many a woman heartbroken and lonely, and otherwise constructive relationships between black men and women devolve into contests to see who can get over the hardest on the other. Selling love (or sex) as a commodity is yet another bitch slap to the already fractured institution that is the black family.

Of course, the reason that these ridiculous depictions of black life are so powerful is simple. It's the same reason that action movies, and not thoughtful documentaries, are the blockbusters. It's why porn is a $12 billion a year industry and PBS barely scrapes by. There is a legitimate and ongoing argument as to how much the marketplace really controls its own desires. After all, no one watches WWF wrestling for the artful technique—they watch it to see someone get hit with a chair. And the eclipsing of the American movie industry by the porn industry in terms of revenue certainly suggests that maybe, just maybe, people are interested in sex. On the other hand, what's being made available to the consumer is largely dictated by corporate America. Whether the proverbial chicken came before the egg here, however, is an entirely different discussion. What we can agree upon is that there is an inherent tension and excitement in viewing conflict, sex, and drama.

The sea change within hip-hop is the idea that what was being talked about on records and shown in videos was real. We as consumers are now expected to believe that the subject matter being presented to us is either true or representative enough of real life that similar situations routinely occur. When the Clipse rhyme "He was talking shit, I put a clappin' to that boy," there should be no doubt in the audience's mind that what Pusha-T intends to do is end a black person's life because he was disrespecting or insulting him. This is a matter-of-fact statement said without even a twinge of remorse or guilt.

There is a perverse pride in being willing to literally take a life as punishment for being challenged. 50 Cent became famous before his first album even shipped on the strength of having been shot nine times. In his own rhymes, he speaks proudly of this experience, touting his survival as proof that he really is a hard motherfucker. If you get shot nine times and still live, according to hip-hop, you deserve some credit. You should be celebrated for being so close to bulletproof. Without that backstory, as well as the continuing blood feud with Ja Rule, Fat Joe, and others, it is unlikely that 50 would have generated the continued interest to make his first two albums the multiplatinum successes they were.

The fact that black people, and particularly poor black people, kill one another, steal from one another, and degrade one another has roots that go much deeper than hip-hop. Poor people of every race, ethnicity, and national origin throughout history have engaged in all manner of depravity not just to survive, but because of the oppressive frustration of their situation. It's nothing new. Palestinians send suicide bombers to Tel Aviv, the Irish Republican Army blew up planes, and if you've ever been to a Brazilian slum, well, the less said about those hellholes the better.

That said, the crime rates and murder rates for African American communities are simply astronomical compared with those among the rest of American society. According to FBI statistics for 1993–2001, the crime index for nonwhites hovered between three and four times that of the white population. Murder rates for nonwhites were between five and seven times those of whites. Keep in mind that the FBI classifies Hispanics, West Asians, and Middle Easterners as whites. According to the Bureau of Justice, at midyear 2003, there were 4,834 black male prisoners for every 100,000 black males, compared with 480 prisoners per 100,000 persons for the U.S. general population, a tenfold difference in the rate of imprisonment.

So where does hip-hop fit into what are obviously socioeconomic problems? Simple. Consider for a moment the idea that entertainment does in fact affect and influence people's lives. As members of the hip-hop community, we frequently wrestle with this idea, because it inherently suggests that artists have a responsibility to say certain things and, more important, *not* say other things. It's the razor's edge between censorship and prohibition of free speech, a right we've been denied for so long that the very idea of muzzling what we have to say is cause for revolt. It's why when people blamed Tupac's lyrics for the murder of a state trooper, or N.W.A.'s lyrics for gang violence, we're so quick to ask why no one indicts Arnold Schwarzenegger for those ridiculously violent *Terminator* movies. No difference, right?

Wrong. The very reason hip-hop's perversion into crass materialism, celebrations of thuggery, and tantrum-throwing antiestablishmentarianism (try that as a Scrabble word) is so dangerous is because it is presented as a reality. Gangsta rap, that wonderful subgenre of the culture that emerged from the West Coast (unless you're from the East Coast and you argue that Kool G Rap was its originator), was branded by many of its artists as "reality rap."

The very ethos of the movement stems from the idea that the subject matter represents real life for this group of people. If you believe for a moment that the depiction of a leather-clad robot from the future sent to kill John Connor and the depiction of a black person sent from the ghetto to kill other black people have the same effect on their intended audiences, then either you're pitifully naive or your self-delusion has taken on Michael Jackson–esque proportions. Yes, Michael, there is something inappropriate about having children in your bed, and yes, America, there is something wrong with glorifying murder, mayhem, and malaise to people who will emulate every facet of their favorite rappers, from their pink New York Yankees baseball hat to the way they pronounce the word *there* as "thurr."

The problem stems not only from the adoption of this reckless culture but from the conditions that amplify its message. With so many black youths living in single-parent households in which that single parent often works two jobs, there is frequently no one to teach the nuances of social interaction and appropriate behavior other than the TV and the CD player. And since the vast majority of these single parents are women, there's a void of male role models. So when our young consumer switches on the boob tube and sees Jay-Z leaned up against a Bentley, "all the wavy light-skinned girls" loving him now, it's fairly easy to decipher how Jay becomes his operational role model.

The problem is compounded again by the economic forces behind the hip-hop machine. While the face of hip-hop is almost uniformly black, the finance is almost uniformly not. Once you get above the A&R reps, the corporate decision makers tend to be white. And their responsibility is not to the black community. It's to their shareholders.

With four major record companies dominating the ability to get product on the airwaves, there's precious little incentive for them to deviate from a plan that has been, for the most part, making their shareholders happy with a minimum of risk. With the advent of music piracy and the declining of corporate profits through music sales, taking unnecessary risks by signing "positive" artists who will probably not turn out to be blockbusters is a much less attractive proposition than signing a new 50 Cent.

The fallout of rap that furthers the negative stereotypes of African Americans can be seen in the bleak picture in which black America finds itself. One need only venture down to any inner-city high school to see the effects. Young black men dressing and acting like carbon copies of their favorite rappers abound. They don "Rest in Peace" T-shirts and get tattoos of dead friends' names wherever they fit. And this is not a fate limited to my generation.

Our children will be born into the same cycle and suffer the same fate. As they get farther and farther from the American dream, they will be relegated to societal obscurity, trapped and powerless in a little ghetto box that they do not control and can never leave. This is an unacceptable fate for an entire race of people. What is even more unacceptable is that we stand by and watch our communities destroy themselves in order to boast an image that most rappers themselves can't even live up to. The idea that entertainment doesn't affect real life is one we must expose for the folly it is. If proud parents can point to an R. Kelly CD and explain how his *12 Play* album is responsible for the birth of their baby boy, isn't it time we realize that the sobbing mother shouldn't have to point at a hip-hop CD to explain why her son is in the ground?

SCARFACE

THE INTERVIEW 2000

Scarface was crafting haunting tales of southern
ghetto strife back in the early 1990s, long before Dirty
South became the marketing catchphrase du jour.
His candid depictions of Houston street life, pic-
turesque wordplay, and earnest delivery earned the
respect of rappers and fans alike. He knows the business of music and the business of drugs personally.

I love niggas who step out of the shoes of illegal business
and make something profitable as well as legal about
themselves. 'Cause, man, if you look at the statistics in the
federal prison system and state prison system, dude, you
learn a whole lot, and you figure out what it really is, man.
You start looking at an even bigger picture than the one
that's been painted in history. It's just a new way of enslav-
ing a motherfucker and capitalizing on that shit. Ninety
percent of the niggas in the federal penitentiary is in that
motherfucker for drugs, and they get a longer sentence than
a nigga who cut a motherfucker head off and pulled their
arms loose and raped children.

You get more time for some hard crack than you do for

some soft white, especially if Bobby got caught with ten X pills and a couple of joints of weed—then he gets a slap on the wrist. But you catch the homeboy Leroy and he got one rock and no weed, they try to throw the book at that nigga. They give a motherfucker a year a gram and ten years for each rock. 'Cause I got a homeboy that got jammed up for selling to a motherfuckin' snitch and they gave him thirty years. And the motherfucker that was with him that didn't have shit to do with it, he got twenty-five years for conspiracy. That conspiracy law, man, we need to fight that shit. That's a cold-blooded motherfuckin' law that they got for niggas. They give a motherfucka who don't get caught with much more years and more time than they give a motherfucka who get caught with everything. You can have a hundred kilos of cocaine, man, and they give you fifteen years or less, depending on the color of your skin. You get caught with one kilo of hard, you gonna get life when you a nigga—life.

And them motherfuckas talk about "stop the violence" and "war on drugs." If you really had a war on drugs, if you really wanted to war on drugs, then war on drugs like you war on terrorism. 'Cause it's only a few spots in this world where they can manufacture and process and ship drugs into the United States. If you really wanted that shit to stop, go send you a few bombers over to that motherfucker and destroy it and it's over. So it's a conspiracy. Them motherfuckers need to pick that thirty up. The government needs to get thirty-five—they need to get life—'cause they put niggas under immense pressure.

I know what's going on in the world but it'll take more than just me talking about politics to get into that shit. I'm telling you. In order for a nigga, not a black man . . . in order for a nigga to get into politics, man, he gonna have to take these motherfuckas to war. In the situation that we in, dude, we ain't near 'bout ready to go to war. We ain't ready for no war. We ain't got enough niggas that understand. They think of the Mercedes-Benz and the Six and a house and wife and kids. They made it, but still a motherfucker controlling that. Motherfuckas taxing 40 percent of a nigga's money. That's damn near half. It goes up the more money you make.

If I was making five dollars an hour, I wouldn't have to pay 39 percent of the tax bracket. You can hide as much as you can, but when them motherfuckers come after your ass, they'll find you. And I don't see why the fuck they need my money anyway. They can print their own goddamn money. I tell you what, dude. I'ma make a movie about that shit. Niggas need they own government. Niggas need their own economy. At least give a nigga a chance, 'cause right now we in somebody else's world. That's incredible, right? We the only motherfuckers that ain't got no spokesperson for us. Who's the black leader? It ain't one.

The only way to fuck with them is to fuck with their money. It's like playing chess—you gotta create a force move to make a nigga step out there. You know, and the minute you start fucking with the money, you start getting some results. But that marching shit—out. You stop buying Nikes and Benzes and Cadillacs and clothes and shit, stop buying Toys R Us and Sony and all that shit and start fucking with niggas that do the same shit, then we've empowered each other. [They] don't understand how powerful our dollars is. Minister Farrakhan did a Million Man March where they fucked the economy up for a day. We need to do a Million Man March for a couple of years.

I know that we need our money. I know we need that. So I'm probably getting ready to join a real politically incorrect band of niggas and go out and demand shit. And I wouldn't even mind being assassinated by one of them radical-ass skinheads. At least [then] I'd know I went out for something I believed in.

I'm not a fucking rapper, dude. I'm a businessman, dog. It ain't no different than a motherfucker that does work with his hands. Let one of them motherfuckers make a song and sell a million records, or get up and come to this motherfucking office and find the next shit. Or go in their goddamn community and blend in with the hardest of the hard. I'm a bad motherfucker 'cause I rap for a living. 'Cause I run a major southern record label I'm a bad fucking guy. America paints that fucking picture, man, and as long as we wear the skin that we're in, man, we gotta deal with it, unless we're ready to go to war for real. The revolution will not be televised . . . will not be televised, will not be televised. The revolution will not be televised. I guess when a nigga grow up, though, I realize what should have been. I realize what could have been. And changing that shit don't mean marching.

When I got a fucking problem I wanna be able to depend on my government. Our government to defend me. They'd rather lock these niggas up and go defend Israel and Pakistan. The motherfuckers won't defend me. They won't defend the taxpayer, but they'll go defend the motherfucker that they in trades with, or they trying to get trades from. It's things for things in this game, man.

THE BUZZ

Like Method Man says: Roll it. Light it. Smoke it. Or maybe you're the type to just get your drink on. A bird in the hand is enough hits to get you through the morning. We can't leave home something for the express train of getting over. But nothing eases the pain forever.

THE BUZZ

BY MARK ALLWOOD

Don't wanna be another number
I got a fuckin' gang of weed to keep from going
   under . . .
    —2Pac, "Picture Me Rollin'," from *All Eyez on Me* (1996)

Man, ain't nothin' wrong with smokin' weed!" my room-mate joked, quoting Ice Cube's now infamous cult classic stoner film *Friday* (1995) while taking the healthy-size Dutch Masters blunt from me and inhaling deeply, fire in his eyes, clouds of bluish gray smoke encircling his lanky frame. Resuming his sidesplitting rendition of Smokey, the perpet-ually stoned, comical character immortalized on screen by Chris Tucker, he continued: "Weed is from the earth. God put this here for me and you! Take advantage, man! Take advantage!"

Swallowing the bitter remnants of my ninety-nine-cent double deuce of Icehouse and ironing the Nautica golf shirt I was planning to wear for the evening's festivities, I couldn't help but think about how many times this scenario had repeated itself over the years in various ways, with var-ious participants engaging in various topics of conversation.

Probably about as many times as we played that bootleg copy of *Friday* that we kept "forgetting" to return to my brother's roommate, who was just next door.

The first time I really caught the unmistakable potent scent of marijuana I was attending one of my earliest rap concerts at the old Omni in downtown Atlanta, at the "Nitro" tour with LL Cool J and Public Enemy. It was the early nineties, back when big-arena hip-hop concerts took place regularly, and just before a series of violent incidents would put them to rest for close to a decade. I remember actually closing my mouth that day trying not to inhale any of the secondhand fumes floating up to the rafters, fearing that the smoke might damage something inside me.

Funny that that memory would stand out. My first introduction so closely linked to my first dabblings in hip-hop. It's a parallel that would soon define not only me but my entire generation and culture.

My first time ever smoking was during the sweltering summer between my junior and senior years in high school. A shy, fresh-faced Long Island transplant in Lithonia, Georgia, long before it became cool to be from the South, I found it difficult to fit in. As the younger brother of a popular class president and aspiring revolutionary, and little cousin to the school's star basketball player, I had a hard time finding my own identity amid a sea of pretty girls dating well-known upperclassmen who drove cars. I didn't have a car yet. Not like it mattered—I was so awkward back then. To me, these men were like gods, and my adolescent world spun on their axis. Damn, I wanted to be like them.

I knew one of my older relatives smoked. His discovery of Bob Marley led to his flirtation with Rastafarianism, which led to marijuana, or herb, for spiritual enhancement. When I heard another relative had tried smoking, too, I figured, "Why not? It can't be all that bad."

We used to hang out by this neighborhood swimming pool. Usually when we came out here, one of my relatives smoked and I amused myself by looking up at the infinite black sky with its many bright stars. I had always loved astronomy. But this particular day, I didn't feel like being a sideline player. "Let me hit that," I demanded, and took the blunt from his hand. And so it began. Like many other first-time smokers I failed to get high that night, but the quiet kid was beginning to emerge from the shadows.

I grew up in the eighties as one of those unsuspecting middle-class kids living under the banner of Nancy Reagan and the White House's half-assed "Just Say No" campaign. I made a commitment, then a tender, naive eight-year-old, that I would never do any drugs . . . ever. Marijuana, cocaine, heroin, any of it. After witnessing the rampant alcoholism in my family, I didn't have much desire to drink, either. I'd heard the many stories firsthand of the battles that some of my relatives had with the bottle. I remember one of my uncles taking me to his sobriety anniversary at an Alcoholics Anonymous meeting. He was so proud that he was able to conquer his addiction, one that had spun out of control while he was fighting on the front lines of the Vietnam War.

Then there was my grandfather, who at age seventeen had come to New York City from Cuba by way of his native Jamaica. He'd always had an affinity for Appleton Jamaican rum. As a small boy I would delight in watching him sit confidently at his kitchen table in South Florida, sipping on an Appleton and ginger ale as he recalled working in sugar cane fields in a bygone era, or hearing his tales of being a tour guide for Milton Hershey in a pre-Castro, Mafia-run Cuba.

But smoking weed was different from drinking, for me. Cigarettes, with all their ills, were in abundance at family reunions. But they didn't have the same appeal that "chiefing," as it would come to be known in Atlanta, did. Weed had hip-hop as its soundtrack. The allure of bad boy rebellion and hellified beats was an eerily irresistible combination.

Tupac, who has always personified the most complex, honest, and even disturbing assessments of black America, was best captured in that powerful image of an ice-grilled, shirtless, and tattooed Pac, his "Thug Life" skullcap matching the words emblazoned on his belly, black gat tucked away in his waistband, one hand flipping the bird and the other holding a burning blunt. This image was the ultimate fuck-you to societal norms and white America's establishment.

Smoking became more regular my freshman year at Morehouse. It was the '94–'95 school year and we'd burn blunts with other classmates in the upstairs rafters of the Warehouse, a popular hip-hop den crammed with college kids and locals grinding their troubles away to the dark grooves of the Wu-Tang Clan, Biggie, Junior M.A.F.I.A., Black Moon, Pac, OutKast, Goodie Mob, and other hot artists of the era.

Besides making me feel like I was a part of something, weed made me feel free. It's not that I felt confined or didn't enjoy life, but, growing up, simple everyday routines and the repetitive rhythm of life were at times boring to me, and marijuana suddenly made everything that much more interesting and fun. Regular routines suddenly became adventures.

I remember lighting up when Biggie performed at a hole-in-the-wall West End club called the Garage. To this day my most beloved hip-hop memory, it was a sight to see, with Big passing blunts to people in the front row during "Unbelievable" and Puffy stage diving, sharing bottles of Dom Perignon with the crowd. I was there, in a sea of head-nodding hip-hop heads, soaking in his lyrics like a seeker to a priest, Big's brown Carhartt hat pulled so low over his head you couldn't see his smoked-out bloodshot eyes.

> High days are better than sober ones . . .
>
> —Big Boi, "It Ain't Over (Till That Big Girl from Decatur Sang)," from OutKast's *ATLiens* (1996)

By sophomore year, I'd moved off-campus, deeper into the heart of the SWATS (Southwest Atlanta). My two-bedroom apartment became a haven for our ever-increasing partying. The summer of 1996 brought the Olympic Games to Atlanta, and OutKast's *ATLiens* became the soundtrack to my life that year. Three, five, and sometimes ten or more friends would come through: sharing blunts, beers, Black and Milds, and games of NBA Live on PlayStation. It didn't matter that a Red Dog (an aggressive unit of the ATL police department designed to bust drug deals) officer lived directly across from us. It didn't matter that my uncle dropped by unexpectedly from time to time, clearly peeping the empty beer cans, liquor bottles, ashes, and the red plastic bong we couldn't hide fast enough.

What did matter was that I was part of a crew, and we were a deep crew. For the first time I was as cool as everyone I used to envy. I was part of something, a movement of sorts, a "consciousness-shifting experience," I reasoned. I was a part of people who understood what the fuck I was about. My icons, the masters of the mic, the smoothest wordsmiths to walk the planet, were doing what I was doing.

It got to the point where everyone I thought was cool got blunted. Every rapper or hip-hop group I heralded as the second coming: Biggie, Nas, Big Boi and Andre of OutKast, Tupac, Method Man, Redman, Keith Murray, Snoop Dogg,

LL Cool J, and the Roots, among a smorgasbord of others, each bowed to the ominous power of the blunt.

Even so-called conscious rappers like De La Soul, A Tribe Called Quest, KRS-One, and Goodie Mob paid homage to marijuana. I enjoyed the way it made me feel. I felt in tune with the people I smoked with. That haunting sense of alienation and solitude dissipated with each puff. I could come out of my shell. My shyness melted away, and when I coupled weed with enough alcohol, I could socialize more easily. I was no longer trapped in introversion. I was no longer invisible. Up to that point, the most rebellious thing I'd done was bash a few neighborhood mailboxes, egg a few houses, and set off an arsenal of various illegal fireworks. Fire had always fascinated me. Weed was the next level.

> I look in every hip-hop magazine, it seems
> That the blunts are being passed around the scenes,
>   in teams
> —The Pharcyde's Bootie Brown on "Pack the Pipe," from
>   Bizarre Ride II (1992)

It wasn't just me who got swept up in the rush. During the mid-1990s the rate of teenage marijuana use more than doubled in America (*Drug Use and Abuse,* 1995). If you weren't in the know by 1992, then Dr. Dre's *The Chronic* (with its marijuana leaf emblazoned on the cover) made it official.

That same year, Newark's Redman let the world know that a similar phenomenon was taking place on the East Coast. His legendary "How to Roll a Blunt" from his 1992 debut, *Whut? Thee Album* was the instructional manual I used in rolling my first L, a sloppily put-together, falling-apart mess of a thing that I constructed that sticky summer night in Lithonia. I can only imagine the corporate board meetings at all the top cigar companies after realizing why their sales had skyrocketed during those first years of the 1990s. Some dumbfounded employee must have been charged with informing a room full of equally clueless executives that these newfound sales came from urban youth who were splitting their cigars open, dumping out their precious tobacco, and then refilling the leaf with marijuana. "They're calling them blunts," he must have professed.

A decade after the "Great Blunt Explosion," these same companies began to cater to their new clientele with ready-made skins that came in flavors like Sour Apple, Champagne, Strawberry, Honey, Jamaican Rum, Cognac, and Wet Mango. Now there are even brands like Blunt Wrap, featuring Snoop Dogg, Too $hort, and other MCs in the ads, for which there is no dumping necessary, just the flavored wrap to roll your own "tobacco." But getting buzzed didn't start with hip-hop, or hippies, or rock and roll, or the jazz age. People have been indulging in intoxicants for centuries.

It's got millions of names: *Cannabis sativa*, weed, bud, herb, dank, dohja, hydro or 'dro, haze, lamb's bread, and countless more. The earliest known reference to its use dates back to about 2800 B.C., when Shen Nung, a mythical Chinese emperor and pharmacist, allegedly shared his knowledge of the plant with his subjects.

In India, it took on a much more religious and spiritual function. The Atharvaveda, one of the oldest books of Hinduism, includes it as one of the five sacred plants. And practitioners of the Rastafarian religion, founded in Jamaica in the 1930s, have long since used herb for spiritualism, often passing around huge clay water pipes called chalices during long marijuana-fueled drumming sessions, also known as nyabinghis. The Bible contains stories involving alcohol. Ancient Sumerians called opium the "plant of joy." Homer alluded to the mixture of opium and wine in the *Odyssey*.

The Incas chewed coca leaves long before Europeans turned the plant into a much more dangerous powder called cocaine. And at the height of the 1960s counterculture movement, Dr. Timothy Leary tried to convince people that LSD was the "gateway to true enlightenment."

Cocaine exploded during the 1970s disco era, and the black community at large was certainly not immune to its effects. Coke continued to flourish in the early 1980s, giving rise to a crack epidemic so horrendous, no one could have predicted its effects. More and more individuals were caught in the vicious cycles of violence, depravity, and fast money that laid the groundwork for music that captured the harrowing tales of addict and dealer.

Marijuana use became more dangerous. Instead of simply smoking a joint, users were now burning weed laced with cocaine or PCP (called "wools" or "primos"). Even today, especially in Miami, users are known to smoke "dirty weed," marijuana blunts laced with cocaine. Miami native Trick Daddy has rapped about the allure of "stank," so called because the cocaine alters marijuana's fragrant smell into a horrible odor. And in Texas and places like Los Angeles, Philadelphia, and New Jersey, people get high by smoking "wet," lacing cigarettes with embalming fluid or PCP. Unlike those living in other major cities, for the most part Atlanta residents are not known for lacing their blunts. But one day while I was enjoying the annual Atlanta University Center California Club picnic at Washington Park off MLK Drive, two teenagers who could not have been more than sixteen paraded through the large crowd, loudly advertising their product: "We got that dust and that weed, shawty," one said in a thick southern drawl. "That dust and that weed!"

In the late 1990s, "sipping syrup," the act of getting buzzed off codeine, was made famous by the hit "Sippin' on Some Syrup" by Memphis's Three 6 Mafia. In fact, the infamous DJ Screw, who innovated the South's prized "chopped and screwed" style of mixing, allegedly died from the concoction. The new millennium ushered in the Ecstasy bandwagon begun by the rave scene, and suddenly popping pills became as in vogue at a party as rolling, lighting, and smoking. Songs like B.G.'s "Hennessy and XTC" sprang up, and Missy Elliott even slyly alluded to the erogenous drug in her album title *Miss E: So Addictive.*

But I can't attribute my use to hard times. Sure, I went through issues growing up like everyone else, but I wasn't enduring any monumental stress. Besides moving to a different environment and having a difficult time adjusting at first, I didn't have a tortured upbringing, see death from fighting on the front lines, or have a fiery quest for enlightenment. In the midnineties weed and hip-hop had given me identity, an identity lost in the shuffle of my adolescent migration down South.

I'd left New York at a young age. Hip-hop, with its New York roots, became my lifeline, my link to a life I wished I had. As a teen, I often wondered if life would have been different for me if I'd stayed in Long Island. A childhood friend of mine from Freeport had begun to DJ parties with a crew of his buddies, and I wondered how involved I would have been in the New York music scene had my family stuck around. So I hung on to what I thought was being a pure hip-hop head. I didn't really listen to anything else.

My brother first introduced me to hip-hop, lending me tapes from groups like Public Enemy, 2 Live Crew, De La Soul, and KMD from time to time. He was more of a house head then, though, listening to some of everything. But I didn't know about other music. I knew hip-hop sampled, but I didn't know the jazz greats from which producers were sampling. Although soul and R&B were cool, all I wanted to listen to was hip-hop and a little Mary J. Blige. I wanted to live and breathe hip-hop. What better way to get lost in the music than to lose yourself in blunted reality?

> People killing, people dying
>
> . . .
>
> I think I'll elevate my mental
>> —Q-Tip of A Tribe Called Quest, "Steve Biko (Stir It Up),"
>> from *Midnight Marauders* (1994)

By the time I was old enough to hit the clubs and relive the wild party tales my older brother and cousins wielded like a golden carrot before my hungry eyes, hip-hop was all anyone was playing. But by then times were changing, and the skyrocketing violence in the music was starting to show itself in my day-to-day reality. My party days read like war stories compared to my brother's carefree party-hopping years. The atmosphere in Atlanta was increasingly violent.

It seemed like there was a fight every week at the Warehouse. There were shootouts outside of clubs, during Freaknik and trips to other college towns like Greensboro, North Carolina, with me and my boys dodging fistfights and ducking bullets in parking lots becoming routine. Even my freshman class in college was wilder and unrulier than anything the incumbent collegiate order had ever seen. We were known knuckleheads. Guys with top-ranking SAT and ACT scores and scholarships were getting kicked off campus for fighting and selling weed. Book-smart kids wanting extra cash thought they were going to come down to school and sell drugs. Of course the neighborhood dealers weren't having that, and some students were killed in the ensuing drama. There was a rumor that the local dealers were gonna shoot Morehouse students at will, so we stopped wearing Morehouse gear.

We, a brash bunch from the likes of Houston, Little Rock, Philly, Chicago, Oakland, Denver, Jersey, D.C., Albany, Georgia, and the like, were embracing the very thing we were trying to escape. I remember this one guy—his father was a famous New York attorney and he came from a well-off family. He came to my door telling me he had glocks for sale. Granted, this is the same guy who had sold my friend and me a bag of oregano we thought was weed after a Morehouse–Clark Atlanta basketball game. Who knows if he really had guns for sale, but needless to say, things were getting out of control.

It's interesting that teenage marijuana use skyrocketed in the early 1990s, when black-on-black crime was at its worst. Between the mid-1980s and 1993, homicides of teenage African American males increased by 158 percent (*Uniform Crime Reports*, 1994).

> There's only so much time left in this crazy world
> I'm just crumbling herb, I'm just crumbling herb
> —Sleepy Brown, in OutKast's "Crumblin' Erb," from
> *Southernplayalisticadillacmuzik* (1994)

The 1992 Rodney King case, resulting in the L.A. rebellion that left more than forty people dead and parts of South Central Los Angeles in ashy ruins, reminded me of Nino Brown's off-kilter proclamation in Mario Van Peebles's 1991 crack war opus *New Jack City:* "Times like these, people wanna get high. People wanna get real high, real fast."

Despite my high times, I did manage to graduate in four years. Later, I would go on to cover the hip-hop icons I idolized, writing for magazines and papers across the country. I would move to New York City, hip-hop's birthplace, and comb its streets for the stories of its musical players. Drug use is still pervasive. It's in the music at the industry mixers, where there's usually an open bar. Some artists even smoke during their interviews. Some offer their smoke to you. Others don't.

Still, something is obviously not working. I remember when, during my junior year of college, it suddenly dawned on me through the clouds of blunt smoke in our living room that one of the participants in the cipher was a neighborhood kid we played basketball with. He couldn't have been more than fourteen or fifteen. After realizing our mistake in letting him, my friend and I questioned his motives for wanting to smoke with us before sending him on his way. His response was a shrug, and the kind of look that said he was just imitating what he had picked up or heard somewhere, sometime. Maybe from a relative, maybe from a rap song. No rhyme, no reason. And I couldn't help but wonder if his mother or father knew where he was or what he was doing, or if they even cared.

The forces that have driven hip-hop to become a weed-centered culture are many and complex. As the first post–civil rights generation, we experienced the dashed hopes of the Black Power movement, the neoconservative backlash, Reagonomics, the crack epidemic (courtesy of the CIA and their Contra allies), the decimation of the inner cities, and the staggering increase in black-on-black homicide.

People are jailed by the boatloads for selling, buying, possessing. A slew of nonviolent offenders, black and brown, pack American jails. Russell Simmons leads marches against New York's mandatory minimums while the Supreme Court outlaws medicinal marijuana use for patients on their deathbed.

How much does that play into my own bouts with weed?

Depending on the setting, you can't break out a blunt like you would a beer, even though alcohol has been found to be far more destructive. There's way too much controversy still attached to *Cannabis sativa*, a controversy that hasn't receded, with a proliferation in hip-hop and mainstream society at large. I do know one thing, though.

As rap music and all its negative excesses continue to replace black culture, many of our youth are being lost in the shuffle. A friend of mine who moved to the suburbs of Atlanta shortly after I did recently found out his youngest brother, now fifteen, has taken to smoking blunts and Black and Milds and hanging out with wannabe Crips gang members. For the most part, Atlanta has never been a gang city, so I can't help but think some of these kids get their ideas from videos like Snoop Dogg's "Drop It Like It's Hot," in which the legendary West Coast MC and former Crip brags about hanging a blue flag from the left side of his back pants

pocket. This activity is not in crime-ridden Atlanta neigh-borhoods like Summer Hill (in the shadow of Turner Field), Vine City (which is in part of the AUC next to the Georgia Dome), or Simpson Road, but rather in suburbs to which parents move their kids to avoid such trappings. Maybe one day I'll have a solution.

LUTHER CAMPBELL

THE INTERVIEW 2003

Club owner. Producer. Artist. CEO. No matter what area he has worked in, sex has always been at the center. But at the same time, Luther Campbell is far more complex than what he chants over 808s on record. From his rap-inspired porn and music business to his legal battles to preserve his exploits under the First Amendment, Campbell was a poster child for censorship issues and a right-wing target for exposing hip-hop's ills. Some say he's a hero. Others say he's a misogynist. You make the call.

I never thought I'd be like this Hugh Hefner or Larry Flynt. I thought I'd be like Berry Gordy. I was him in some ways because the way I came up was similar to him. Manufacturing my own product. Distributing my own product, carrying the whole South when there was no South.

When you look at this business today, you see Luke written all over it. I created having girls in videos, this whole life for hip-hop outside of break dancing in the alley with spray-painted shirts and things like that. I brought hip-hop to life and it's still stuck where I left it at. They've done a million videos with girls. And a million videos with explicit lyrics that they weren't doing before. Everybody owns their own company. I owned my own company, but at the time no one owned their own company. You would never think that a New York artist would do an up-tempo song. You'd never thought in a million years they'd be saying what 50 Cent says on a record. I went to court for that shit.

The Jimmy Iovines, Barry Weismans, the Steve Rifkins of the world, don't have shit on me as far as knowing this business. I can stand toe to toe with any of them. The only thing they have on me is that they're white and they can sit at the table and sit with other white men. I've set the standard for what they are doing in this business. If I don't do nothing else, it will still be stuck with muthafuckas running down to South Beach with girls. They'll keep doing videos with girls running down the beach. Riding in boats with girls in videos, drinking champagne with girls in videos, talking about girls and what they can do and all that.

I actually just decided to get into [the adult entertainment industry]. I've been primed up to be the next Hugh Hefner. If you look at it from a film standpoint, you will see that the most successful mags are *Hustler, Playboy, Penthouse,* and what you see in those magazines are white women, blue-eyed women, and they're based in California. A lot of the girls who end up in those magazines are women who couldn't get into the film industry. So their angle was to get into adult entertainment and work their way back. The adult entertainment industry's music was rock and roll. The difference now is you find all types of women: black, Latino, Asian. You find all different types of women in adult entertainment.

I look at it as going from pop to urban. Ten years ago you wouldn't be excited about Jennifer Lopez. You'd want to see someone looking like Britney Spears. Ten years ago you wouldn't see a black girl in a beer commercial or in Victoria's Secret. Now, being me going the road that Hugh Hefner went, I think it's time to step it up a notch and be a leader of this industry.

I tape everything. I got sued all the time. Everybody wanted to say somebody was raping somebody. I tape in the room. I remember a time in Alabama, a girl was in the room, on the phone, talking to her girlfriends, saying, "I'm going to get this muthafucka." I had a tape on it. Got downstairs the next morning, she said, "I just want to be dropped off by the police department." I put that tape out and I said, "Okay, let's listen to something while we have breakfast." Busted her, slammed her. Dropped her off at the nearest Greyhound. It's protected me. I tape every goddamn thing. I wired up my damn house and tape the phone calls if a woman's talking to another man. If I feel like someone is full of shit, I put some cameras on them. I tape all my shows. I don't tape for pleasure. I tape for profit and protection.

There are a lot of people who are in my industry who walk by [you] every day. People have high respect for them and they don't know who they are. Now, who's running those Web sites? God only knows who they are. They could be married. They could be in church praying with you. I look at it like that. If I ever do get lucky, then the person I'm with will know me and will accept me for me. I let them all know up front.

In the case of the fiancée that I had, she understood what I was doing but she just couldn't handle it. Then there was another young lady—she was a doctor. I was extremely attracted to her. She admitted that she couldn't handle it. I'm a professional person. I run companies. It's just unfortunate that I'm in the adult entertainment industry. I tell them to come by the office and see what I do, come on down the road and see what I do. And see in that whole trial period . . . see if they can deal with it.

But it's not that they can't deal with it. It's this peer pressure from their friends. Most single women and most single men don't want to see someone else happy. For me it's extra added. Now it's more ammunition. How could you date him? He does this. They defend me in the beginning and what we have in the beginning, but it takes its toll. I always say you have to be not shallow-minded and be strong. If I do end up with someone it will be a strong relationship, even in these times with these bullshit relationships that people have.

What people don't know is they think that I like the dancing girls, the wild shit. But I don't. I like nice girls. If you look at any women I seriously date, they're laid-back and conservative. It's hard for me, really—the women that I'm really attracted to . . . they're nerved out about me.

I think I'm a better man because of the two lives that I live. I can be wild and fulfill all my curiosities, but at the same time handle my business. One girl will be lucky one day. She'll have the best of both worlds.

THE LOVE

We know what it is. We know how it feels. We know how to do it because we see it everywhere. Tight pants. Low tops. Bikini lines close cropped. Hands on ass. Palms over nipples. Sweat, moan, and groan. Sex is easy. Love is hard. How many of us can tell the difference?

REMOTE CONTROL:
ROMANCE VS. PROMISCUITY IN MAINSTREAM HIP-HOP

(PARENTAL DISCRETION REGRETTABLY ADVISED)
BY LISA PEGRAM

Have you ever seen the average American male with a remote control? Regardless of age, race, background, or class, he will flip. Some will meander. Some will browse. Some will charge like horses through endless channels. But they all flip. Women do it, too, but on the whole not quite at the rate of men. We attempt to read the menu, pick a show, and commit to it, secure that all options were efficiently reviewed to maximize viewing time without the worry that a better program may have been missed. Our stray point is at the commercials.

When I was in college, and the one girl bad-ass enough to kick it with the dudes when all the hos were dismissed . . .

> I rock rough and tough with my Afro Puffs
>
> —Lady of Rage

. . . I silently witnessed the sacred ritual as they took turns waxing many variations of one sermon: "Ain't no ass better than new ass." The congregation was mostly the brothas on athletic scholarship, imported like pandas to Liberal Arts USA from concrete jungles. Their WASP jock teammates and hippie "trouble men" hallmates brought offerings to the pews as well, and all kept the King James remix of Snoop's *Doggystyle* on their nightstands. Every man prayed to pimp like the brothas, even the brothas themselves. The communion hymn was "We Don't Love Them Hos" and when Pastor got good and right he'd holler: "Show me a fine-assed woman and I'll show you a man who's tired of fucking her." Let the church say Amen.

But I digress.

The remote control as not only a device but a philosophy represents American society's increasing appetite and commitment phobia. One of the main rituals in American life, the consumption of media, is in itself an act of promiscuity. Cable, satellite radio, DSL. Flip, flip . . . flip. We are on a collective pilgrimage for the quicker, sleeker, and smaller, and the better catered to our needs. Options, options. Love 'em and leave 'em. We surf hundreds upon thousands of channels and sites like squirrels hoarding nuts. The problem is, too often our eyes are bigger than our stomachs. This appetite is a symptom of our greater avarice, and its repetitive nature pushes "the flip" far beyond technology and into our social interactions.

ENTER HIP-HOP

Why is there more lust and obscenity than love and romance in mainstream hip-hop culture? The simple answer: mainstream pop culture as a whole in this country is more openly lustful and obscene than it has ever been. Everyone is showing his or her ass, not just black folks. On the surface, hip-hop is no different from any other art form trying to survive in the age of the bare midriff. Future pop pioneers of all shades have loaded up their wagons and embarked on a manifest destiny of The Ass: The Final Frontier. Sex sells like ketchup—it is the essential condiment. As a country, we are bursting at our puritanical seams with taboo. The thread is about to snap, and, of course, black music is a usual suspect. We have always gotten the rap for contaminating the young American public with our seething, lusty inclinations.

Peel back a few layers and you will find hip-hop compromised even further by the minstrel masks that American audiences still can't seem to let black entertainers shake. The proof is in the sales. Ever since always, our principal roles in the great American drama have pretty much been limited to Jester, Delinquent, Servant, and Sex Object. Not much room to stretch or grow without risking the dreaded flip. These images are what audiences demand for their money, and mainstream art is subject to the whims of the mob. Combine this with the history of a people who have been time and again sabotaged out of healthy romance and portrayed by the media as incapable of it, and we find ourselves inundated on all sides, all in our own way internalizing the messages these images imply.

FLIP . . . THE HISTORY CHANNEL

There are two sides to every coin, and here's the first: African Americans have not fully healed from the emotional erosion of slavery, Reconstruction, and Jim Crow. We simply haven't had enough time to do so. I dare anyone to say there would be no long-term psychological effects from such devastating blows. The Bad Old Days lasted centuries and ended only less than one century ago. The institution of slavery deliberately deformed the black family with long-term encoding. To attempt to reconstruct a home when both the man and woman have been scarred because of each other's absence is a helluva knot to untangle. We are still in exodus. Many of us have seen the glory, but many are still on the road.

FLIP, FLIP . . . THE LIFETIME NETWORK

Pussy don't fail me now,
I gotta turn this nigga out

—Missy Elliott, "P***ycat" (2002)

We inherit and internalize the types we are cast in, along with the power methodology of our society. For boys, money is power. For girls, sex is the one thing men can't refuse. It is a simple equation of supply and demand. If you want him to stay and you're (literally) sitting on a pot of gold? Give up the ass before he flips the channel! After centuries of being cast as mules, breeders, and straight-out sex objects, black women face the extra challenge of battling for basic respect from their partners, greater society, and ourselves. We were reduced to bitches and hos for ages, good for only one thing. How long did it take before a little part of us started to believe it? I live in Washington, D.C., where the ratio of women to men is 6:1. The tricks women will pull to keep a man in this town make dating look like Cirque du Soleil. It is hard to move forward when everyone around insists that you shake your ass or be dismissed.

GOOD NEWS BREAK

I'd like to take a moment to say, everybody loves Mary J. Blige so much because she manages somehow to keep it real and still be successful. Yeah, she's a singer, not an MC, but hip-hop is a major shareholder in black music today and our sound as a whole is filtered through it. Mary is a pop diva and one of the first of the Hip-Hop Generation who speaks more about the romantic despair, disappointment, and joy of young women than the tricks they turn to earn it. Mary sings the millennium blues—she wails, she moans, and the crowd goes wild. She's like that little girl in the church choir with the raw voice who shuts her eyes, unhinges her jaw, and brings the house down every time. We learned along with her that you can't lose a love you never had. And when she finally did find love, we all cheered. *One* win for the home team.

(We now return to our regularly scheduled programming, already in progress.)

FLIP . . . ESPN

And now . . . the brothas. God bless the American black man's heart!

Black men have faced the most obstacles in obtaining the "American dream," replete with all the glamorous trappings of capitalism at its best. Money. Power. Sex. For the first time, more brothers than a few have access to all three in ways they never have before. The almighty dollar has evened out the playing field, and hip-hop is one of the most lucrative musical movements of all time. Lock a starving man in a banquet room and what do you get? I can tell you he won't waste his time contemplating the significance of the mere olive to the whole. *Devour* is the operative word. Cars, mansions, gear, bling, women. Deprivation followed by excess often leads to delirium. For example, a recent group of military officers were subjected to extensive training and denied water for an extended period of time. When they were finally given water, two of them were so thirsty they drank until they drowned. Literally. Cars, mansions, gear, bling, women.

Drowning.

FLIP . . . FLIP . . . FLIP: MONEY TV

The issue of class is an important one in this examination of how black people are portrayed in the media, because the prevailing images suggest that black people are all of one caste, and therefore predisposed to the one set of cookie-cutter "ghetto experiences" that fascinate mainstream white audiences. Guns Up, Hos Down, the image is that now wealthy rappers keep it real by staying destitute in morals. You can take the nigga out of the ghetto, but you can't take the ghetto out of the nigga. But there is also the reality that the closest many black people get to the ghetto is on MTV. That is not to dismiss "ghetto life" as unworthy of representation, because it is real and its voice should be heard, but ghetto life is about more than just drive-bys and pimp slaps. And it shouldn't be the only voice heard. There is little evidence in entertainment to suggest that there are scores of black people who don't live "ghetto lives," and in a variety of ways. The few times that non-ghetto life is depicted, it is a standard "black upper-middle-class" template packed with sexual stereotypes that ultimately bring them down to a level just as base.

FLIP . . . FLIP: AMC

Just when you thought racism couldn't get any more racism-er . . .

—Foxxy Love, *Drawn Together* (Cartoon Network)

Remember, there are two sides to this coin. The aftershock of slavery is the chicken, and here's the egg: white America has always had a sore blind spot where intimacy between black folks is concerned. It is like a ten-year-old, all squeamish and grossed out at the sight of us kissing. For centuries the tendency has been to mute that channel, distort it, or block it altogether. Admitting that black people pine to be cherished, find "the one," get their hearts broken, and fall in and out of love treads dangerously close to recognizing them as "the same as me" in some people's book. In a society drunk with taboo, mysterious sexuality is a welcome distraction, and often easier to swallow than similarity. Much to their chagrin, even many über-liberals harbor some vestige of distinction between "us" and "them." (I may hang a quilt on my porch and hide you in my basement till it's safe to run free, but please don't move in next door.) The entertainment industry has long been a tool to perpetuate this neurosis. It is also fed by greater Western culture's historical proclivity of eroticizing people of color in general. Black, Asian, Latino, and other native cultures have all encountered this fixation on "uncivilized sexuality" and suffered artistic stigma and limitations because of it.

(Damn. If it's that deep, white sex must be kind of a lemon once you drive it off of the lot.)

You can't separate the image supplied from the audience that demands it. Reaching back to blues and ragtime, rednecks and bluebloods alike have craved to be black on Saturday night despite the political climate. They have always been fascinated by that deliciously nasty X factor the music employs. Can't get that nowhere else, so white audiences opted to cheat on their boundaries and keep black music as a honey on the side. The magic ingredient: funk. For all its strengths, white America was and is hopelessly square. Life may be riches or rags, privileged either way, but it sho ain't funky. Imagine the spark that first hit ignites for white youth. *Was it a snarling dusty guitar? Tiptoeing keys? A coronet that plays the notes between notes? A belly rub in silver eyeshadow and four-part harmony, or that hippie song your aunt used to pop gum to on the porch, all remixed and pimped out phat like a classic ride with hydraulics?* Black folks make everything funky—love, pain, joy, struggle, defeat, triumph. The Funk is the Force. Unfortunately, all art is subject to interpretation. Funk, in all its complexity, has been underestimated and misrepresented by mainstream audiences in every genre of black music to date. Hip-hop is heir to that legacy.

FLIP . . . THE ETYMOLOGY OF FUNK AND ROCK AND ROLL

The word *funk*, once defined in dictionaries as body odor or the smell of sexual intercourse, commonly was regarded as coarse or indecent. African American musicians originally applied *funk* to music with a slow, mellow groove, then later with a hard-driving, insistent rhythm because of the word's association with sexual intercourse. This early form of the music set the pattern for later musicians. The music was slow, sexy, loose, riff-oriented and danceable. (Wikipedia: http://en.wikipedia.org/wiki/Funk)

Jazz tunes from the early twentieth century had titles like Buddy Bolden's "Funky Butt." As words like *funk* and *funky* became more popular by mid-century when used to describe R&B, the terms were still deemed off-limits for the genteel set.

Rocking is another term with loaded meanings: Southern American gospel singers initially used the word to describe their experiences of being swept away by the Spirit. Yet by the 1940s, the term was also used to describe dancing and, barely layered under that, sex. Rocking songs were dubbed by the recording industry as "race music" and were therefore rarely played for white audiences. DJ Alan Freed broke away from this and began playing this music for his white listeners; he's credited by many with coming up with the term *rock and roll*.

If there was any question that white audiences perceive black music as sexual, just look at how they dance to it. The carnal response to black music is a key factor in the modern sex object stereotype. It is rooted in the ecstasy that the drums, bass, and minor notes inspire. White audiences can't seem to get enough, and still today are quick to use a tight groove as license to show their ass and call it dancing. Sure, black music has a nasty side like anything else, but that is not all we bring to the table. Throughout time black music has also been about struggle, faith, joy, pain, and much love. We can't help but sing deep—that's how we roll. Unfortunately, sometimes the music is interpreted as sexy even when it isn't just because of its rich sound. In *Lady Sings the Blues*, Billie Holiday talks about the trippy California audiences that would beg for that "sexy dance tune about the black bodies swayin' in the breeze" (otherwise known as "Strange Fruit"). She was appalled in that moment of all others to find herself a sex object. Come what may, black music always hits "the spot." It is that ingredient that seduces audiences and sells records.

FLIP . . . BEHIND THE MUSIC

Marvin Gaye's dream was to sing ballads like Frank Sinatra, but the industry refused. It wouldn't sell big because it wasn't "believable." He was told to sing pop and make panties fly; that's what makes money, and money is the North Star. Make enough of it and down the line you can record whatever you want. Only "down the line" is a tough row to hoe. In 1965, after much pop success, he recorded

Vulnerable, an album of gorgeous, buttery ballads in tribute to Nat "King" Cole, but it would not be released until 1997, well after his death. Gaye did go on to succeed at making important music about the jacked-up world around him: "What's Going On" was a number one hit in 1971, and "Mercy Mercy Me" (The Ecology) and "Inner City Blues (Make Me Wanna Holler)" topped charts as well. Once again, Motown had initially refused to release the album *What's Going On* because it had "no commercial potential," but (fortunately for Marvin) in the wake of the Vietnam War mainstream audiences were ripe for political criticism. His commentary was the perfect soundtrack, but lust took hold again soon after as disco emerged in the 1970s with the decadent 1980s fast on the horizon. Later in his career it was "Let's Get It On," "I Want You," and "Sexual Healing" that delivered sales to help revive the stamina of his youth.

Russell Simmons once said it best: "You can't go platinum unless you get the suburbs." Suburban trends still demand that black images be urban and full of dark, gritty grinding that ain't got nothin' to do with Starbucks. Gangstas, pimps, and hos. Even though many black people contact that way of life only on MTV, including the artists portraying it, it is a comfortable fit into the archaic stereotypes that continue to segregate us. Sure, all artists create an image, an alter ego to serve as their public face to some extent. The difference between successful white artists and artists of color is options. White artists have room to choose from a host of roles and even reinvent themselves time and again while their audiences remain loyal. The public is used to seeing a variety of white images in the media. From Marilyn Manson to Martha Stewart, they do it all. Madonna won her fame with raunchy shock factor, but when she decided to become spiritualist Madge and settle down like a proper British lady, she earned more than $50 million with her Reinvention tour alone. Then she combined the two and flipped back to a sultry sexy mama persona with *Confessions on a Dance Floor* and went platinum again. I'm afraid audiences would not extend Lil' Kim the same courtesy should she move to go natural and abandon her pasties in search of Justice, Light, and Modesty.

All of this works because money is made by sales to the mainstream masses. The reality is that the mainstream masses are white. Go figure. Can't argue with capitalism—look at the numbers. To the entertainment world, the rest of us are secondary audiences. Our wants and concerns about how we are depicted and what we want to hear or see have little credit. Supply and demand. I was watching *Tyra Banks: True Hollywood Story*, and this industry guy was gushing about how her biggest success was that she brought a huge audience to a network that before *America's Next Top Model* had no audience at all. I was stunned. UPN has always had an audience. A black one. Despite "U People Network's" somewhat minstrel lineup, black folks all over the country have tuned in since it first aired. That comment dismissed the whole black market. Not until *Top Model* was the network deemed valid, because until then white people weren't watching. Sobering thought, but not a shock.

**FLIP . . . FLIP . . . FLIP: STYLE CHANNEL
(OOOH! *AMBUSH MAKEOVER!*)**

Back in the day we got away with croonin' about love, romance, hope, and life because politics blocked access to the music. Whether the music was live or recorded, the thrill was in the chase. Once they found us, they took a seat and ordered the special. Now that mainstream audiences have full access to black music, the chase must be remixed to keep 'em coming back for more. The industry projects depravity as the "black factor" that secures the market. Today we sell

YOU, not your music. That way you talk, dress, and walk is fabric for a fan's costumes. They want to be you because you are nothing like them. Make them wanna be you and they will buy the costume. They will buy YOU. A costume ain't a costume if it looks just like them. It's an outfit.

Imagine if the dominant image portrayed of white people by the media was the type of folks you see on *Jerry Springer.* If you were a Springer fan, it might be difficult to imagine that articulate, respectable white folks existed. Even if you encountered one, you might just think they were a fluke, a ruse, or simply not as entertaining as what you were used to, and take your dollars somewhere more "authentic." That is how the entertainment industry brands artists of color. You settle for one of a few predictable roles just to work and keep booties in the seats, the album/film strikes gold, and suddenly your continued success hinges on your dancing that jig. That is as true now as it's ever been. Josephine Baker to Beyoncé is more of a hop or a skip than a jump. Dorothy Dandridge to Halle Berry ain't so far of a stretch, either. Berry got the Oscar, but for what role, and what compelling roles have you seen her in since? Now ask yourself the same question about Charlize Theron.

FLIP . . . E! CHANNEL

Speaking of Oscar, here we are live on the red carpet, where Love is made, laid, betrayed, and passéd. Just ahead, Jamie Foxx, who won a nod from the Academy for his stunning portrayal of the music icon Ray Charles. Soon after breaking this formidable barrier, Jamie released the equally stunning first single from his debut album. The title: "Unpredictable," with a heavy emphasis on the "DIC," which makes it anything but. Verse by verse, Jamie proves in explicit detail that the more things change, the more they stay the same.

The heavy dose of lust attributed to mainstream hip-hop culture is the same prescribed to every incarnation of mainstream American black music to date. Young white audiences have always patronized our cutting-edge styles and used them as a vehicle for rebellion and experimentation. The protest from parents, politicians, and critics has always been, "It is evil, lustful, and entices the pure to sin." We've heard it all before and are likely to hear it again. In earlier times, black music was able to maintain some modicum of dignity because the times themselves were less vulgar (at least where sex is concerned). It was considered nasty just because it was black. That was then, this is now. Romance is lacking in hip-hop because it is lacking in American culture as a whole. In this remote control dynasty, 50 percent of marriages end in divorce, and that record has held strong for the Hip-Hop Generation's entire lifetime. The concept of true love sometimes seems "retro" these days on all fronts. Flip to the E! channel any day and I rest my case. Anyway, it all boils down to black folks shaking their moneymakers then, now, and, if we don't do something about it, forever.

FLIP . . . BRAVO

Art reflects life. Hip-hop is black music is popular culture. A renaissance. It is our blues, our jazz, our rock and roll, and our generation's birthmark on the American experience. It was born and raised in a project village among distant relatives and negligent neighbors and still not only survived, but thrived. I give props to our people for being so talented, determined, and business-savvy. Between remote controls and global communication, hip-hop is like the British Empire: the sun never sets on it. We've conquered quantity, now what about quality? As the music industry's genie of the lamp ("Phenomenal Cosmic Power . . . itty bitty living space"), we need to figure out what we are doing with that power.

Individually, we have learned to succeed. However, our sense of the greater good weakens with each generation. How we agree to communicate with each other across gender lines is also about community. Black love is like the Washington Monument, impressive but heavy, and sinking fractions of a centimeter every year into the camouflaged swampland beneath it. We have freedom of speech when two generations ago you could swing by the neck for speaking truth. Now we take that gift and translate "Daddy's home" into "Guess who's back in the muthafuckin' house with a fat dick for your muthafuckin' mouth?" Folks were crucified in the battle against calling a grown man "boy" or a grown woman "gal." We turn around, pair that medal of honor with platinum shackles and coiffles, and use its power to exercise the right to call each other "ho" and "dawg." So in the end, are we choosing to be a bitch and a buck after all? And let us not forget that the veterans of those fights are still living. They are our grandparents, our parents even, yet we claim not to understand why they can't look at what we've accomplished, despite the billion-dollar profits, and be PROUD? Ungrateful is ungrateful.

These days, intimate relations for all people on all fronts are a less than savory state of affairs. I'm not charging hip-hop with the total bill, but it damn sure ordered more than water and a side salad. We can do better, and, with multimillion-dollar record sales, we can afford to leave a fat tip. As the keepers of our music, we have got to take a stand about how we will allow ourselves to be portrayed to the world. A line must be drawn and protected. What are they gonna do, outlaw black music? Been there, done that, seen how successful it is. How could we of all people dare *not* use the music to inspire other folks (and ourselves) to get some real good lovin', as long as we've been denied it? It's like coming out of the desert to the sea and choosing to stay dry.

In the abundance of water the fool is thirsty.

—Bob Marley

Remote control exists in our insatiable need to flip and in the hand that programs the hundreds of channels we choose from. Our shared prejudices act as antennae in our reception of that programming. "When it comes to environments and individuals, it is up to environments to adjust because they are bigger with more resources," said Professor Kianda Bell of American University. We all saw *Crash*. No American is immune to the baggage that saturates the foundation of our environment, but we should work on getting over it already. The media is the lens through which we view ourselves and the world, but just like cable, we pay a lot to flip for hours and still find nothing decent to watch. Maybe we should all just turn off the box and read a book.

ICE-T

Hip-hop's triple threat, Ice-T began as one of the first in L.A.'s hard-core rap scene. Musically he morphed into a lucid gangster/pimp persona at large, which somehow translated into major TV and film roles. Ironically, he tends to play hardened, street-savvy cops. Always one to push conventions, Ice-T ventured into heavy metal with 1992's "Cop Killer," a song protesting the police brutality that was unveiled by the Rodney King beating. The song drew a conservative-pushed campaign for censorship, enraged law enforcement, and ultimately caused Ice-T to be dropped from Warner Brothers. Outspoken and politically brash, Ice-T is as praised for his wit as for his musical past. Now an old G, by hip-hop standards, here Ice-T muses over the trajectory of his career.

The show (*Law and Order SVU*) turned out to be cool for me. I've been on it three years. When they called me to do this show, I kind of immediately told them I couldn't do it, 'cause I didn't really want to pull fourteen hours, sometimes seventeen hours a day, every day. That's a lot of work,

[but] they pay per episode, so that's kind of how they got me to do the show. I said fuck it, I'll try it and relocate out here. I've been out here for three years. It's been cool, [but] it's definitely been an adjustment, 'cause I was going through stuff in L.A. I had been with my girl for going on sixteen years, and a year ago we separated. As a man I think you go through different zones, and the cool thing about me and Darlene's relationship is we kind of like grew away from each other by me not being around that much. Of course, a woman's gonna want a cat that'll be there for her, and in this lifestyle you just can't be there. The good thing about us, by being together for so long it was very smooth. Nobody's mad, everybody's cool. It was just like, "Yo baby, I'm gonna do me. You gonna do you. Just keep it gangsta." But then being out here by yourself, that's another zone in itself, too. It's a different game, but it's cool. I got a new girl now so I'm happy. It shouldn't be totally about relationships, but at the end of the day, basically that's what it is. Whether you're gonna be happy with yourself or with somebody else.

I'm pretty mellow right now considering I've been in the game like twenty years and I'm still in it. I still be on the streets and ten-year-old kids be screaming "Ice-T!" I'm like, "How the fuck do y'all know who I am?" I'm an old-school rapper, but somehow through films and television, the resurgence of hip-hop, *Pimps Up, Ho's Down*, whatever, these little kids know who I am. That's gangsta to me, 'cause a lot of my peers they've forgotten.

I crossed a lot of boundaries in my career. When I first got into rap, I didn't think you could make no money rapping. I was rapping for the fuck of it in the club after we had hustled all day and got paper, and I would just run up in the club and say what we did that day on the mic. Next thing you know I'm in a movie called *Breakin'*, 'cause they came in the club we was partying in and that led to a record deal, which led to what they called gangsta rap. I tried to rap early like the rappers did, like, "Hey, go [to] the party and hands in the air" and all that. My friends, we were so thug, they was like, "Nigga, what are you rapping about?"

But nobody rapped about bitches and hos and guns and drugs and shit, so I was like fuck it, lemme try it, and the crowd kinda dug it. I used to pay my way on the mic. We would walk in the clubs and they'd be like "No rapping," and we would throw the DJ five hundred dollars and I would have the mic all night. Sitting in the booth, talking shit about what we was drinking and shit in L.A. You gotta do that if you want to get over anywhere. First you gotta be a star in your own town.

Then I got a chance to do *New Jack City*, which was the first like real big hip-hop rapper going into acting, and then doing the TV and the rock, I kinda like spread myself across the culture for a while. And I think one of the things that gets me a lot of respect, though, is people know it wasn't easy for me. They know that every time I did something somebody was yelling "Shut it down!" I'm an outspoken cat, and I'm glad of the things I said in my career, 'cause it would've been a waste to go so far and to have said nothing.

I was influenced by Melle Mel and *The Message*. That was the record that let me know you could say something on a record versus just party. Eminem will tell you the first rap record he ever heard was *Reckless*, and to me that was an honor. I call Eminem the bastard son of a thousand gangsta rappers.

What I do is gangsta rap and it's apolitical. It's basically written from the point of view of a gangster, but now, honestly, truthfully, though, sometimes I just hear too much and I'm just like, C'mon. There is an art to it. To me the art is making it visual like Biggie could do it. Like I feel 50 Cent. It's not everybody that can pull this shit off.

It's another form of rap. It's an acquired taste. Nobody knocks on your door and makes you listen to it, and the trip is, no matter how hard you make it, it ain't hard enough for somebody. Somebody out there thinks M.O.P. is soft [laughs]. Do we gotta step out the record and murder you in your house?

The first kinda hip-hop scene that we had in L.A. was more of a big dance party scene run by Uncle Jamm's Army. It was more like a techno, funk scene. Bobcat was part of that, who ended up being a DJ for LL. They used to throw big parties and actually pack the L.A. Sports Arena, seven thousand kids dancing, and Egyptian Lover was like the first DJ on the West Coast to scratch. While the New York kids were breaking, the kids in L.A. were popping. We didn't have a name for it—it was like street dancing. I was like the first person to rap in L.A. on a stage like New York rappers with lyrics, because then they were like chanting. It was different.

I used to rap over New York beats and they would diss me, like, "Yo, you doing that New York shit." But what happened was I started rapping about the L.A. scene, and truthfully, there were gangs out there, so instead of rhyming about partying, I just came on the stage like, "Yo, what sets in the house? Throw your rags up, just banging on the stage." And they was like, "Oh, this is us!" And that's when "6'n the Morning" and all that shit jumped off. Now I remember for a fact when I came to New York in the early eighties and I was rapping like that, the New York cats told me I couldn't rap like that. I came out here to try to get my record *You Don't Quit* played. "6'n the Morning" was the B side. Scott La Rock, Red Alert, was playing it at Union Square and Latin Quarter, [but] a lot of New York cats was like, "You can't call girls bitches." New York really wasn't on that shit. The women out here had niggas in check. So we came with the hard shit. The first group out here that really came hard to me was a group called Mob Style. But they was down with Alpo—them was some real gangsters out of Harlem. They was talking crazy, 'cause their album cover had triple beams and coke, but eventually New York caught on and started doing it.

It's all good. It's family to me. I'm happy to say it moved on, 'cause a lot of the genres of hip-hop . . . the hard core is what's really been going the longest.

THE CANE

All bitches are the same. And they better have our money. Big brims. Blinged canes. Controlling her makes him "The Man," even if it kills them both in the end.

CASHMERE THOUGHTS

BY MICHAEL A. GONZALES

-1-

Diamond in the back, sunroof top
diggin' the scene with a gangster lean
—William DeVaughn, "Be Thankful for What You Got," from
Be Thankful for What You've Got (1974)

Ever since I was nine years old, I've wanted to be a pimp. Of course, at the time my innocent mind knew nothing about the mathematics of street culture: the money, honey, or viciousness of the scene. In my brain, "the Game," as the art of hustling was called, was all about styling, profiling, and swaggering like an Afroed blaxploitation superstar.

In the early 1970s, when I first peeped the true players chilling in front of the Shalimar barbershop in Harlem at 123rd Street and 7th Avenue, life just wasn't the same afterward. Having seen *Super Fly* that summer at the Loew's Victoria on 125th Street, a decaying bijou a few doors down from the Apollo Theater, I wanted to be as in vogue as the peacock pimps I passed on the block.

Even though a few years before I had bugged Mommy for

a Black Power beret and a dashiki, by 1972 every kid on the block wanted to be down with the loud suits, feathered hats, and candy-colored platform shoes that defined that funky flared soul generation. The last ambassadors of black elegance, those brothers were slicker than a can of oil.

The Shalimar was a mack daddy lounge with a barbershop of the same name next door. The men who hung in front of the spot, with their sleek Cadillacs painted in screaming colors and sporting flashy hubcaps, were a sight to see. But, unlike the pimps in parodies of recent years (no matter how much I enjoyed *Pootie Tang*, it was still a joke), these dudes were as serious as James Brown's cold sweat dripping on his good foot.

My stepfather, whom I called "Daddy," had been cutting hair at the Shalimar since I was a kid. The air inside the shop smelled of stale cigarettes, and there was a colorful LeRoy Neiman poster of Muhammad Ali taped to the back wall. On the cluttered counter was a small FM radio that was always tuned to "Stereo in Black," WBLS, and the freak flag soul of the Jackson Five, James Brown, and Stevie Wonder blared through the shop. Underfoot, the worn linoleum was the color of piss, a floor from which I came to sweep the naps a couple of days a week after class.

From eleven A.M. until eight P.M., Daddy styled the 'dos of Harlem luminaries that included smooth balladeer Billy Eckstine, b-ball hustler Pee Wee Kirkland, gangster legend Nicky Barnes, and "that evil, one-eyed son of a bitch" Sammy Davis Jr. (as Daddy called him). Although he was only five-six, he handled himself like a giant. The palms of his hands would be blood red from the lye in the perm mix (anyone who has seen the classic conk scene in *Malcolm X* knows that the harsh ingredients can burn like hell). After thirty years in Harlem (the earlier of which he'd spent creeping down desolate streets at dusk and sleeping on cold tar rooftops as an abandoned adolescent), he still had a Rican accent as thick as mondongo.

In addition to the other four jabber-jawed haircutters in the shop, there was a shoeshine dude named Gee Whiz and a fine-as-cherry-wine manicurist named Duriella du Fontaine. Having known the honey-complexioned Duriella since she was a dimpled child with a Kodak smile, Daddy had given her the job after she graduated from George Washington High School.

"Duriella's a good kid," he explained to Delroy, the beer-bellied Jamaican barber who clipped heads next to him soon after he'd hired her. "She wants to make a little money before going to secretarial school."

"Don't you think she might be kind of young to be around this crazy crew of bad boys?" Delroy sighed. "I wouldn't want my daughter around some of these fools that come through that door."

"She's a good kid," Daddy reassured him. "Got a good head, a good brain. This is not forever for her, just a small stop before she goes back to school next year. Don't worry. Everything will be fine. Her mama raised her right."

It was love at first sight from the day I saw Duriella's hypnotic hazel eyes. A redbone chick with swaying hips and buxom breasts, she could make a blind boy see and a mute man holler. "You're so cute," she'd say when I brought her a pocket full of Hershey's kisses or cellophane-wrapped peppermints from my grandma's crystal candy dish.

Pretending to be shy, I savored her attention. When I'd come in to sweep the joint or run errands, I'd silently stare at du Fontaine's flawless face and create scenarios of a better tomorrow, when Duriella would be my wife. As far as I knew, she had no man, which made her the perfect prey for wolf whistles and lewd remarks every time she stiletto-stepped down Seventh Avenue.

Four days out of the week Duriella cooed to the barber-shop crew, but come Friday afternoons she only had eyes for one customer, and that was the sharp-as-a-tack mack who went by the moniker Deacon Blue. Dark as the night, with gray eyes colder than a Mr. Softee cone and a wiry frame that moved like a serpent's, Deacon Blue was a slick-talking son of a preacher man.

Hailing from the mean streets of Detroit, with smooth soul in his strut and satin in his language, Blue reminded one of a cool Motown groove with Marvin Gaye on the mic. The Deacon reeked of Brut and charisma, and everything in his wardrobe, from his wide-brimmed fedora to the spar-kling sapphire on his pinkie finger and stylish shoes on his feet, was some shade of blue. With his suits custom tailored by a cigar-chomping Cuban who had a thing for Italian silk and double-knit polyester, Deacon prided himself on having the finest vines in the hood and a skill with knives and straight razors that was the stuff of Harlem legend.

After getting his hair conked in Daddy's chair, Blue would slide over to du Fontaine's side of the shop and plant himself in the hard plastic chair to have his nails clipped and buffed.

"Baby, I'm too cool to be a genius, but I'm smart enough to wanna make you mine," he proclaimed to her. "A fine bad bitch like you needs a pretty bro like Blue to show what to really do."

Dressed to thrill in brown suede go-go boots and a match-ing mini, Duriella fluttered her long lashes. "You already got enough girls," she joked. There was a musical lilt to her voice. "There's no way I could fit in."

Every time Deacon dipped into the sanctuary of the Shal-imar, he tried to verbally snag his prey from a different an-gle, dazzling her with promises of diamonds, pearls, and trips around the world. He was determined, and sweet

Duriella was just young enough to fall victim to the bullshit. A few months later, I walked into the Shalimar on a winter afternoon and there was a different foxy lady squatting where Ms. du Fontaine usually sat.

"Where did Duriella go?" I asked Daddy.

Always a smart-ass, another barber named Eddie Mitchell blurted the answer before Pops opened his mouth. "Ain't gonna see that one no more . . . She done joined the Deacon's congregation."

From the radio, the mellow voice of Frankie "Hollywood" Crocker introduced Issac Hayes's cappuccino-smooth "Cafe Reggio"; Daddy's face tensed. "Don't talk to my son like he's some hustler," he screamed, stabbing steely ice picks into Eddie's chest with his wild eyes. "He's nine years old! He don't need to know about stuff like that!"

"Sorry, Carl," Eddie mumbled shamefully. Closing my eyes, I envisioned a smiling Duriella du Fontaine lounging in the front seat of Blue's aqua-hued Eldorado as it sailed down the tarred ocean of 125th Street. She was clad in the fiercest furs, and her smooth neck was dripping with diamonds.

It wouldn't be until watching *The Mack* a year later that I fully understood the kind of parallel black metropolis that Deacon Blue and Duriella du Fontaine existed within, and it wasn't the pretty city in my dreams. "Don't be sorry," Daddy replied to Eddie's apology. "Be careful."

-2-

Give a bitch some dough,
she subject to go crazy.

—Pretty Tony, *The Mack* (1973)

Spring 1973. The orange-hued poster for *The Mack* hung in the lobby of the Tapia Theater for two weeks before the movie finally opened. As a fan of graphic illustration, from album covers to comic books, I was enticed by the image of a bold brother wearing a snow white fur coat, matching hat, and shades, and carrying a gold-handled walking stick. The man was flanked by girls handing him money, a gold-colored Caddie was in the background, and the teaser text stated, "Now that you've seen the rest . . . make way for [large boxy letters] The Mack." Twenty-five years later, comic book artist Bill Sienkiewicz would sample the same style for RZA's 1998 *Bobby Digital* album.

A live-action Harlem version of the Fat Albert gang, my crew was inseparable. A motley medley of black boys that included Kyle, Beedie, Marvin, Daryl, and my little brother, Los (who was called Perky in those days), we all lived in the same prewar building at 628 West 151st Street.

There was always a double feature at the Tapia. Paying seventy-five cents each at the door, the entire crew would troop in at noon and get lost in the cinematic sauce of krazy karate flicks, bugged-out American International movies about dogs robbing banks, an adorable killer rat named Ben, and crazy cracker movies called *Macon County Line, Grand Theft Auto,* and *White Lightning.* And, of course, there was the boogie of blaxploitation.

As a generation coming into our own, most of us separated from our fathers, we began to look at these so-called black action flicks as the perfect Saturday-afternoon surrogates for the men we didn't have at home. Stepping into the theater, the gang walked across the hideous carpet, a multicolored nightmare covered with space-age designs and soda stains. An ornate chandelier (from the theater's more glorious past—when it was still called the Dorset) hung from the lobby ceiling.

After flirting with the pretty concession chicks while buying popcorn and Cokes, we rushed to the middle seats on the left-hand side of the theater to watch *The Mack*. A mushroom cloud of reefer hovered over the theater. Simply breathing was enough to get you stoned. Yet, from the moment Max Julien's sad face filled the screen, I observed a kind of existential indifference about the character of Goldie. Stepping out of prison into a world ripe with crime, this former car thief and drug addict soon reinvented himself as the coldest pimp in the Bay Area.

Outside the few blocks that was Goldie's entire universe, the rest of the world was just part of the game on the road to fame. But as much as Goldie seemed to relish his reality, he still chided a small child who wanted to be like him. "I don't ever want to hear you say that," he scolded. Handing out dollar bills, Goldie encouraged the kids to stay in school.

Slouched in my seat and sipping on a Coke, I was instantly seduced by this shadowy world of gambling spots, players' balls, and the establishing of a stable of hot hookers. I was intrigued by the image of Goldie training the chicks to shoplift and later putting them out on the ho stroll. Watching the black barbershop scene with the rival pimp Pretty Tony, I was instantly reminded of how the Shalimar was filled with the same kind of bad-ass sarcasm and player insight.

Twenty years later, *The Mack* has become a classic signpost for pimping in pop culture, being an obvious influence on Snoop Dogg (on his debut *Doggystyle* he speaks the lines: "You ain't no pimp. You a rest haven for hos"), Quentin Tarantino (the crazed white pimp character Drexl Spivey in *True Romance*, while watching the blubbery bare breast scene from *The Mack*, says, "I know I'm pretty, but I ain't as pretty as two titties"), and countless other artists.

Yet the fact that at the end of the feature "the mack" is

penniless, motherless, and ho-less is never even mentioned by those who romanticize the pimp lifestyle of the film. And while *The Mack* (much like *Super Fly* and *Willie Dynamite*) could be seen as a cautionary tale advising against the dead-end world of crime, for most viewers that significant message failed to penetrate.

-3-

It safer to be a drug dealer than a pimp; at least a drug dealer doesn't have to worry about a kilo of coke shooting him in the chest.

—Ice-T

According to mack legend, the first black pimps in America can be traced back to the southern plantations of yesteryear. While some blind, guitar-plucking joker was lounging on a log, laying down the Brer Rabbit rap to the lil' nappy-haired pickaninnies, a Barry White–size buck was in the slave quarters, scribbling down the rules of the Game.

Noted author Cecil Brown, who waxes poetic about old-school outlaw (pimp) culture in *Stagolee Shot Billy* (2003), has this to say:

The slave master was perceived by the male slaves as not working and having control of all the women, both black and white. After the Civil War, when blacks came into the cities, they adopted that role for their own employment.

In other words, it was as if they were merely trying to crack the capitalist codes for survival in a world of supply and demand.

Though it's been more than two hundred years since the party days of black folks' emancipation, in the words of Oaktown native Too $hort, brothers still believe they were "born to mack." The cult of pimpdom looms large in the public imagination. From cartoons to cars, the Technicolor sparkle of Planet Pimp has spread like a virus through the psyche of America. As with drug addiction, some brothers just can't say no.

Regular men who work nine-to-five slave jobs are mystified by the pimp's power and awed by his noir narcissism. As comic Chris Rock pointed out in one of his routines, we want to know, "What do pimps say?" To this day, I find pimp poetics endlessly fascinating. In fact, the only other people I know who have as much voodoo in their verbal game are rappers, black homosexuals, and preachers. As pimp laureate Iceberg Slim, an author, once said, "I sexed more hos with conversation than I ever did with penis or tongue."

For many hip-hop hedonists, including myself, the fantasy of pimping is as euphoric as a dozen red roses delivered to your girl on Valentine's Day. At home, as wives or lovers scream over the roar of the television, we slip into a trance of an alternative lifestyle that includes lushness, loot, and sexual promiscuity.

In the minds of most men, the pimp aesthetic represents a sense of power without moral conscience. While we might understand that it's wrong to slap a woman or place her in dangerous situations simply for the love of money, in pimp mode these rules of restraint no longer apply. To swipe a phrase from the title of the autobiography of underrated scribe Chester Himes, "a pimp's life is one of absurdity."

For the so-called square or lame fantasizing about the Game, there is a constant allure of the siren songs blaring from the battered jukeboxes stashed in the black under-world. The problem with turning these desperado aspirations into reality is a matter of anger and viciousness. Without a doubt, the brutal behavior of a true pimp can be viewed as chauvinistic and misogynistic—although in player parlance, neither of these words exists.

A bona fide pimp isn't about trying to get booty. He just wants to get paid. Most true pimps must have genuine hatred in their hearts, for the lame world and for their own whores. Iceberg Slim told an interviewer from the *Los Angeles Free Press* in 1972, "The career pimps I knew were utterly ruthless and brutal without compassion. They certainly had a hatred for women."

These days, the simplistic images of pimpdom perpetrated in the rap videos lead one to believe that all it takes to get a degree in pimpology is a gaudy goblet overflowing with designer champagne, the riotous roar of the latest rap soundtrack, and some bling-bling gleaming from your wrist.

-4-

I made pimping a full-time job,
so bitches wouldn't have to rob

—Big Daddy Kane, "Big Daddy vs. Dolemite," from
Taste of Chocolate (1990)

As his big black limo rolled through the sprawl of downtown Los Angeles in the summer of 2000, legendary rapper Ladies Love Cool James lounged in the buttery backseat. With his muscles bulging and trademark Kangol tilted to the side, he resembled a b-boy Adonis with a permanent smirk. LL moistened his thick lips with a quick wipe of his tongue and became more relaxed than the mack, and just as cool.

Dressed in a stylish crimson and ivory FUBU sweatsuit and white Nikes, LL clicked on the radio. Ironically, as we passed a quartet of men returning from the Gay Pride Parade, the piercing roar of LL's labelmate Jay-Z erupted from our car's speakers. As the post-bop bang of "Big Pimpin' " blared, LL nodded his cap-covered head and stared out the window. Yet when the reigning king of New York City recited the now classic line "Big pimpin', we spending G's . . . ," LL laughed uproariously.

"If you ask me," LL said, "Jay-Z sounds like he is doing more tricking than pimping."

-5-

Dressed to kill her physique is ill
face belongs on a dollar bill

—LL Cool J, "Fast Peg," from *Walking with a Panther*

(1989)

Winter 1999. Many men talk about being pimps, but very few ever mention being a trick. Who are these men who have no problem paying for sex, whether getting their "knob slobbed" in their office, or waiting for the Rolexxx (a favorite Miami strip spot) girls to perform, or getting a dirty "wall dance" in Detroit? Yet in the days before rap, "tricks" were thought of as victims, hence the name. Whether one was "tricked" out of a few drinks at the bar or a fistful of twenties in some hotel, the bottom line was that "pimps got paid and tricks got played."

Hip-hop has helped to make hypersexuality a part of our personal lives. Whereas once a man might have been content to fantasize about the bodies of beautiful girls in the pages of *Playboy* or *Players* (whose parent company, Holloway House, published both Iceberg Slim and Donald

Goines), they were now flocking to swing clubs, strip spots, and brothels with no shame in their game. A female friend recently confessed that her ex-boyfriend could get an erection only with hookers.

Certainly, one must also wonder who these women are who ply their bedroom skills into sex-trade thrills? Like snowflakes, no two whores are alike. There are those who hump for the easy cash, others who need loot to re-up their drug stash, and more than a few who believe their options are severely limited. Many of the minority strippers/working girls I've met in N.Y.C. hailed from depressed communities all over the world. Most of them are just "poor" women trying to make a buck. For them it's just a job.

These days in New York, the culture of whores has predominantly moved from the streets to underground black booty clubs and aboveground apartment houses. In Manhattan-based spots like the now closed Medallions in Midtown (which was directly across the street from DJ Premier's legendary D&D Studios) and Hot Cocoa's wild parties at the Mark Ballroom in Union Square, loud rap music provided the soundtrack for the evenings and early mornings.

Unlike the more upscale strip clubs like Flashdancers and Scores, the black underground places had the feeling of Sodom and Gomorrah with a hip-hop soundtrack. As The Notorious B.I.G. or the latest R. Kelly blared from the speakers, a diverse multitude ranging from homeboys to hip-hop insiders to movie stars crowded into these spots. One night, I peeped an ebony and ivory screen-team checking out the sweaty hoochies at a Cocoa party. "*Money Train* is in the house!" the ecstatic DJ screamed.

Walking around like wet-dream brokers in various states of undress, the big-booty black and Latina girls who work these clubs reminded one of the freaky dancers in a Hype Williams video: short skirts, high heels, thick thighs, wild weaves, and lusty lipstick. These chicks channeled everything they've learned from Lil' Kim, Foxy Brown, and Trina. Spending all their cheese, the brothers felt as though they were living the street dreams that Nas rapped about.

Leaving the club one night, still horny after watching fine naked sisters parading through the spot, I needed some one-on-one attention. Picking up a *Village Voice*, I sat down in a late-night dive called Infernos and flipped through the back pages of the paper (which were filled with a rainbow coalition of hos). Making a rash decision, I called a brothel called Lush Ladies from my cell phone.

Lush Ladies was an "in-call" spot, which was a modern way of saying a brothel. The building's neighbors, I later learned, were paid off so they wouldn't complain about the traffic of single men steadily filing through the front door. I made an appointment for two A.M. and downed two dirty martinis before venturing into the night.

Located, ironically for me, around the corner from an ex-girlfriend's apartment, the Lush Ladies pad was a medium-size residence in the east twenties—an upwardly mobile neighborhood filled with yuppies straight out of a Jay McInerney novel. I was met at the door by a buxom white chick named Savannah, who inquired in a southern accent if I was a cop. As an added precaution, she frisked me thoroughly. I was of course clean.

As she guided me through the spacious apartment, I heard the blissful moans of a satisfied customer from behind a closed door. "Take off your clothes and I'll be right back," Savannah said.

"How is this done?" I asked. Savannah snickered as she walked out the door.

There was a framed psychedelic pop art picture in the room, painted by Peter Max, showing a silhouette of a woman's angular face and the word *LOVE* boldly painted in blue letters. After stripping down to my boxer shorts, I took a seat in a black leather La-Z-Boy next to the full-size bed.

In a matter of minutes, Savannah returned with five fly black females. As each negligee-clad chick was introduced by her given moniker (Fire, Dream, et al.), she politely said hello. Overwhelmed, I chose an Amazonian light-skinned babe with almond-shaped eyes, named Peg. She wore silver hoop earrings, and her thick black hair flowed to her broad shoulders.

Peg was a curvy chick who couldn't have been much older than nineteen, with skin the color of butterscotch. When she spoke, I could see her silver tongue ring. With thick, smooth legs and an ample ass, Peg wore a crimson-colored teddy with matching mules that strapped around the ankles. She lit a cinnamon-scented candle on the dresser and turned off the lights. Lounging across the bed, she asked, "So, why did you pick me?" For such a gorgeous girl, her voice sounded insecure.

"Well," I began, and sat next to her. Peg smelled as though she had taken a bath in rose petals. "I thought you were the most attractive." From a neighboring room one of the girls blasted *The Miseducation of Lauryn Hill*. The luminous music seeped through the wall. "Where you from?"

"So what are you looking for?" Peg asked, lustfully licking her full lips.

"Looking for?" I asked. "What you mean?"

"I mean, you want a golden shower or S and M, or—"

"Naw, that's too freaky for me. How about just regular sex. Or is that extra?"

She pulled the teddy over her head and tossed it on the floor. Peg smiled, and opened her fleshy legs. From the next room I heard fingers snapping, and then realized it was Lauryn Hill and D'Angelo's "Nothing Even Matters." I gently licked sweat from her neck, and Peg moaned.

Reaching under the pillow, she pulled out a condom. With slender fingers, Peg slipped on the rubber. Before moving her hand, she placed my prick into her mouth. I felt the stud of her tongue ring moving thrillingly along the shaft. For the next half hour, the world was a beautiful place.

After I came, we lay in a heap on the crinkled sheets. There was a warm feeling between me and Peg; I felt a tenderness that I wanted to believe went beyond the purely trick/whore transaction. I looked at my watch. There were ten minutes left in my hour. Rubbing Peg's full breasts, I gently kissed her nipples and cherished those few moments before I would again be walking the lonely streets of the city.

Though that hour with Peg will live forever in my sexual memory, I did feel a slight shame as I trekked to the subway that chilly night. The image of pimps is all about making loot, but here I was, two hundred dollars broker than when I awoke that morning. Moments later, standing on the downtown platform waiting for the Brooklyn train, I reasoned that while paying for pussy was far from the worst thing on the planet, I would rather be clockin' dollars than giving them away.

-6-

Time to separate the pros from the cons,
the platinum from the bronze,
that butter-soft shit from that leather on the Fonz
  —Jay-Z, "Brooklyn's Finest," from *Reasonable Doubt* (1996)

It was a humid Indian summer afternoon in October 1997 when I first hooked up with Jay-Z. For months I had blasted his debut disc, *Reasonable Doubt,* inside my book-cluttered office. Feeling the cool sea of Jay's complex storyteller style splash against my earholes, I savored the brutal poetics and mean metaphors that described the drug rings, pimp dreams, and player schemes of his hood.

From the hot ice of the brother's voice and the buttery bop of his metaphors, we knew Jay-Z was a pimp before he even showed his true colors on "Cashmere Thoughts." Much as there was with my favorite eighties microphone fiend Big Daddy Kane (who was also an early mentor to young Shawn Carter—the nigga's real name), there was a genuine gritty humor and smoothness to his style.

Riding alongside Jay, one could almost imagine the young wannabe MC in his Brooklyn bedroom, blasting Big Daddy ("Twenty-four sev chilling, killing like a villain," he spat on the seminal single "Raw") while absorbing the blaxploitation beauty of Kane's lyrics.

In Kane's day, with crack controlling the wild streets and weak minds of chocolate cities across America in the late 1980s and early 1990s, the potent drug became the new mack. Unlike in the pimp/ho golden years from a decade past, the streets where one's stables once strolled had become overrun with a different kind of fiend.

As director Spike Lee revealed in *Jungle Fever,* with the drug-addicted hijinx subplot of Gator and Vivian, addicted chicks were sucking dick at a discount. "You know what a pimp is these days?" my homeboy Smiley joked after seeing the flick. "One crackhead and his crackhead girlfriend." Still, that didn't hinder Kane from setting the foundation for future microphone macks.

Perhaps what Jay-Z learned from those many hours of listening to Big Daddy Kane was how to lyrically articulate like a mack (whose affected speech patterns, if fused with the hard funk of James Brown/George Clinton/Rodger Troutman instrumentals, would sound like a song) without behaving like a minstrel.

As Jay-Z zoomed with me up Brooklyn's notorious Myrtle (Murder) Avenue in a black Range Rover, I caught glimpses of the stark backdrop visuals that propelled his aural pimped-out persona: sweaty Bed-Stuy black boys playing basketball and clamorous corner boys chugging cheap brew, older women tiredly dragging themselves (stooped shoulders, aching feet) from the subway station and pretty young girls pushing baby strollers down the soiled sidewalk, crack fiends fluttering in doorways, and police sirens screaming in the distance.

"This ghetto is a part of me," he said, turning down the radio. "But I refuse to record a song about people getting killed every two minutes. That's not real. We have cookouts, family picnics, and our friends. All of us are just trying to maintain our balance in the anarchy that surrounds us.

"When I was younger I used to be rolling up this block, riding real slow and playing a Donny Hathaway album real loud," he confessed. "I thought that was the coolest thing in the world, because it looked like a movie. You know, like a character from *Scarface* or *The Mack*."

Moments after telling the story, he parked the ride in front of his former stomping grounds, Marcy Projects. Although he no longer lived there, his sisters still dwelled on the fifth floor. After greeting a few of his homeboys, including protégé Memphis Bleek, he directed me into the building's dank hallway. Stepping into the elevator that smelled of urine and reefer, Jay pressed the button and the doors closed. "You know, everything I come across in my life is used as material," he said. "I would have to say the one writer that inspired me the most was Iceberg Slim."

A pimp is really a whore who's reversed the Game on whores.

Iceberg Slim, *Pimp* (1969)

Nobody does a better mack daddy impersonation than Fab Five Freddy. "What's up, player?" he asks, his voice a cool growl. "Ain't heard from ya in a while, player—hope you ain't slacking in your pimping." Once dubbed "the all-purpose art nigga" by his buddy Russell Simmons, the Bed-Stuy native (born a generation before Jay-Z or The Notorious B.I.G.) has been involved in everything from fine art to fine honeys, from filmmaking to breaking beats.

Although the average rap fan might remember Freddy as the first face seen on *Yo! MTV Raps* back in the golden year of 1988, his extensive résumé includes working as a painter (alongside buddies Jean-Michel Basquiat and Keith Haring), directing rap videos (Gang Starr's masterful "Just to Get a Rep" and KRS-One's "My Philosophy"), producing feature films (*New Jack City* and *Wild Style*), and starring alongside Billy Dee Williams in a series of Colt 45 commercials.

While Freddy and I had been acquaintances for years, we didn't become true friends until I'd seen him a few times at those off-the-wall Hot Cocoa parties in the late 1990s. As I sat in the chair in the semidarkened room, waiting for the perfect baby-oiled booty to glide across my lap, I'd spot the fashion-conscious Freddy rapping to some hot honey across the room.

At six-two, Freddy towered over all the girls and most of the guys. Wearing his trademark sunglasses and hat, Freddy was as flashy as a riverboat dandy. "As a child growing up in Brooklyn, I was inspired by revolutionaries, be-bop musicians, and urban outlaws," Freddy says, between puffs on his cigarette. "For me, these men were the foundations of coolness. They've become the models for everything I've tried to do in my career."

In addition to the jazz cats and graffiti rats (he tagged BULL on the porcelain subway walls) that populated Freddy's neighborhood during his formative years, he also met his first pimp when he was a teenager hanging out on Reed Avenue.

"A friend of my father's was a dude named Paul Chandler," Freddy remembers. "One day, he introduced me to a real flamboyant guy who was wearing these tight clothes and dangling jewelry. At first I thought he was gay, but he said he was a pimp. Being a pimp wasn't as popular as it is now, so I was a little confused at the time." At the suggestion of Chandler, young Freddy popped into a local shop and picked up a copy of Iceberg Slim's first book, *Pimp.*

Since that night in the early seventies, Freddy has had the opportunity to meet and speak with a few true players. "Every great pimp I met was proud of themselves, but they would all tell you they'd much rather be doing something else with their game. Iceberg was blessed because he became a best-selling author, but that's only one cat out of thousands."

While Fab Five is a fan of Snoop and Jay-Z, he says, "The age of the true classic pimp is dead. That subculture exists more on records than on the streets. The pimps on parade one sees in music videos are far from the real thing."

-8-

Pimp juice is color blind

—Nelly, "Pimp Juice," from *Nellyville* (2002)

A few months after the debut of 50 Cent's video "P.I.M.P.," which featured player of the decade Snoop Dogg and his mack mentor, Bishop Don "Magic" Juan, me and my homegirl Sheila were caught up in the madness of Greenwich Village's annual Halloween parade.

Standing on Sixth Avenue and Tenth Street, we were passed by screeching drag queens dressed like Hillary Clinton and Martha Stewart, midgets in clown suits walking on stilts, countless witches, ghetto youngbloods dressed like Morpheus from *The Matrix*, and a long-haired Asian kid wearing a watermelon on his head. "Yo, that nigga got a watermelon on his head!" blurted one of the Morpheus crew.

Wiping laugh tears from my peepers, I turned around and saw two college white boys dressed in gaudy fake pimp gear. Everybody wants to be a bad-ass mofo, I thought: to be large and in charge; to be able to pull the finest freaks while bragging about the eight times you were blasted; to be able to ice grill a chill through the hardest dude and have pockets fatter than Albert.

One square had the nerve to be wearing white platform boots with a goldfish in the heel (a direct bite from Antonio Fargas's brilliant Flyguy pimp parody in *I'm Gonna Git You Sucka*) and a red hat with a leopard-print band, standing next to his homeboy, who was dressed to depress in a purple coat with a zebra collar and crushed velvet pants. He looked more imp than pimp.

I wasn't bothered by these white chocolate boys who had obviously overdosed on MTV; not at first, anyway. Obviously, they believed that the secret to ultra blackness (as perpetrated by rap's latest stereotypical Stagger Lee—the biggest, baddest nigga on the block—50 Cent) could be achieved by simply donning razzle-dazzle threads and a funny walk.

Indeed, the myth that the codes of black cool could be broken by simply pretending was older than Norman Mailer's seminal 1957 essay "The White Negro." Back then, the pale faces of Mailer's bohemian Greenwich Village desired to blow the blue notes of Charlie Parker, strum the bass like Charles Mingus, or bang tight skins with the fierceness of Max Roach; the new millennium white boys, on the other hand, desired to represent Thug Life. Praying at rap's jiggy altar, they imagined themselves as paleface versions of Tupac, Jay-Z, The Notorious B.I.G., and 50 Cent.

As someone who had often imitated the flair of white blues boys Jimmy Page, Tom Waits, and Elvis Presley (not to mention the number of black men who wish themselves to be Italian mafiosos, no matter how many times those godfathers utter the words *nigger* or *spook*), I could understand how a little race reversal could be good for the soul. Yet, while these not-ready-for-prime-time pimps in front of me looked more like Kid Rock on crack than uptown macks, I was taken aback when I noticed that their young "hos" were two attractive black women. It was at this moment that racial complexity reared its ironic head.

Although Slim had insisted that white boys didn't have what it took to be true pimps, popular culture was now schooling them otherwise. Although the word *urban* was once code for ghetto blacks, it has now become a synonym for *cool*.

Gazing into the glowing glass at the latest hip-hop video, be it the city-slick boogie of Diddy and Jay-Z or the country bumpkin bump of Nelly and the Cash Money Millionaires, these suburban kids were experiencing what Cornel West referred to in his essay "Black Sexuality: The Taboo Subject" (1973) as "the Afro-Americanization of white youth."

In other words, blame it on the pop cult boogie of black folks once again: charge the slick-boy-slim players swarming the twilight streets of Times Square for inspiring Harvey Keitel's character Sport Matthew in *Taxi Driver*; claim too many hours of blaxploitation caused Quentin Tarantino to create the white Frankenstein pimp Drexl Spivey in *True*

Romance; and now hip-hop could be held responsible for inspiring a generation of ivory-skinned pimp posers.

Watching those wannabe down beige boys and their dark-skinned ladies, I didn't care that "when white kids and black kids buy the same billboard hits . . . the result is often a shared cultural space where some humane interaction takes place," as West had written. All I could think of was how historically white men, while afraid of black male sexuality to the point of committing brutal murders for imagined acts, had had no problem raping black women for centuries. I thought of the stories I had heard of the troubles of brothers accused of "reckless eyeballing" some ivory-skinned cutie in Bensonhurst or of black men being chased to the other side of the Mason-Dixon line for dating a white girl.

These tales were not ancient history but had happened within my lifetime. Finding myself growing angry, I emotionally blurted, "I wonder what those girls' fathers would think if they saw them?" Yet, as a b-boy intellectual who understands that Planet Hip-Hop was integrated many years ago, and white boys—who now fondly referred to one another as "nigga"—were the music's chief consumers, it is still difficult to accept. And the excuse that the borders of cultural representation and marketed urbanity have blurred isn't enough to keep it from being insulting.

-9-

Farewell to the night, to the neon light
farewell to one and all

—"The Fall" (an old prison poem)

Six months before his death from cancer in the winter of 1992, my stepfather, Daddy, and I sat in his favorite Rican restaurant on 116th Street and rapped about old times.

King Heroin once ruled with an iron needle a community, a community now destroyed by crack. Ten years later, gentrification would sweep those neighborhood addicts into the East River and restore the area to its former glory. El Mundial was one of the few remaining old businesses in East Harlem. Daddy had eaten at that spot since the early sixties, and all the waiters knew him by name.

"Hey, Carl," yelled Jorge, the restaurant's chubby career waiter. He hugged Daddy's frail body with macho affection. After seating us next to the plate-glass window, Jorge brought us both glasses of homemade red wine.

Close to eighty years old, Daddy had lived life to the limit, working hard and playing harder, and was now suffering from bad health. Still, for his age, Pop Duke was a trooper. Regrettably, most of his Harlem friends had already gone to that Nigga Heaven in the sky. Daddy's old eyes, once so sharp, were now permanently bloodshot. His olive-colored skin was pale, wrinkled, and dry as sand. Dressed in a crisp white shirt embroidered with neo-deco designs, starched black slacks, and black patent leather shoes, he sat stiffly at the table and buttered the warm bread.

"You know who I was wondering about?" I said. "What ever happened to that pimp that hung out at the Shalimar back in the day?"

"Which one?" Daddy asked. After years of puffing filterless Camels, he was left with a voice as scratchy as broken glass. "There were a few of them, you know."

"I was thinking about that dude Deacon Blue. You remember that cat, right? Everything in his wardrobe was blue. He stole Duriella du Fontaine from the shop."

Sounding like a rusty crank on an antique Model T, he laughed. "You still remember that, huh? Shit, I saw that Duriella not too long ago. She looked terrible—no front teeth and skinny as a table leg. She was so pretty back then, but she ain't so fine no more. You know, smoking that stuff."

Staring out the window as though wishing he had bottled some of his better days, he watched a group of wild boys shooting dice on a battered tenement stoop across the street. Black Sheep's "The Choice Is Yours" blared at a vociferous volume. One cool Kangol-capped kid leaned against a wild-styled Rammellzee graffiti masterpiece and puffed a cigarette.

"But what about Deacon Blue?" I asked again. Even before Daddy answered, I was sure whatever had happened to Deacon Blue was not a happy ending.

The inevitable ending of most cats in the pimp game is serving time in jail or being murdered, either by a jealous rival or by some cuckoo for Cocoa Puffs chick. Many others have destroyed their own flesh and spirit with drugs, and only a few live to tell the tale.

"Some people are better off getting a nine-to-five, because this pimp game can blow your mind," Bishop Don "Magic" Juan once told me. "I know dudes in the game who just lost their minds. A pimp friend of mine from Chicago got so high on angel dust, he killed his own baby."

Although Iceberg Slim claimed in a 1973 *Washington Post* interview that he had made attempts to save young men from the streets with his own examples of drug addiction and prison in *Pimp*, many readers simply ignored the less glam parts of the text.

"It's almost impossible to dissuade young dudes who're already street poisoned, because without exception they have no recourse but to think they're slicker than Iceberg," said Iceberg Slim.

"Last I heard, Blue was working as a skycap for American Airlines," Daddy said with a cruel chuckle back at El Mundial.

It was difficult to envision that once proud player president dressed in his dandy sapphire suits being forced to lug suitcases. Undeniably, like rapping, pimping is a young man's art form. "Ain't nothing worse than an old pimp," Daddy said.

"Except for an old whore," I replied. We both snickered, our red wine spittle staining the ivory tablecloth. It was the last day I can remember hearing his laughter.

Special thanks to Darius James, Garry Harris, Fab Five Freddy, and Barry Michael Cooper for deep discussions and mack daddy inspiration.

LUDACRIS

THE INTERVIEW 2005

One of a number of Atlanta-reared rappers, Ludacris flipped a stint as an A-town disc jockey into a label imprint for Disturbin' the Peace with Def Jam South. His combo of comedy and lurid sexuality made for club hits appropriate for head nodders and rump shakers alike. With his chorus-driven hooks, colorful genre-bending videos, and fun-loving persona, Ludacris achieved a level of fame that would lead to countless A-list guest appearances (Jermaine Dupri, Missy Elliott), an almost Pepsi endorsement (conservative Bill O'Reilly foiled that one), and lofty acting roles (*Crash, Hustle & Flow*). But at the bottom of it all, he has to thank God for his success.

I think it's important to thank God each and every day for waking up. My mother and my aunties, even I myself, went to church back in the days. It's not the cards you're dealt but how you play your cards. You've got to be spiritual. You got to believe in God, that's what's up. How do you stay centered? I'm as strong an individual as anybody. You've got to overcome the odds. It's just about self-motivation and how strong you are.

The weak don't last long. You've got to last. I kind of brushed it [Bill O'Reilly] off. I heard things here and there. And then it turned into something a lot bigger than I thought it would be. It was a learning situation. You always have your haters. I always knew he was a hypocrite.

Karma comes back around. You saw what happened to him recently, and there you have it. That's how it felt. I never wished anything bad on him. I knew it would come back around, and that's how you do it. I learned a lot from the situation. There's still a lot of discrimination to this very present. I don't know why he did it, but his kids probably love me. They probably have all my albums. They probably listen to it in the house—I have no idea.

"I'm Bad" by LL Cool J way back to the day. I remember every word to that song back then—I had to have been in the fourth grade. I was loving it. It was the confidence in the song. The cockiness. Him saying he's the best. It was the flow. It was everything. His delivery, all of that.

The streets can try to knock you down every now and then. I'm talking about self-motivation and self-confidence. He had that self-confidence; you could hear it in people's voices sometimes about how confident they were. Going through a hard period, to hear someone and how confident they are, is self-motivation.

Pimpin' can be pimpin' the system. I'm pimping the industry. The way I'm juicing these contracts, the way I'm juicing these individuals. That's what pimp culture has to do with the music industry.

The greatest changes I've [seen in hip-hop are] people are experimenting with it, taking it places. Some people don't like the way it's going. Like the collision course, Jay-Z merging with Linkin Park—it's just a lot of experimenting going on. If you don't like it, don't listen to it. If you do, respect it for being something new. I can't speak on what other people aren't feeling. I just know what I feel. I'm a real modest individual, but I think I'm the medium between God and the microphone, so I love what the hell I do, all four albums.

THE CROSS

On our knees. Hands clasped. Two hundred scriptures a day and twice as many prayer meetings. But do we really have faith, and if so, what do we have faith in? One soul's God is another one's stone. Who's right and who's tithing for nothing?

A CHRISTMAS STORY

BY YTASHA L. WOMACK

It's ten A.M this snowy Sunday morning. I'm cruising through Chicago's aptly dubbed "wild hundreds," on the city's far south side, blasting Boolumaster's morning hip-hop mix on my way to church. Jay-Z's "Excuse Me Miss," backed by the Neptune's banging beats, is giving me a better rush than the competing gospel station. Five hours earlier, I was dancing to the exact same track at a bourgie north-side club with more posers than partiers. But for now hip-hop is the score for the video through my windshield, a familiar blur of snow-capped Baptist storefronts, liquor stores, and beauty supply shops. Churchgoers and weary workers fresh off the night shift hold down the bus stops, a motley crew of stone-faced winterland mummies comforted only by memories of having survived worse winters.

It's like clockwork. I can close the club down dancing until four A.M. Sunday morning, nap, wake up for meditation, and by nine I'm flipping through pantsuits and Sunday dresses for the morning service. My girlfriends, many of whom don't even kick it on Saturday nights and still don't make it to church, find my commitment mind-boggling. I just call it balance.

What began as a rote family tradition blossomed into a quest to know God as an adult. One ordinary day, when office monotony was getting the best of me, I remember hearing a clear voice in my head. An awesome calm overcame me, and, while I felt no pain and nothing was physically wrong, this voice resounded with urgency. It insisted that I leave work and head straight for the hospital. For some odd reason, instead of tossing the thought aside, I followed its plea and soon discovered that I needed emergency surgery. Apparently, the anger I'd harbored against exes, others, and myself for a career start turned sour had morphed into something that was making me ill.

Part of me wanted to cry, but a bigger part surged forth, ushering in a peaceful sense of confidence I'd never felt before. An old lesson I'd learned from my metaphysical teachings suddenly made sense. Get rid of the anger and proclaim your perfect state of health. For the next few years, I worked on releasing anger. After that surgery, I began meditating. Another whisper urged me to change my diet, too. My physician marveled at my improvement and I stood thankful and became ever watchful of "the voice."

That voice, on that long-ago day, was God. Was it the first time the spirit spoke? No, but it was the beginning of an awareness of a power greater than myself that whispered to me on a moment-by-moment basis, an ever-so-slight nudge I'd felt off and on my entire life but never felt like listening to. I took classes at my church, Christ Universal Temple, one of the largest New Thought churches in the nation, headed by Rev. Dr. Johnnie Colemon, an African American woman who for some forty years had taught metaphysical interpretations of the Bible. She was among the first black students to study at the Unity School of Practical Christianity and would later found the Universal Foundation for Better Living. The teaching is nondenominational, emphasizes prayer, meditation, and listening to the silence, and centers on five basic principles: 1) the Omnipresence of God, 2) the Divinity of Man, 3) the Power of Thought, 4) Practicing the Presence, and 5) the Law of Demonstration. The belief that your thoughts and feelings combined create your experiences is a core lesson in the philosophy. Change your thoughts and you change your world, they teach. While they also teach that everyone is a divine expression of God, the charge is on both a conscious (thinking nature) and subconscious (feeling nature) level to be fully aware, moment by moment, of our oneness with the one presence of God. Jesus is the example they teach from.

I, too, began to practice "experiencing the silence." "Listen and obey," she once told me. But the challenge became not so much to hear God speak but to follow the directive. That, I found, was the hard part. Rarely did I ever feel like doing what the voice urged me to do, even if it was as simple as making a phone call.

But equally as challenging was accepting the awesome concept that God and I are one. "God is in you as the ocean is in a wave," the teacher in my Basic Truth Principles class reminded us. While I affirmed what I thought I knew as fact, it didn't take long before my classmates and I admitted that we didn't get it at all. Sure, Jesus said, "This and greater things shall you do," but what does that mean? And how in the world am I supposed to do that? How am I supposed to be greater than Jesus Christ?

So I'm at church. I plop down in my regular seat, right next to Mrs. Boolumaster, the affectionate mother of the DJ whose mix had me charged on the way here. I hurriedly stuff money in a green tithe envelope and glance at the church bulletin as the choir begins singing.

Today's sermon is "The Grandmothers of Christmas," to be delivered by guest speaker Dr. Samuel Chand, a native of India and professor at the Interdenominational Institute in Atlanta. It's an overlooked area of the Bible, Chand says, lost in the sea of "who begot whos" that Matthew illustrates in his dismal tour of a cemetery. Out of the some forty-two generations in Jesus' lineage, only four women are mentioned, he notes, an indication that they were in some way very special.

History lesson: Aspects of Jewish and Christian culture at that time, like other cultures of the day, did not regard women as equals. Many early writers of the books that would later compose the Bible did not want women teaching spirituality or serving as roles of authority in the Church. Fathers technically owned their daughters and sold them to their husbands for a dowry. Whole families would be recorded without any mention of female siblings. "Even Jesus' sisters weren't mentioned," one minister shockingly shared, noting that his brothers are listed, though glossed over by most readers. In fact, many writers of the Bible didn't bother to name the women they were writing about. So if a woman was even mentioned in this limited line of reasoning, she was practically the equivalent of a modern-day superhero and did something so great, it obliterated sexist conventions. The fact that Mary Magdalene, for example, was even referenced at all as frequently being in the company of Jesus probably meant she was much more than a random follower. But that's me talking. Back to Dr. Chand.

This should be interesting, I think, whipping out my notebook and pen. And what began innocently enough, as a new Christmas spin on holy women, quickly unravels into the scandalous domain of the soaps. The first grandmother of

Christmas, he says, was Tamar, a twice-widowed Caananite who wanted a child so badly that she dressed as a prostitute to trick her father-in-law into sleeping with her. Umm, I think.

The second was Rahab, "the harlot" (Some names just stick, says Chand), who owned a brothel on the famed wall of Jericho. "This isn't getting any better, is it?" remarks Chand, who forewarned us that the stories would be PG-13 plus. The third, Ruth, was the distant descendant of Lot, whose two daughters got him drunk in order to sleep with him and bear children. And the fourth, Bathsheba, was minding her own business, when King David spotted her, forced her to sleep with him, and subsequently killed her husband.

The congregation, while intrigued, is equally appalled. Though I'd heard these stories before, his blatant phrasing makes the tales a little too real. "It's stories like that that give me hope today," Chand says. "God can use who he chooses to use," he professes.

It's a side-curling joke in the comedy world that even the hard core in the rap world will thank God at the Grammys. Jada Pinkett, while hosting the BET Awards with hubby rapper turned actor turned world phenomenon Will Smith, joked that artists shouldn't thank God if they can't perform their songs in church. The audience fell out laughing. Hip-hop artists have more biblical metaphors in their music than some gospel acts. But what seems borderline blasphemous to the majority makes perfect sense in a world where every block has a church and a liquor store, ministers rival pimps in flash, and every family hardship is weathered by an unwavering faith in the Almighty. The joke implies that God is choosy, judgmental even. A young man or woman whose brash pride in being a thug is lyrically and rhythmically intriguing enough to make millions cop his or her music, catapulting the performer into the fame of a childhood fantasy, is supposedly beyond God's scope.

Ask anyone who witnessed this kid's hard-knock life and they'll testify that he or she is a walking miracle—the ultimate testimony that there is a higher power, 'cause there's no way in hell this child of the ghetto, talented or not, was supposed to escape the winding tentacles of poverty and low expectations—a schemata in which the tales of a hustler's life and imminent death often resonate more strongly than those of the mothers or fathers who worked three jobs to keep them from it. The God-given talent to speak in rhythms with a truth that makes heads nod and an unwavering faith in something greater than themselves, greater than the transparent-walled block that birthed them, was this person's salvation, and they know it.

DMX affirms that his gift of rhyme is heaven sent in "The Convo." In a heart-wrenching dialogue with God, the Almighty tells him he gave him a gift of rhyme. In fact, DMX credits God with helping him see the light and ultimately abandon a life on the downward spiral. "Put down the guns and write a new rhyme. You'll get it all in due time."

8 Ball and MJG in "Thank God" thank God for everything from family to slavery's end, to having a second chance after a life of hustling. But they didn't overlook their divine ability to share their tales. "I was blessed to be a storyteller, CD seller," says 8 Ball.

But the acknowledgment of that blessing, the muttering of a mere thank-you at the Soul Train Awards, the adornment of a blinding diamond cross or Jesus piece, a moment of prayer at a concert, like those emotional outpourings at a DMX show, become fodder for even the cheapest joke. It's total hypocrisy by mainstream standards. Can a person who talks about ass shaking and bloodshed, the blunted life, the glitterati, and the "get yours" mentality have a relationship with God?

It's the more recent version of an old theological question that predates Moses, a never-ending crusade by the haves, so to speak, to draw a line between the so-called wicked and the righteous, with everything from the color of the skin to the loot in the pocketbook as dividers. Bottom line: some people are worthy of God's blessings, and some just aren't.

Keeping it real for America's youth, for all its rhetorical value, in many ways equates to living a paradox. Tired of watching politicians, business leaders, artists, and even their own parents living as hypocrites, many youth have a pride in lifestyles that previous generations worked to hide. Instead of sweeping the dirt under the rug, as our grandmothers encouraged, today's youth wear its grimy smudge with honor. Challenge them and they'll lift up your rug, revealing your own sludge and dust, too.

Face it, even the so-called holiest in the Bible had some seriously maligning personal issues. The four mothers of Christmas, Tamar, Rahab, Ruth, and Bathsheba, are just the tip of the cesspool. Most biblical icons were living contradictions, and it takes a reflective honesty to cut through the sanctimonious bull and admit it. Solomon was the wisest man in the world but made the incredibly unwise, egomaniacal decision of having ten thousand wives. Moses killed a man shortly before accepting his mission to lead the Israelites to the "Promised Land." David murdered a woman's husband and forced her into his harem. And Paul's sexist leanings resonate through the Church to this day.

The truth is that many of the men and women in the Bible were as conflicted as they were spiritual. Each a great person with inner turmoil. But these misgivings have been glossed over in the name of oversimplifying spiritual text. You can't be as great as Jesus, traditional church doctrine states. Oddly enough, it's hip-hop artists who seek, in their own way, to prove otherwise.

Reconciling the soul and all its myriad issues with your higher self is a struggle that can span a lifetime or two. "Mama raised a hell-raising, heavenly son," Tupac once said. Traditional church doctrine dictates that we live a perfect life to be in God's favor, a credo the rap world and its fans rebel against. The fact that men and women in the Bible could do great things in spite of their problems is a source of inspiration and a theme that rappers have steadily incorporated on various levels into their music. They compare their struggles to those of Jesus and Moses, with haters equated to Jesus' persecutors and their impact on the music world paralleled to the parting of the Red Sea.

"I got to be God's favorite/I been through so much in my lifetime," N.O.R.E. chimes. And it's the hip-hop world's acceptance of biblical characters as human with relatable struggles and not dead Europeanized relics of the past that has listeners intrigued. It's the reason Nas can bear the cross, Jay-Z doubles as the omnipotent Jayhova with Roc-A-Fella as the holy trinity of hip-hop, Lauryn Hill can be visited by angels who usher her birth of Zion, and N.O.R.E. can be God's favorite. Busta Rhymes can predict the apocalypse, Ras Kass can question God and Satan, Tupac can hail Mary before licking shots, and Common's pimp stick can morph into a Moses-like staff. Even Wu Tang's eclectic clan refer to one another as gods (a Five Percenter term, but you get the similarity). Kanye bore a thorned crown on the cover of a magazine and even that was passed over, generating minimal controversy. These references go by with little questioning because, well, we understand.

Whether you're a Five Percenter, in the Nation of Islam, Buddhist, Yoruba, a Black Israelite, or a born-again Baptist, you are aware of some spiritually tinged cultural beliefs commonly referenced in African American life, beliefs not entirely different from those in the sea of islands, nations, and cultures that compose the African diaspora. Ask a deacon, a broker, schoolteacher, drug dealer, and bum and they'll all agree that it was God (call it what you wish depending on the religion) that got us out of slavery, it was God that helped us survive Jim Crow, just as she ended apartheid and ushered in the end of colonialism in Africa. And it's God who's guiding us through these questionable times now.

It's a widely held belief among many in the African diaspora that we are the lost tribe of Israel, Jesus was black, God is always with us, and some great day everything is going to be restored to its rightful place and this hellacious plague of racism, poverty, sexism, and classism will end. We'll emerge as great kings and queens like the great Songhai and the world will become the utopia it was created to be. Now, what you think it is that's going to rescue you—a space ship, the second coming, a diamond-encrusted cross hanging from your neck, meditating with crystals, a pack of roots, or an individual realization of our oneness with the universe— will vary. But these core beliefs give rise to the incredible plethora of religious analogies that hip-hop's stars drop with the authority of a Harvard theologian.

The pain of slavery bore both spirituals and the blues, one form thanking God for carrying them over, one questioning why we bear the cross. Whereas the brewing frustrations of the seventies and eighties gave birth to hip-hop, a hybrid art form that embraced, in an odd sort of way, both. Sex, religion, violence, and youthful passion are mixed together in stories that are almost folkloric. Replace the word *gun* with *sword* and you'd think you were listening to a reenactment of *Beowulf*.

Call it a throwback to Africa's unity-of-life theories or homage to those obligatory church visits, but hip-hop, for better or worse, embodies both righteous ideology and the torn souls of the maligned. Its confusion disguises itself as irony. In this effort to evolve, there is no line between the sacred and the secular. In OutKast's "B.O.B." video, the duo gives credence to Atlanta's stripper culture and Baptist church scene with equal reverence, intercutting gyrating strippers with well-dressed parishioners who just seconds ago were with the same strippers. "Hello ghetto, let your brain free/Believe there's always more," Andre 3000 says.

Then there's Busta Rhymes's "Make It Clap" video, a thinly veiled ode to strippers partially shot in a church, with the dreaded rapper himself starring as the con artist preacher. Whether it's a pointed commentary on the hypocrisy in church is less important than the obvious fact that Busta had no qualms talking about smacking asses in the house of the Lord.

The most popular religious-infused hip-hop song was Kanye West's "Jesus Walks." A surprise club banger that led to Grammy nods and an almost Stellar Award (the gospel show recanted when they discovered the single wasn't on a gospel album), the song was West's proof that, as he'd boasted he could, he could make a hot radio single about Jesus. In the song, West claims that despite his personal mishaps, Jesus walks with him. In fact, he walks with everyone, including hustlers, dealers, murderers, and strippers,

West specifies, and anyone else who feels out of step with their divinity. The three videos for the song feature a range of striking images, from a Klansman chopping wood for a burning cross to a black Jesus, played by a poet I know, dancing and hanging out with neighborhood kids. The message: Everyone has problems. Despite this, anyone can aspire to and live greatness.

While there's nothing revolutionary about this message, it was unique in its packaging. Unique in that it didn't attempt to relay messages of inspiration through any of the typical means—that is, using familiar gospel music sounds, or even using church or gospel radio as a vehicle. This song was not tailored for a gospel music audience. It wasn't tailored for underground rap audiences, either. Unlike Christian rap, "Jesus Walks" was written by an artist who doesn't claim to be overtly religious, although his constant references imply otherwise. In fact, much of his music teeters in irony, bouncing between intellectually conscious and deeply flawed, surely reflecting the contradictions experienced by most, including legions of hip-hop fans. And in what could be called pure marketing genius, West touched on a long-held history of people of color and church affiliation, highlighting the awkward though universal relationship between salvation and sinner, the physical world and the spiritual world, all factors that have come to define a culture.

The formula was beefed up for the song "It's Impossible," complete with "I can do it" mantra, gospel choir hook, a mean bongo, and a playerific verse by Twista. It reminds me of when Boolu mixed the track for Ol' Dirty Bastard's (a.k.a. Big Baby Jesus) "Got Your Money," a play on the economics between pimp and prostitute, with the lyrics to Kirk Franklin's gospel hit "Stomp" in a radio mix. There's something pleasingly guilty about bridging these contrasting elements into one. There was no denying that the off-kilter combo was hot.

However, it's the eerie line of the spiritual divide, this inner turmoil between heaven and damnation, the lore binding violence and religious-inspired comeuppance, that hip-hop often teeters in uncomfortably to the shock of rap lovers and ministers alike. Was it arrogance, ignorance, or a challenge to religious piety that urged Notorious B.I.G. to want to "smack" the Virgin Mary? What about when Big threatened to slit a priest's throat? How can Nas flip Jesus, using the Prince of Peace's own age, into a metaphor on the rounds of bullets fired at an enemy? Violence and Christianity are bound by a bloody past eons older than rap music, and the carefree acceptance of this by music makers is compelling, albeit disturbing.

Wars, slavery, the Holocaust, and most battles in world history were waged in the name of the cross. "You yell stop the violence but the cross you're still using," said KRS-One in "The Truth," his attack on Christian doctrine and the irony of wearing a cross. "If Jesus Christ was shot in the head with no respect/We'd all have little gold guns around our neck." While KRS-One sheds light on the irony, other artists, just as presidents, priests, warlords, and others did before them, use religion to somehow justify the violence in their songs. "In the beginning God created thugs and other drugs," Pastor Troy hurled. Or take Snoop in "Mac Bible Chapter 211 Verse 20–21," in which he decrees that God said he'd send "a G with street ethics" who'd issue a Gangsta Ten Commandments including "Thou shalt kill a snitch" and "Thou shalt check a bitch."

On the other hand, hip-hop also professes that everyone is a spiritual being, harnessing religious anecdotes as an affirmation of survival with a backbone hovering in the supernatural.

"I bear the cross/If Virgin Mary had an abortion I'd still be carried in the chariots by stampeding horses," Nas boasts in "The Cross," stating that no one can stop his destiny of greatness, or ours for that matter. In "Fear Not of Man" Mos Def dismisses conspiracy theories. "God is sufficient over plans they prepare," he affirms.

"Yea, though I walk through the valley of the shadow, I fear no man because faith is the arrow," Mos Def says in "Know That." Lauryn Hill evokes the power of the word and the golden rule in "Lost Ones." "Don't you understand universal law? What you give out comes back to you raw."

But there's also a strong tendency in hip-hop music to somehow be Jesus or Moses, and to use those inherited spiritual gifts to uplift humanity. It's a birthright they both embrace and fear. And the anguish they feel in pursuit of the intangible is all too often compared to the nailing of Jesus to the cross. From Tupac to Jay-Z, countless rappers have made uncanny references to being crucified, either for their allegiance to the disempowered or for their efforts to make big money. It's arguably one of the most controversial religious twists in hip-hop, yet it's the one theme that fuels the most passion among fans.

KRS-One, Tupac, Nas, and Lauryn Hill are the reigning gods and goddesses of Christian-based metaphors. KRS-One, or the Teacha, as he's often called, has a straight, no-chaser, heavy-handed style more reminiscent of a Bible-toting pastor than your typical rapper. He's as enlightening as he is shocking, discussing complex religious concepts by twisting spiritual metaphors and analogies in ways that compel his listeners to seek out reference materials to fully understand what he's talking about. While some artists are content to make a biblical reference here and there, KRS-One clearly embraces hip-hop as a platform to teach spirituality to the extent that some criticize him for being "preachy." Referring to the

Temple of Hip-Hop, the Bronx-born rapper believes that hip-hop is a tool of empowerment, claiming that at its root, hip-hop is spiritual, and he's been ordained to uplift the masses. "I'll give you the gift, but use the gift to uplift," he writes, indicating that God has anointed his mission.

In his musical career, KRS-One has criticized the traditional church for its racism and hypocrisy, pointed to the dubious righteousness of rap artists, taught the metaphysics behind biblical stories, explored inconsistencies in the Bible, all while constantly pressing others to pursue a quest for knowledge. "You gotta read the Qu'ran, Torah, Bhagavad Gita, the Bible, Five Baskets of Buddha, Zen/ And when you've read them shits, read them shits again," he says in "Build and Destroy." Whereas his career began with Kris highlighting the ironies in Christian philosophy (in addition to underscoring political criticisms, conspiracy theories, and advocating the study of black history), his music soon morphed into a Christ-based ministry. "Instead of reading the word of Christ, be the word of Christ/Instead of following God's word, be God's word," he says in "I Will Make It." In fact, his 2002 album *Spiritual Minded*, a play on his critically acclaimed *Criminal Minded*, was actually a hip-hop gospel album including appearances by gospel great Hezekiah Walker.

Tupac and Nas are the reigning kings of Christ-like personification. Tupac, clearly haunted by his (ultimately self-fulfilled) prophecy of an early death, compared himself to Jesus quite frequently. Referring to himself as a modern-day martyr for the disenfranchised, Pac had his own inner turmoil about which path to follow, bouncing between revolutionary and thug, a vulnerable take that would later characterize his work. As if he was being pulled by opposing forces, Tupac's efforts to cross-section his own life or that of the characters he personified read as a cry to the spirit world for help. Sometimes the characters he gave voice to (when he wasn't talking about himself) were too far gone to the dark side for redemption, shouting out prayers he knew would go unanswered. Other times it's as if Tupac was a sacrificial lamb, waging a misunderstood battle for true freedom against forces even he didn't understand.

"Hail Mary," an oddly layered song, on one level tells the story of a vengeful madman poised to kill, saying a final prayer before his pending death to fall that night—a death he anticipates because of the violence he's perpetrated before. And when death doesn't come, he says the prayer knowing his dangerous life can end only in peril. "Hail Mary" lines the chorus. But the song opens with a decree to follow him. "God said he should send his one begotten son to lead the wild into the ways of the man/Follow me." However, it can also be argued that the song is about leading a people's revolution, like Jesus, that would also result in a life cut short. To underscore the parallel, Pac was depicted on a cross on *The Don Kulluminati*, the album released before his untimely death.

Nas clung to spiritual questioning, expressing a desire to be like the early mystics, in order to possess their knowledge and powers. While he expresses that he has the potential of the greats, in "One Mic" he asks God to show him how to do things his son did. Nas intertwined his day-to-day life and decisions with the pressures felt by Jesus and others, doing so almost as a means to somehow transfer their spiritual gifts to himself. He often links his mission to that of Tupac. But Nas's references ultimately humanized Jesus, with attempts to show direct parallels between our quest and that of the Wayshower.

In his most dramatic attempt, Nas's "Hate Me Now" video featured him as Jesus on the day of the Crucifixion. A thorny crown atop his Caesar, Nas carried a wooden cross through an angry crowd of "haters," who nailed him to it. In the song, a rousing anthem with heavy bass and sonic chords, Nas challenges those who don't believe in him or support his rise to stand in awe of his personal overcoming. It's a theme that resonates with anyone trying to do better for herself who also feels knocked by friend and foe alike. One controversial version of the video featured Diddy nailed to a cross beside him. (Diddy allegedly consulted with his pastor and decided he didn't like the depiction, and when the video was released anyway, he allegedly attacked a music executive with champagne bottles.)

Whereas Tupac and Nas wield the cross to explore their own demons and aspirations, Lauryn Hill, a.k.a. L-Boogie, uses biblical imagery to encourage her listeners to seek enlightenment from a different vantage point. Although Nas's and Tupac's quests are thematically consistent in their struggle, they are inconsistent in actually embracing redemption—musically, anyway—with both hopping from murder to salvation, misogyny to heaven in a single verse. Hill, on the other hand, maintains a position of spiritual balance in her music, although it's clear she had internal conflict as well.

"Forgive Them" reiterated one of Jesus' final statements on the cross, asking God to forgive those who've hurt her "for they know not what they do." Her conflicted decision to keep her firstborn child was affirmed by angels in "Zion." The refreshing take on uplifting her audience in "The Miseducation of Lauryn Hill," backed by heartfelt vocals and her strong songwriting ability, garnered more Grammys than any hip-hop album to date. It was a one-of-a-kind approach that despite its success was never repeated by hip-hop luminaries. "You can hear God in her voice," Common once said.

Even her follow-up *MTV Unplugged* album, a critical success that confused many fans with its stripped-down acoustic sound and lyrical gymnastics, showed a woman looking to the Bible not only for self-exploration but to teach and encourage her listeners to rebel as well. Each song is riddled with biblical references and points to a personal evolution clearly rooted in the spiritual quest she feels we're all on. In the song "Adam Lives in Theory" Lauryn uses Adam and Eve as metaphors for humankind's utter confusion. But she differs from other hip-hop artists who've acknowledged spiritual questioning in that she feels a responsibility to her audience in the same way a minister would to his congregation. "I'm not going to give you something I haven't tried and tested first," she told the *Unplugged* audience.

Nas cried for one God to show him how to do the things his son did, and it's a sentiment echoed far too often in headphones across the globe to be dismissed as sheer arrogance. To be Jesus, to somehow overcome the cross they bear and be resurrected into an enlightened life is the beleaguered goal of today's rap icons? It's sad that the very prospect of such an inquiry would make for the perfect *SNL* parody. Yet their path isn't all that different from most.

"These things and greater shall you do," Jesus said. And again, I ask, what does that mean?

It's one of those questions that only the one who seeks can answer. And in contemplating this, I try to be lighthearted about this juke-off called life. Frankly, I don't truly know what experiences anyone, including today's hip-hop stars, needs to live in order to cultivate his or her own sense of awareness. We're all on a spiritual journey. No path is greater than another. Although spiritual evolution is a personal experience, it's comforting to know that others, in their own way, are asking the same age-old questions that the early mystics who studied shamanic wisdom, Zen, Gnostic Gospels, Confucius, Buddha, and every other spiritually enlightened view posed so many years ago. We are each subconsciously yearning to hear the voice and praying that once it's heard we'll have the strength to follow. So if sporting a diamond-encrusted cross or making a shout-out to God is a step along that quest, who am I to question it?

I've learned not to be judgmental, an effort that's not particularly easy for a fixed Aquarian like me. But I figure that it's challenging enough living my own purpose without aimlessly pointing fingers at someone else. I usually listen to music that resonates on a deeper level, music I don't mind seeping into my subconscious and popping up somewhere in my life, and sometimes that means listening to the raw aggression of a street-birthed beat. But even in those hip-hop songs I wouldn't play before my mother, I still see light. I see a need for greater love and compassion that extends from the artist to the industry to the eager listeners at large. And when that same artist thanks God for an award, I watch and think, "Well, on some level he knows." Then I go about my day.

BILLY DANZE (OF M.O.P.)

THE INTERVIEW 2004

Billy Danze and his partner in rhyme, Lil' Fame, make up the Mash-Out Posse (M.O.P.). Street anthems such as "How About Some Hardcore" and "Ante Up" have made them in dens of debauchery worldwide. Their music is for street soldiers, for men and women in the ghettos of the world, trying to make it whichever way they can. That struggle has many casualties, many loved ones lost, many closed caskets. They know death, and they know what it does to people, especially themselves.

As far as music, it always inspires you to do one of those joints like "Dead and Gone" that we did or "Blood, Sweat, and Tears." It helps you keep going. You gotta move because this person that passed would always wanna see you shine or do your best at whatever you're doing, so I just take it like that and run with it. In between our first, second, and third albums, we lost a lot of people. I lost my mom. Fame's mom passed before my moms. My sister actually brought it up to me the other day that they were like a year and a month exact apart. My homie Boo Dang, we always talk about him on the joints. My little homie Bremer. A lot of people, man. When I was a little younger, I was fourteen, while my pops was in the hospital dying I lost my brother. Then I lost my pops maybe three months after that. Then maybe four, five years after that, I lost my other brother, and there's still more. Like my grandmother, my uncle, then my other uncle, then my aunt. Not all of what I just told you was in the correct order, but it's always been something for a nigga to deal with. But I got kids now so I need to move on and keep living, because I'm sure they would want it that way. I keep them with me. I ride around with obituaries in my car. I got them all planted up on my wall. These people are very important to me—not was, still is. These people help me keep moving every day. It could've pulled us down, but it pushed us. We understand that no one is gonna be here forever, so you enjoy them while they're here and you miss them while they're gone, but you just keep moving forward. That's all.

I'm not an artist, man. I'm just a dude that knows how to put words together and enjoy doing it. The people we lost in hip-hop, some to a lot of people were not as important as others, but to me, all of these dudes that we lost . . . I've actually kicked it with like from Pac to Big, Freaky Tah, Big L. All of these dudes, I knew these dudes. They were all good dudes. So everybody's life is important, man, regardless if they're an artist or not. I get a little bit upset if I hear a Big L joint and people not so excited about it, and then you hear Biggie or a Pac joint and people going crazy about it. Because at any given time they all could've went in the booth together and rocked and made a bangin' song. My hat's definitely off to Freaky Tah, Big L, Pun. Goddamn! Pun was my dude! I would see Pun anywhere and this nigga would just be glowing, had all the fat guy jokes. Pun was full of life, man. The hip-hop community, these people [now] are all trained anyway. They're all puppets. Not that I don't love 'em, but they're all puppets. That's pretty much it, though, man.

THE COFFIN

Pour out a little liquor for the dead homies. The war becomes clichéd within a nation at infinite war. Why do we lose so many? Why do so many choose to lose? Life is getting shorter for those who never get to learn what it means to live.

COUGHING

BY SUHEIR HAMMAD

The war is over, for now at least
It'll be more dead people after this
So I'm glad to be alive and walkin'
Half of my platoon came home in coffins

> —Eric B and Rakim, "Casualties of War," from
> *Don't Sweat the Technique* (1992)

N.Y.C., JULY 2004

Thank you, Rakim. For laying down in lyrics all those years ago a rhyme that speaks to our era. Hip-hop is being exported once again. Not only as easy-to-digest hooks and half-naked women. Not only as the best walking commercial the diamond industry could have asked for. Not only wackness. Violence. Stunted growth of our men and advanced sexual maturity of our girls. Now hip-hop is wholesale leaving the States. In uniform. Freshly minted Marines. Real guns, not the props in video after video. Real bombs. In a sick 360, the youth who grew up alongside this music and culture we love so dearly are being all they can be. In Iraq. In Afghanistan. In Haiti. In Guantánamo. And on hundreds of military bases around the planet. What? They couldn't be fly in Brooklyn?

No. They couldn't. Young folks are killing and dying all over the world to the soundtrack of my life. But wait. Biggie and Tupac grew up under Reaganomics. And the Bush agenda (which is available for all to read on his Web site) is an extension of these policies, both domestic and foreign. There it is. The fatalism, which has been married to hip-hop culture for two decades now, can be directly traced to the decisions made for us as children by our government.

What is more of a living coffin than a jail?

Blacks are incarcerated nationally at a rate of 1,547 per 100,000 black residents. In some states, the black rate of incarceration reaches extraordinary levels. In Alaska, Arizona, Connecticut, Delaware, Iowa, Oklahoma, Rhode Island, Texas, Wisconsin, and the District of Columbia, blacks are incarcerated at rates that exceed 2,000 per 100,000. The lowest incarceration rate for blacks, 570 in North Dakota, exceeds the highest rate for whites, 440 in Arizona.

—Human Rights Watch

When prison has become part of a culture's fabric, how far away is war? My generation has barely survived the War on Drugs and the War on Gangs. Wars that were waged in neighborhoods like the one I grew up in, all across the United States, some of them places that would seem to have nothing in common with 1980s Sunset Park, Brooklyn. And now we have this ever expanding, color-coded War on Terror. Will we survive this one?

PALESTINE, AUGUST 2004

To enter Bethlehem from Ramallah, I have to take a car to the Qalandia checkpoint. I hand in my American passport to the young Israeli soldier and try to fix my face so I am deemed friendly and not threatening. Each day's experience is different. One day I get an American from Connecticut. His daughter is studying in Brooklyn, he tells me. Another day I get a young woman who may or may not have a broken heart.

She asks a question I have no one answer for: "Why are you here?" The answers are many, and I quick-think that none of them will satisfy her.

"I'm going to an orphanage in Bethlehem, to visit with the orphans," I tell her. It's not good enough, but it's all I have. So I let her take her time, flipping the passport this way and that, as if a secret plan will fall out of the pages. She lets me through.

My friends and I visit the orphanage and the Dheisha refugee camp. Both places are bursting with young people with nowhere to go. The Israelis are building a separation wall. The *New York Times* still calls it a "fence." One need only make the trip here to see what a "fence" looks like to an occupying power. By the time we get to the community center in Bethlehem where the Palestinian rap group DAM is holding a hip-hop workshop, I am ready to see humans make music with their mouths.

We watch and listen to young Palestinians rhyme in Arabic. Beatbox. Constructing and dissecting their lyrics to perfection. Cipher. I ask one of the young people if he knows where the word *cipher* comes from. No.

"It's the cipher, *habibi*. The zero in Arabic. A closed, ever-forming circle." The idea that this fundamental aspect of MC craft has its origin in an Arabic word brings a shy smile to his face. Because language is more than sound. It carries the cultural weight of the people who created it. And like the cipher, we are enclosed in this space.

When progressive rappers like Mos Def, dead prez, and

Talib Kweli have come back from trips to African countries, Cuba, Japan, they have often talked about the fascination with hip-hop that they find in what would appear to be far-flung locales. Here is Talib in "Gun Music": "We got tribes in Africa that listen to Pac / fighting with brothers who pump Biggie like they live on the block." And you know what I heard, over and over again, from hip-hop heads in the Occupied Territories and within the 1948 borders as well? Another line from the same song: "Israelis got tanks and Palestinians got rocks / Inmates got shanks and dirty cops they got glocks."

The young men from DAM (which means "blood" in Arabic) don't speak English as much as they speak hip-hop, or "rrrap," as it is pronounced, with that pretty roll of the letter found in most Arab mouths. And they have a million questions about their favorite rappers. "Is it true dead prez is blinging now?" "Is Mos too big a star now?" "Is there anyone saying anything new? Anything real?" Yes, y'all. Travel halfway around the world and you will meet the same near-manic desperation to "keep it real."

What I realized is that Talib's lyrics connected so gracefully the prison system, war, and "real." And that is what these young men responded to. I did not meet one man in the Territories who has not been to jail—not one between the ages of fifteen and fifty. Cigarette burns. Broken teeth. Broken lives. Torture in the Iraqi jails? Every Palestinian man I talked to told me to track the origins of American misconduct in Iraq to the Israeli jails.

That thing with the hood and the dogs? Palestinians had been there. The humiliation of being naked and dragged through the prison? Done that. I tried to explain that American jails could be just as bad. That there were riots all the time. That there is a movement in the States to eradicate all jails because the system is fundamentally . . . fucked up. But it was my word against all the videos streaming into the living rooms of at least the Palestinians who live within the 1948 (Israeli) borders. Jail is portrayed, in the videos of Ja Rule and 50, as a brightly lit video set. Their ladies are always decked out in Choos and Dior, just waiting for them to come home and get back to the good life.

If there are no bars, is it still prison?

If you ain't laid down in a coffin, are you alive?

I think a generation, a nation, that became accustomed to the longing, the missing, that occurs when so many are jailed becomes a fatalistic one. By my late teens, when my parents moved my family to Staten Island, most of the young men I grew up with in the BK had either been killed, shot into paralysis, or jailed. Even today, my friends and I count them out, just in case we missed someone. Maybe some others escaped the enclosing circle. Maybe someone else made it out. But no. We can count the men who escaped on one hand. And in Shaolin, my new friends were getting picked up every day. The drug game, they called it. But even games have rules, right? Who made them up? Who keeps changing them?

> I'm ready to die
> All y'all motherfuckers come with me if you want to
> —Biggie Smalls, "Ready to Die," from *Ready to Die* (1994)

N.Y.C., AUGUST 2004

When Biggie died, it was different. Tupac had belonged to the world, but Biggie belonged to Brooklyn. And that morning, the phones did not stop ringing, remember? Lovers, sisters, homeboys—we called to check on each other. No. Most wouldn't believe it, unless they had MTV. And those who did have MTV and the Internet, which I didn't, were taping and copying information for the rest of us. No. I mean, Pac wasn't even cold in his grave yet, as my mama would say. Now "they" gonna take Biggie out, too?

I didn't join the procession. To those of us who struggled with his music the way one struggles with family, his coffin wasn't big enough to hold him. He wasn't just a hero to most of the women I knew, women who loved and lived the culture as much as any of the men, women who found little breathing space in his lyrics about bitches and hos. For real. We, I, loved him. But not simply. We, I, loved him 'cause he represented neither the best nor the worst in us. Just the hustle, the decision to get by, not fly, not drown. In death, all of that evaporates, right? We are left with the essence of a person. The intention. And we, I, want to believe that after it all, Big was another survivor of the real war, the War on the Poor. And he came out swinging. Some of us got hit in the neck. All of us in the heart.

I wonder how many of the young folks who took over Bed-Stuy's streets to say goodbye to Big are in the military right now. Since the army employs more young people than any institution other than McDonald's, the number must be high. And so the music, the language, the swagger, and the "ready to die" mentality is being integrated into America's imperial plan. Does this bode well for the rest of us? "Y'all motherfuckers come with me if you want to."

Too heavy-handed? Too much information, maybe? Maybe. But hip-hop's relationship to death comes from her life experience. Can we create a world, a language even, in which the worth of lives is more than how much money can be made off them? How many we can spare for collateral damage? Can hip-hop be a part of that building? Yes. Maybe we need this exportation, this movement away from what has become an industry. Maybe it is the youth of Brazil, Cuba, South Africa, and Palestine who can reflect back at us where we really are. Where we want to go. After all, no matter how disenfranchised folks in the States are, we are still subjects/citizens of the most powerful military and economic power the globe has ever known. My generation has yet to learn to carry this weight, which we did not ask for, with grace.

I pronounce the word *coffin* the way I do *coughing*. It's the Brooklyn in my mouth. When I was a kid, my parents taught me that we say "God bless you" after someone sneezes, or coughs, because in that instant when we have no control over the sneeze or the cough, we are close to death. So close, in fact, that when we come back from it, we greet each other with the name of God. A "welcome back." Always, the difference between life and death is a breath away.

Images of coffins coming back from Iraq are rare to come by in our corporate, for-profit media. It is easier to get an idea of American deaths in Iraq from foreign media outlets. But the coffins are indeed coming back. The boots, empty. The uniforms, like skeletons, void of life force. And the dead Iraqis? In the tens of thousands, and we are likely to never know even an approximate death count. Our government thinks it's better if we do not know. We can keep shopping (get out and buy the new rap CDs!) and dying from lack of health care. We can keep blinging while AIDS ravages Africa. We can keep dropping it like it's hot while bombs get dropped in our names.

It is bigger than hip-hop.

TOO $HORT

THE INTERVIEW 1996

The West Coast's first rap star, Too $hort had three
sellout indie albums in the early 1980s, long before
1988's *Born to Mack* solidified his underground
legacy. Hailing from Oakland, Too $hort writes that
music evokes the attitude of an unapologetic player.
His songs, with their slow, looming bass, raucous
words, and West Coast swagger, were bumped more
in car tape decks than on the radio. Merging a simplistic rhyme scheme and knack for humor, his laid-
back rap style inspired a league of wannabes. His
music is meant to be bumped, the soundtrack for
those from west to east who love to front in their
rides.

I f you've been around [in the rap game] you get a little
clout. You can show your face here and there. Things seem
to roll a little easier when you're recognized.

I was famous before I had any money. So therefore I'm sitting there and everybody's goin' "Too Short! Too Short! Let
me have your autograph!" when I'm living in a little one-
bedroom apartment with my rope chain and a Cadillac I

bought with my last money just to hold on to an image. I learned to respect the fame, but the hardest thing in this business is learning to respect the money. It's not just [trying to] make it over and over again but doing the right things with [the money you have]. I look at Death Row, Ruthless, Def Jam, Luke Records, Rap-A-Lot, and all the other rap empires, and I know what I want. I'm learning to become either a label or at least a major production company where I would sign maybe five to ten producers, hire a bunch of musicians, and we just make music for whoever wants it.

My personal theory is that rappers don't really lose it lyrically, they just don't pay attention to the production. That first album, when you was broke, came out the bomb, but then [with] that next one you've got some jewelry. You got a car. The girls want you. And then you go in the studio and you got the ego and the ego can't make records. Records gotta come from within.

I like to deal with subjects like bein' a player and sometimes little things about what's goin' on in the community. But if you're a Too $hort fan you know that I get off into it. It's not lyrically complex. It's slow as hell. I really don't try to make records that'll ever be played in the club that you can dance to. I never really try to make a radio hit because I find that that can really throw you off track. I just keep it slow with a lot of bass, and a lot of explicit language. I gotta uphold the image. There's a lot of pimps and players on the mic, but if you listen to them you can honestly feel that they don't really know what they're talkin' about. They're just feeding off something they heard from somebody else.

I moved to Atlanta because it's a complete music town from R&B to rap to bass. So this is where I thought I should be. Not in L.A. and not in New York. I decided to be somewhere where I could get in there and work. I was feeling uncomfortable in Oakland based on the fact that I had threats coming in from this way and that. Now I ain't scared to get killed and I ain't scared to kill a muthafucka, but why should I have to turn gangsta? I ain't never sold dope. I ain't never done drive-bys. So why should I have to strap every day because some nigga is mad at me? That's bullshit.

THE WHIP

A key in the ignition turns. Rollin' through the hood at five miles per hour so everybody sees you. Check your mirrors at the stoplight 'cuz somebody with a gat wants to be you. You are what you drive. The story keeps spinning like those rims you can't afford.

RIDIN' DIRTY

BY ROBERT JOHNSON III

Cars say a lot about the people who drive them. The vehicles we choose to twist speak volumes to the other drivers, passengers, and pedestrians that make up our world. The great American car culture has been solidified in our collective psyche as a mix of sex, style, status, speed, and power. The old adage "the clothes make the man" can just as easily apply to that man's car. Automobiles fulfill dreams of success, pride, and respect. They give us the ultimate choice: freedom to go as we please in our home away from home. How would we manage without them?

However, car culture approaching the 1980s was on a collision course with a fast-growing pop culture juggernaut: hip-hop. This juggernaut would make car culture its own, and the masses would follow hip-hop's lead. The irresistible automotive accessories such as chrome rims and full entertainment systems would come to permeate middle America, from the hood to the 'burbs, all because hip-hop became the definition of cool.

When MTV introduced Xzibit, the exuberant Westsider, as the host of *Pimp My Ride,* the show that turned automotive pumpkins (i.e., lemons) into stagecoaches in under a half hour, it became an instant smash. On the show, selected contestants who own the very worst in buckets and hoopties are given a free overhaul, conducted by a Los Angeles–area detailing outfit. This overhaul generally includes the most innovative paint jobs, rims, engines, leather, velvet or suede interior, and decorative extras more likely to be found in a bachelor pad: record players, aquariums with freshwater piranhas, and so on.

Every episode I see, I think about the full restoration I "planned" in my postcollegiate days for my cherry red 1967 Volkswagen Bug, complete with thirteen-inch chrome Daytons (wire rims). Years before the Bug, there was my 1974 Delta 88, a monster machine that comfortably seated eight passengers. I imagined pimpin' a blue "bowling ball swirl" paint job and Chrome Cragars deep-dish rims onto that whip. Everyone I have ever known has dreamt of what their car would look like if they had the dough to spare.

But if you don't have the dough, what do you do? Get a ninety-nine-dollar paint job by Earl Sheib, the McDonald's of auto detailing? Drop the chassis and put a homemade kicker box with two ten-inch speakers in the trunk? The list of "hood" accessories is endless. The designs are always creative, extremely competitive, and still personalized because they're made by folks at the bottom of the socioeconomic ladder, folks who have had to make something out of nothing every day. That is the essence of hip-hop, and this is what we bring to American car culture.

Yours truly came up in the automotive capital of the world, Detroit, Michigan. As the city that boasts the oldest freeway in the United States, the Davison, Motown, it's safe to say, has loved cars for some time, and so have I. "Motown" derived from the "Motor City" did not apply to me, because I had no motor or any other parts needed to be "rolling." This led me to the bane of my young existence:

public transportation. Looking back, my first objective in life was getting any kind of action from a cutie checking for what I thought was game. My second was to get off the bus.

I lived on the west side of Detroit and went to school on the east side. Translation: two hours of my afterschool years from sixth grade to my junior year of high school were spent on the bus. I went from the Lafayette, to the Grand River, to the Schoolcraft. Boy oh boy, it went on forever. All this time, I walked past drivers, waited at the bus stop watching drivers pass me by, and rode the bus looking at rulers of the road until a *ding* announced my stop.

The bus slowed just as the Corvette I was admiring sped off toward its destination. As far apart as we were on the automotive field of life, those on the bus and those in the hot cars whipping past had a common goal: to get from point A to point B. But the other side got to enjoy the journey.

Although I did enjoy the camaraderie of kicking it with my crew on the bus, I equally hated the many misadventures that came with it: the fights, the robberies, the heat, the rain, the snow, the breakdowns, the overpacked buses that forced me to wait for the next bus (which was too packed also), the unpleasant smells, and, most important, the time. Time kept on ticking.

With such comical handles as "the Iron Pimp," "the Freight," or even "the D.O.T." (for Department of Transportation), one could never be taken seriously as a regular bus rider. Thus, I quickly hypothesized that if my second objective was achieved it would drastically affect the first objective, because the whip meant freedom. Freedom to skip school, freedom to get to her house and get freaky on the basement couch before her mama got home from work, freedom to go where I pleased whenever I wanted.

The first time I got a ride home with a friend, at sixteen,

on the same route I used to take the bus, I got there in like fifteen minutes. Then and there, the seed was sown. I had to get a car as soon as possible, by any means necessary.

My first ride, a Mercury Lynx, was about as unofficial as you could get. I had no insurance, no registration, and stolen plates. But at least it ran. Yeah. You couldn't tell me shit! I was off the bus and that was all that mattered. Or so I thought.

The cat and mouse game I played in my Lynx, maneuvering through the potholed streets of "the D" and ducking the Blue Pigs while scooping as many ladies as I could, was a rite of passage that ghetto youngsters were experiencing all across the country, unbeknownst to us, all with the same soundtrack, which reflected our daily struggles and aspirations, sometimes all in one verse: hip-hop.

"EVERY SINGLE WEEKEND"

"Case of the P.T.A." put the then next-generation rap stars Leaders of the New School at the forefront of hip-hop, introducing an explosive, energetic, and later-to-go-solo Busta Rhymes. LONS was a crew out of Long Island whose debut album, *A Future Without a Past*, articulated the roller coaster of high school life, addressing issues ranging from the quality of their education, the bully problem, and the "feminine fatt." The second single was "Sobb Story," a *Cruel Intentions* sort of song that versed how an automobile can be a catalyst to all drama that high school can bring. As they ran down the list of situations ranging from working like a slave for a down payment to getting played by "friends" with cars who never scoop you when you are hoofin' it, the song created a de facto Ten Commandments for owning an automobile in one's teenage years:

1) Thou must get a car.

2) Thou shalt not roll, see a friend walking, beep, and keep driving. Thou must pick them up.

3) Thou shalt watch for leeches, for when thou gets a first car everyone becomes thy best friend.

4) Thou shalt not be a leech.

5) The girls with Gucci and Fendi won't allow thee, if on foot, to get friendly. (These are still the ladies thou wants, even when knowing that they will only bring drama to thyself.)

6) Thou shalt always get snaps on the petro (gas), unless it's thy homies.

7) Thou shalt not hog the radio or play a record or song over and over again (a commandment I breaketh regularly to this day).

8) Thou whip shalt have style and/or character.

9) Thou shalt keep thy game trump tight. For a car is a car—the function of thy automobile is transportation.

10) When thy ride is down and gone, remember that I knowest thee and thee knowest Thou!

Learning the commandments of owning a car was major, but one masterful tune would coincide with drivers hiding their shame "around the corner" and "down the street" in hoods worldwide. In 1989, Sir Mix-A-Lot created a work of genius in "My Hooptie," a classic anthem dedicated to the eyesores of ghettos everywhere. A "hooptie" can be any rundown car that saw its glory some years (if not decades) in the past.

Hoopties can have as much style and character as a brand-new car, or can be devoid of it completely. They are generally recognizable by such attributes as the primer gray (ready, but not totally ready, for a paint job), cardboard taped over smashed-out windows, missing hubcaps, or mufflers held up by bungie cords. But the most important fun fact is that hoopties are unreliable as hell! Their batteries die. The starters don't always work. The locks are selectively broken. They'll get you where you want to go, but getting back is often another story.

My Lynx barely ran. But with a tape deck, a cheap amplifier, and some six-by-nine-inch speakers, I was the king of my world. My friends would crack jokes and talk shit whenever we climbed in and rolled out. I felt like the homeboy of mine who couldn't afford Adidas and thus wore the Payless Shoe four-stripe knockoffs with argyle laces. Necessity made us inventors, which in turn gave us extra pride in any possession, even if it was less than perfect. Just like the jean jacket outfit with Mickey Mouse airbrushed on the back, the rhinestoned Starter hats, or the gold chain with the Cadillac hood ornament as the medallion, anything we owned had to be contrary to the norm, whatever it was, even a hooptie.

"LET ME RIDE"

Until 1991, the East Coast controlled the direction of hip-hop. In a little over a decade since the genre's inception, New York had produced the majority of artists who would have a meteoric impact on the music and trends that would come to define the culture, socially and politically. But just as hip-hop spread from the Bronx to Queens, through Brooklyn, and so on, it also spread from New York to Cleveland and all the way to Oakland and beyond. As Chuck D recalled, "Rap was the urban CNN." A flood of "reporters" nationwide were telling it like it was, no matter where they were from, emerging with topics and personas ranging from pro-black to pimping, gangster life, and even preaching.

Nowhere was hip-hop's dominance more evident than in the musical chronicling of adolescent automotive adventures from the Atlantic to the Pacific. On the 213 side of things, Friday, Saturday, and Sunday cruising the streets of Watts and South Central gave inspiration for Kam's "Every Single Weekend." Kam's words were the experience of so many teenagers in the late eighties and early nineties: beepers beeping before the cell phone era, the blowing of (what we thought was) ridiculous cash, dating and designer clothing, fronting in whoever available's cars, the ducking of the police, the showing out for the young ladies, and, of course, getting twisted on malt liquor.

LL's "The Boomin' System" snatched the beat of En Vogue's breakthrough hit "Hold On" to make a downright gangster anthem dedicated to "all the brothers who like to front in their rides." A night in the life of any fella armed with "the jam that you're lovin', that don't get no airplay" as the bait, and the boomin' system as the icebreaker, he is on the prowl and loving every minute of the adventure. The second verse, evidence of his success, explains that he is now in the company of beautiful women and is participating in a late-night American pastime: cruising. He even manages to drop a product endorsement for a German beer, inviting Mary Jane to enter the party and show that New Yorkers roll hard, too, proving throughout that a dope ride is the ultimate chick magnet.

Miami's L'Trimm even blipped on the radar with "Cars with the Boom," cosigning that women love cars with sounds. Many tapes were made to accommodate this phenomenon because the fellas respected it and the ladies loved it. Can it be that it was all so simple?

There were also cuts that had nothing to do with rolling that became riding anthems. Too $hort's "Freaky Tales" wasn't as lyrically complex as anthems from the period coming from the East, but that 808 bump sealed the deal. Teaching an important lesson in what was heard lyrically versus simply what was heard, $hort's boomin' system kicked out pimp tales of his sexual exploits in East Oakland. No trunk rattle, no hiss of open wires from the bass, for those were unacceptable and showed a lack of sophistication in ghetto terms.

More songs followed, coming out of Los Angeles, Houston, Seattle, and Miami. MC Breed's "Ain't No Future in Yo Frontin' " got it. Bone Thugs-N-Harmony's "Thuggish Ruggish Bone" got it, as did OutKast's "Southernplayalisticadillacmuzik."

Avid hip-hop fans seemed amped at the similarities and differences in a culture that had come to represent the consensus of our generation across the country, everywhere except for in New York City. Why was so much of the music that everyone loved nationwide despised by both fans and critics in the Big Apple? And why was so much of the music New York revered seen as just okay by the rest of us?

Was it just the ego that came with birthing the culture that started in the Bronx but was spawning up across the country in ghettos everywhere, and the originators not wanting to lose ownership? Was it a hip-hop caste system centered in the five boroughs, that deemed everyone's music and regional culture less than worthy the farther you got from New York, geographically? Was there a common denominator that could bring us together, or did the 1990s set us up for a civil war?

"AIN'T NO FUTURE IN YO FRONTIN' "

And then there was "The Chronic." The Left Coast had for the first time shifted the paradigm of what and where hip-hop was. Props to every MC on the album for creating a classic with rich stories of rollin' in a six-four with sixteen switches, gang banging, and macking chicks, and fierce lyricism and a diaspora of skits, from the revolutionary "If I gotta die for this little African to have a future, I'm a dead muthafucka!" intro to "Little Ghetto Boy" to "The $20 Sack Pyramid." It's arguably the most hilarious skit punctuated with DOC's raspy voice saying "Uh, I know Doc."

In short, the West had finally struck gold. The production was the product of a Compton DJ, Dr. Dre, who had undoubtedly spent some time on foot before graduating to vehicle status. Dre had spun house parties, knowing what to play, how it should sound, and how the people would react. The album was an overwhelming hit with listeners nationwide, colonizing the car culture "sound" under the banner of the West Coast. Crazy drums, so much bass (but the highs were audible), synthesizers complemented with the craziest gangsters on wax since, well, N.W.A. So gangster that the *Source* magazine, with its East Coast hip-hop bias on its shoulder, eventually had to give props and up it to five mics from the original rating of four and a half.

"A BEAMER, A NECKLACE, OR FREEDOM?"

The automobile became the ultimate invention. Created in the name of transportation, it would "ironically" become a symbol of freedom. Cars move faster than the train of thought, and level the socioeconomic playing field to give the driver a tool to fulfill their personal bliss. They grant us the choice in a land founded on the principles of life, liberty, and the pursuit of happiness. But in 1908, when Henry Ford's Model T first came off the line, white women couldn't vote and the NAACP hadn't even been created. Years later, all citizens of the country still aren't all the way free. There are rules, written and unwritten, that if not "obeyed" can lead to complications.

It's no secret that blacks have had an unsettling relationship with the authority figures of this country since we arrived, but nothing has exacerbated that relationship more than the automobile. In my generation, flashy cars coupled with antiestablishment ideology are two main ingredients necessary for those who would come to exemplify hip-hop, including those most closely aligned to it, young black males. Furthermore, as hip-hop and American car culture grew intertwined in popularity and visibility, all eyes were on us, on and off the microphone, good, bad, and ugly. All the while, haters of every race lay in waiting for an event to say to the world, "See, I told you so!" The more things change, the more things stay the same. As history does repeat itself for those who follow, this is not a new phenomenon.

Jack Johnson, the first black heavyweight boxing champion of the world, was an avid fan of the automobile, and was also the victim of racial profiling in the early 1900s. A colossal man in stature who was unabashedly flamboyant, immensely wealthy for a "negro" at the time, and who had a penchant for white women, he was loathed by white Americans for representing everything vile and repugnant in "successful and uppity niggers."

Unbeatable in the ring by any of the "great white hopes," he was eventually knocked out by the law. Johnson was convicted of violating the Mann Act, which barred the transportation of women in interstate commerce for the purpose of debauchery. Johnson, with a never-ending carousel of fair-skinned beauties, had a new white lady friend, a nineteen-year-old prostitute he was in a relationship with, across state lines, and her mother charged that Johnson "abducted" her daughter. He was convicted in 1912 and sentenced to a year in prison. This would be one of Johnson's many run-ins with the law, as Johnson, a black man in postslavery times, refused to know and remain in "his place" in white society.

A century later, when hip-hop and American car culture became intertwined, all eyes were on rappers, the modern-day Jack Johnsons on and off the microphone. Fast money, pretty women, and foreign cars were the über symbols of success, symbols flaunted before the community by the upwardly mobile and the kings of the underworld (i.e., the dope man), both of whom were influenced by the top tax bracket of wealthy Americans who lived as they pleased, free from the troubles of money.

Not unlike the fashion fads that were Starter jackets, Timberlands, and Chuck Taylors, your automobile became an extension of your individuality and means. Soon the everyday working man began expressing his freedom to buy the best and most expensive cars automakers had to offer. Black males were seen rolling in Benzes, Beamers, six Fos, SSes, and of course the hood-favored Cut Supremes and Coupe DeVilles. And with so many expensive rides in hoods where high-end employment was at a minimum, the local cops almost always assumed that those behind the wheel of these high-end whips had to be up to no good.

DWB stands for driving while black. The LAPD knows it's not a new phenomenon. Back in 1965 there was an altercation between black motorist Marquette Frye and a white Los Angeles police officer that sparked the historic uprising in Watts. After the ashes cooled and social change became the goal, the grassroots movement of men and women who fought injustice, pushing for civil rights on the West Coast, soon formed the Black Panther Party and the Organization Us, with the purpose of creating healthy, blossoming, and self-sufficient communities. If they said "Progress!," then FBI director J. Edgar Hoover said, "Not that far!" Hoover's Counterintelligence Program would prove to be the invisible enemy that would strike from the shadows and do whatever it took to complete the "job," and they did. It was in the interest of national security, it was "legal," and it was the United States government. So the combustible mix of the Vietnam fiasco, a downturn in blue collar jobs in L.A. County, and a vacuum in black leadership became a ticking time bomb in the black community that eventually blew up on all of Los Angeles in the creation of street gangs. This time around, the gangs would rob, steal, and kill while maintaining a flare that helped them multiply, exponentially, making an impression upon all individuals who dreamed of the "fast life." But the audaciousness of a post–civil rights generation, affected by street gangs, Reaganomics, and an "I don't give a fuck" attitude, would create a mentality of a group who would create a song giving a diametrically opposed view to DWB, one that would make police departments cringe even to this day.

N.W.A.'s "Fuck the Police" was an angry tirade against the racist, weak, and amoral cops who prey on young blacks. Recorded in 1988, the song would put N.W.A. (Niggaz With Attitude) on an FBI watch list. Just a few years after its release, Rodney King would be pulverized by numerous clubs and Tasers by none other than the LAPD. This time, the crime was caught on tape, giving N.W.A. the validation among whites that it already had in the hood.

Unfortunately, the police weren't the only predator in the concrete jungle. Registration and insurance are a must to protect you and other drivers in case of an accident or theft, but there are often other types of "insurance" drivers deem necessary. Mack 10 refers to firearms as the "African Express," because he "don't leave home without [one]." In the eyes of some, having a gun is necessary to protect them and their rides from jackers who are out there looking to "come up."

In 1995, in Harlem, New York, an acquaintance of Queen

Latifah's was shot as the rapper/actress was "relieved of" her BMW 750. This would perhaps explain why less than a year later she was arrested for gun possession. Not long after, countless numbers of our favorite MCs would start catching charges for unregistered guns in their vehicles: DMX, Busta Rhymes, Beanie Sigal, Fabolous, Master P, Snoop Dogg, Eminem, and the list goes on and on. In theory, protection is warranted, and a right granted by the United Snakes of America under the Second Amendment, or is it just another "freedom" that gives us a "choice" meant to entangle us in the web of the criminal justice system?

Whatever the cause, this time out black men are being subjected to extensive racial profiling nationwide under the auspices of the War on _____ (fill in the black—I mean blank) A) Drugs, B) Gangs, C) Crime, D) Hip-Hop. The admission of the existence of the hip-hop police unit in New York City, designed to monitor "hip-hop artists" and share information with police departments nationwide, took very few by surprise. It was somewhat similar to the Counter Intelligence Program created by FBI director J. Edgar Hoover to covertly monitor the activities and progress of those deemed "un-American" and neutralize their movements.

As hip-hop has added new vitality to the automotive industry, the by-products have been astounding for all involved. The pros of the marriage of hip-hop and car culture far outweigh the cons, mostly due to another important juggernaut of this land: capitalism. Our generation and all that follow have been aggressive consumers, and corporate America realized that early on, earlier than the rappers who were generally pimped by offering corporations free exposure each and every time they dropped a name in a verse. Thus, at the turn of the millennium, automakers around the world began to embrace us in varying degrees.

On one side, you have Toyota, with their subsidiary Scion,

who have created a car line parallel to the ideals of hip-hop car enthusiasts who demand customization. Aligned with the "socially friendly" side of hip-hop, Scion has thrown parties spun by iconic DJs (Jazzy Jeff, Biz Markie, and Red Alert) and sponsored b-boy events with the Rock Steady Crew. Scion is selling hip-hop multiculturalism and a lot of those hot-looking cars at the very same time. There's nothing wrong with this unless you were a contestant in their NextUp MC contests, where one finalist was shut down because of the "politically charged" content in his lyrics. Boooooo, Toyota/Scion! That's not hip-hop. That's culture pimping.

On the other hand, you have Sean Combs selling one hundred Sean John Navigators, ironically, the same type of SUV that was the getaway vehicle in the infamous club shooting at Club New York involving rapper turned inmate Shyne. Contrary to numerous accounts in the media, Lincoln-Mercury had nothing to do with this so-called partnership, but by brand recognition they were "aligned" with hip-hop's premier tastemaker. They wanted him to design an SUV for his audience. The result was nothing less than a "ghetto fabulous" offering: big rims, tinted windows, a DVD player, TV screens in the dash and headrest (six in total), a PlayStation 2, and, most important: the Sean John logo. That's hip-hop!

Last, you know your culture has truly arrived when Hollywood comes knocking. The *Fast and the Furious* films, set in the world of underground street racing, feature hip-hop superstars Ja Rule in the first and Ludacris in the sequel. Snoop Dogg was featured in a recent Chrysler commercial with none other than automotive don Lee Iacocca, the two rolling in a pimped-out golf cart kitted with an electric blue paint job and rims.

Chrysler was delighted because the odd couple pairing

was given the thumbs-up by audiences both young and old and ended with Snoop's patented "Fo-shizzle, Ica-zizzle" referring to Mr. Iacocca. But as we become the spokespersons and cosigners of the automotive industry, when will we branch out to other arenas in the automotive world? Is Slim Thug the only artist with aspirations of owning a dealership? With so many artists that love to "redline" foreign cars in their songs, where are our Jeff Gordons, a NASCAR driver turned car dealership owner? Will we ever have a Lee Iacocca?

Even with all the drama that comes with the car life, the reality is that we're not too sure of what we would do without it. As blacks have struggled to overcome segregation and inequality, we are still Americans in this land of milk and honey. We want our piece of the pie, too. A family, a home . . . maybe not the picket fence, but definitely the two-car garage, filled with something sick!

I remember when the crime of the day was snatching Cadillac or Mercury emblems off hoods and using them as medallions for our fake gold chains. That small piece of the car made me feel special. Function versus necessity aside, I still feel like a part of something bigger than myself when I pull onto the road. Until I'm flying George Jetson–style, I will be a champion of the automobile, hip-hop, and all that comes with it.

ROB MARRIOTT

THE INTERVIEW 2004

A cofounder of *XXL*, Rob Marriott has eyewitness accounts of hip-hop's juggernauting skies and decadent pits. Author of the pimp pictorial *Pimpnosis*, and with a slew of iconic interviews under his belt, Marriott spins his wheels on the haters and lovers of bling's debauchery.

The argument that the bling culture of hip-hop—with its chintzy, pimped-out glamour and diamond-infested carnality—leads to the moral and economic degradation of its fans is a valid one. It is also stating the obvious. It does not take a genius to see that bling-hop's compulsion for flossing and vulgar self-aggrandizement does little to foster humility or sane attitudes toward resources. Nor does it take much to see that the image of a thug king like 50 Cent, peppered with bullet wounds, clad in designer teflon and dripping with diamonds, poses real questions about the state of young America. Yes, yes, we know, we know: hip-hop is a parade of nigga psychoses—niggerism writ large—conspicuous consumption being the least of its demons. And yes, most rappers and their congregations are too busy gittin' crunk to give a flying fuck about how these ideas and images are affecting the kids or our collective economic security. Still, for anyone to expect rapper types* to burden themselves with the moral and economic fate of the nation defies logic. For me, the acknowledgment that the Negro's bling habit is both wasteful and foolish is not so much a critique as it is a point of departure.

Bling culture, or at least the wanton out-of-control materialism it describes and celebrates, is like violence: American as cherry pie. It was an American phenomenon long before Juvenile and the Cash Money Millionaires coined the phrase. Everyone and everything from Elvis, Marilyn Monroe, and Liberace to media like *Vanity Fair* and *Dynasty* were bling before bling, servicing America's lovejones for flash and cash. Who within the reach of a remote control has not been hypnotized by the elusive specter of the good life? And who more so than poor folk, whose deep abiding love for television† and relative deprivation make them most susceptible?

---

* Meaning young people a) who rhyme for a living, b) whose inspiration is as likely to come from television commercials as it is from any revolutionary agitprop, c) whose own economic security teeters on the whim of corporate bosses and fickle adolescents.
† From my informal survey: the poorer the neighborhood, the higher the TV-per-room ratio.

THE ICE

It's blinging all over. On fingers. In ears. Around necks. Someone's getting rich. And it ain't the dark faces working the mines.
It ain't the writers whose words always rhyme. It ain't the people
who say "I do." No matter who you are, most likely the real king
of bling ain't you.

THE ICE

BY GREGORY L. JOHNSON

From ghetto to ghetto
Jo 'burg to Tampa-'burg
A life is the price for ice that blur sight
—El Juba, "Diamonds"

As my college roommate, Ricky from Chi-town, liked to put it, "Niggas draw heat." Maybe that explains the passion of Jesús (name changed to protect the innocent, or more likely the guilty) for the ice. Or perhaps, like the sparklers he preferred to sport, his raison d'être lies in his origins. A product of uptown New York City, 'Zoos (as a child, his little sister couldn't pronounce "Jesús") still moves to the frenetic pulse of Washington Heights while physically in the depths of Tampa's soupy sluggishness. Seeing major players with weight—whether coppin', sellin', or just throwing it around by flashing bread, whips, and jewels—left its mark on him. He had that distinct big-city swagger that stands out in Cigar City.

I'm sure his family meant well by picking up their stakes and moving south to raise their kids; many East Coast transplants to the Sunshine State often do. They soon found that relocating to Florida only moved 'Zoos a degree closer to the epicenter of the sickness known as the dope game. Since the 1980s, the Bottom's gaudy pink glow as the vice-drenched cocaine capital has in fact dimmed and states like Texas and California have leaped ahead, thanks in part to various Mexican syndicates and mafias. But showers of blow still move in from the Gulf of Mexico—enough keys rain down on the Florida dope-boy network to start thousands of pavé-studded jewelry collections.

And where there are d-boys flush with flow, jack-boys are soon to go. But hey, you couldn't tell my homeboy 'Zoos *shit*. He always thought himself too cool for school, particularly on one summer day in 2000, as the heat made its last sizzling stand before bowing to the breezy fall. 'Zoos tipped his snow white Buccaneers hat to the homies gathered around the spot, stepped into his brand-new air-conditioned Audi, and peeled out to check on one of his many lovelies. As stic-man of dead prez, a wise poet native to the state, once said, "The summertime makes a woman more sexual." Therefore, your game has to be on schedule. And Jesús liked to be on time.

Yeah, 'Zoos was a charming young son of a bitch, no doubt. He kept crisp brand-name gear, white gold chains with stunning Lazarus and Jesus pieces, and a regular rotation of new import tuners—all funded by moving weight. Factor in his dark Afro-Latin good looks and clever, flirty *piropos*, and few young Tampa tenders could abstain from his advances.

As the sun began to drop, the cutie pie had 'Zoos's full attention, and in turn he had shorty just about wrapped around his finger. At some point, 'Zoos's sharp eyes pierced the humid dusk and he spotted a used Buick in the cut, parked behind a thick camouflage of aloe plants and palmettos. "Somebody got out," he remembered. "Then they changed their minds, got back in the car, and rolled out, so I didn't think nothin' of it."

He didn't flash back to the recent theft he had suffered, either. Not more than a few days prior, Jesús had snapped up a high-tech camcorder to kill a little time on one of those long July days. Typical shit, you know: rolling trees and getting blowed, then wildin' and snappin' jokes on camera, jewels out in full force, maybe flashing a little bread as was his wont, though he was too high to recall once he noticed the cam had been stolen.

His mistake, see, was to leave his cam in the car when electronics will fetch you some decent paper at any of many pawnshops. Naturally, someone hungrier and more observant hit his snoozin' ass up. And on that tape was enough evidence of disposable wealth to leave any jack-boy drooling. As he left his lady friend's plantation neighborhood to go fill up his tank at a nearby 7-Eleven, 'Zoos failed to add it all up to the proper sum.

Gas stations have been beloved icons of Americana ever since Rockefeller started dotting the nation's roads with his Standard Oil bulk outlets at the turn of the twentieth century. Still, whether in L.A., Newark, Houston, Baltimore, or Detroit, anyone from the wrong side of the tracks in a city dominated by car culture knows the gas station means something else: potential danger. Get your gas and get it quick, but don't get too flashy with it.

Flossin' was J's favorite pastime, though. His ten-carat, twenty-one-inch white gold necklace with matching cross pendant swung invitingly as he stepped out of his Audi. His three-carat ring and diamond bracelet chimed in, too. He was just beginning to fill 'er up when he noticed a car cruising by. It was the same ride he'd spotted earlier—the ominous Buick (i.e., the "drive-by car" made infamous by legions of jackers and killers nationwide). After making an abrupt U-turn on Waters Ave., this particular Buick pulled into the 7-Eleven.

It was the moment he feared. "The car pulls up into the

gas station and stops on the other side of the island, at the pump next to me," Jesús told me later. "Their car is parallel to my car, pointed in the same direction. Nobody gets out of the car, right? After a while, I'm pumping my gas like, 'Damn. Ain't nobody got out the car yet—what the fuck?' "

'Zoos shook the last drops of gas from the nozzle, hung it back on the pump, and slid back into his ride. As his Audi ignited, the strange Buick pulled a sharp right, blocking off his forward progress. A screw-faced little 'jit—barely a teenager—crept out of the backseat, pushing the door open and clutching a gun with his right hand. With the left, he quickly brought a black mask down over his features.

But the youngblood's evident inexperience at robbery spoiled his plan. The precious seconds wasted while donning the mask were a gift to his potential vic. The bright but brief glint of the large-caliber chrome pistol jutting out of the door frame was all the warning Jesús needed to bail—and fast.

"He should have already had his mask on," sighed 'Zoos. "Luckily, he's putting the mask on and getting the eyeholes aligned and shit . . . that gave me the split second I needed to make my move, you know?" Dropping his seat back to a near horizontal position and slamming the gears into reverse, 'Zoos swung the wheel hard. His tires screeched out a three-quarter donut as he flew out of the gas station at top speed. Bullets greeted his maneuver, splintering his windshield into a mass of spiderwebbed bullet holes and destroying his speedometer. The chase was on.

"I was ridin' in my Audi V-8, and they were in a Buick," Jesús later said with a chuckle. "I took that back cut by KFC, made that turn by the Village Inn, took Dale Mabry to Busch, and gunned that bitch to eighty all the way back to the crib."

Once he got back to the ranch, 'Zoos threw on his Kevlar vest and grabbed the Tec-9 he had stashed under the bed, barely coherent in his frenzy as he tried to explain the situation and rally the crew into action. "These niggas already know where I live," he barked, before his soldiers hit the steamy Tampa night en masse for a safety patrol.

None of his peoples ever crossed paths with the jackers or their deadly g-ride again, though Jesús suspected the jackboys were the ones who also stole his camcorder. "I think them same niggas saw us wildin' out on the camera and figured, 'Damn. We gotta try to catch this nigga,' " he concluded. "So I think them niggas followed me from my house when I went to go see homegirl."

And the desired diamond chain, what of that? Sold to cover an $8,000 business debt—yep, eight g's. That was the market rate for a young minority's life that day. Yet back in Africa, where a black majority works mines and rivers for shine, where those same cursed diamonds were likely born, brown life is even cheaper.

THE PRIMEVAL ELEMENT

Diamonds give you power; diamonds beam force. That's been the buzz on ice since the first primary source (i.e., its first mention in recorded human history dating back to India in the fourth century B.C.E.). A couple centuries later, word of the superhard crystal leaked to the Greeks, who christened the stone *adamas*—meaning unconquerable or invincible, from the root word *adamaos*, for "I tame" or "I subdue." Even then, the ancients honored the diamond as an alpha gem among lesser elements, the kick-ass mineral that could scratch everything but not be scratched by anything save another diamond.

Indians considered the rock to be sacred to their warrior god, Indra, and believed that human souls could reincarnate in such minerals. Indian diamonds were also icons of social status: their clearest, brightest diamonds were reserved for their highest, whitest (or most Aryan) caste, the Brahmins. For centuries, India was the sole source of diamonds worldwide, until, upon establishing trade routes with Asia, the white man got wise to them as well. Sprung off the beauty of this clear crystal, sixteenth-century European nobles employed the stone as one of their many representations of mastery over man and nature. By adding unpolished diamonds to their ostentatious crown jewelry, these medieval powers stunted on each other in a fierce game of one-upmanship. In a scant two centuries, this kind of Western hunger for OPR (other people's resources) drove Europe to bombard Asia, Africa, and America with crusades and colonies, in search of the raw materials that would spur the birth of capitalism.

Unsurprisingly, white rulers and their thirst for diamonds raised their value globally. As the American Museum of Natural History points out, "The implications of the rise of diamonds' popularity in ornamentation are nothing short of revolutionary—as more diamonds reach Europe, [worldwide] demand . . . increases." Conveniently, eighteenth-century Portuguese rulers found a more expedient alternative to the Indian rivers sparkling with ice. The transatlantic slave trade supplied plenty of African captives to work the hills of Brazil's Chapada Diamantina region in Bahia. Portugal's west-side colony endowed Europe with a newfound monopoly on worldwide diamond supply. The unearthing of Brazilian diamond mines established a long, tragic hate triangle between enforced black labor, unspeakable acts of cruelty, and immeasurable white wealth.

THE BIRTH OF A NATION

The victorious Union army of the United States may have hammered out the tombstone for nineteenth-century chattel slavery in the American South and Midwest, but diamonds buried in South African soil cast a spell of fortune that resurrected its vampiric spirit in an early form of apartheid. Young boys playing in the dirt unearthed the 10.73-carat Eureka by chance; while the 47.75-carat Star of South Africa was discovered by a poor black Kaffir who sold the stone to whites for five hundred sheep, ten head of cattle, and a horse. (Given the true value of the stone, this may be one of the earliest and most notorious "nigger deals" on record.) Wealthy interests in London were consulted. They concluded that this dusty, remote outpost in southern Africa hid the come-up of the century, a verdict that lured prospectors from every corner of the British Empire to swarm South Africa.

Among the shady characters drawn to the chase were Barney Barnato, a former boxer and juggling clown turned diamond hustler, and Cecil Rhodes, a grumpy intellectual and closeted homosexual who later founded Rhodesia and became southern Africa's most brutal, ruthless, and powerful colonizer. Rhodes bought the rights to a mine established by the de Beers brothers, forming the De Beers company. Then he began instigating beefs among black tribes in classic "divide and conquer" fashion, and jacking them for land to increase his holdings. Poor blacks were to be "treated like a child," Rhodes argued, forcing them into a Jim Crow–like system of disenfranchisement, pass books, random searches, and company compounds that rivaled the worst prisons. Thanks in great part to Rhodes's skillful exploitation of the natives, by 1887 De Beers rivaled Barnato's Kimberley Central as a top shot caller on South Africa's diamond scene.

With the backing of London moneymen like those of the infamous Rothschild family, Rhodes eventually neutralized his enemy Barnato by buying an alliance with him. Together, Barnato and Rhodes laid the foundation for the modern diamond industry, but it was Sir Ernest Oppenheimer—a well-connected diamond dealer who double-crossed and outmaneuvered family, friends, and enemies alike—who as chairman of De Beers refined Rhodes's diamond monopoly into a science that would make any hustler sick with envy. By hoarding as much of worldwide production as possible, De Beers could escape the inevitable boom-and-bust cycles of the global economy. When ice prices dropped too low, they yanked back on raw diamond output. When prices shot back up to their satisfaction, De Beers loosened their grip, flooded the market with product again, and caked themselves into a frenzy.

There was a drawback to this kind of contrived price rigging. Any significant new raw diamond supplies that surfaced outside the South African cartel's control would be a hard jab to their very fragile balance of power and price. Coming to grips with this cold hard fact, the South Africans developed a "cut me in or cut it out" mentality that would make *The Wire*'s book-smart gangster Stringer Bell beam with pride: scoop up or squash any loose supplies of unpolished rock; kill any organized outside threats with kindness, specifically by offering them a place in the De Beers cartel; and ruin those who refused by deliberately dropping prices until they were put out of business. These policies certified that for nearly a century De Beers made obscene amounts of paper off 80 percent of all diamonds sold worldwide.

THE GREAT IMPRESSION (A DIAMOND IN EVERY HOME)

With their monopoly firmly in place, De Beers aimed their gems to the perfect target consumer, one looking for the gaudiest of emblems to declare their new social status: the American nouveau riche, new players such as Rockefeller, Vanderbilt, Hearst, and Pulitzer, who emerged from the rumble-tumble times of the nineteenth century wealthy due to equal parts of smarts, ambition, and underhandedness.

Though one recent University of Arkansas report suggested that given the 328,000-plus carats mined and refined into 870 million diamonds annually, the value of diamonds should legitimately be no more than thirty bucks a carat in the modern market, De Beers continued to cloud their artificial price structure by establishing value to, and through, the heads of the world's youngest and sexiest superpower.

The new money being blown by these American elites from the turn of the century to the Roaring Twenties did not keep British and South African pockets fat for long: once the Great Depression hit in 1929, the demand for diamonds in the world's biggest market, the United States, plummeted. After the war, De Beers responded by smartening up, opening the market up, and persuading the common man to invest in something eternal during those unstable times. The advertising firm in their employ, N. W. Ayers, launched a 1947 marketing onslaught that is still arguably the most successful of all time. Cleverly, Ayers traded off the jewel's association with ancient royalty like Alexander the Great, the Indian Maharajas, and Maximilian I of the Hapsburgs—the first historical figure to bless wifey with a diamond engagement ring. "Diamonds Are Forever," their new slogan proclaimed, making an engagement ring an icon of stability and a pledge of eternity upon which any worthy marriage should be based.

Ayer and De Beers also carefully researched the engagement ring's most acceptable price point for the American, European, and even Japanese male. In the Old World of Europe, where the birth of the diamond industry was carefully planned, the craze for stones has never really taken root the way it did in, say, Japan, so the pitch varied for each market. American men, ads insisted, should make the small sacrifice of two months' salary; in Europe, the figure was set at one month's salary, not two. Three decades later, in post-WWII

Japan, it was found that the Nipponese male would willingly pay *three* months' salary.

The Japanese hunger for diamonds is yet another feather in the Oppenheimer cap. Yet again, they cunningly spotted an opportunity to not only play upon but shape a culture's collective psychology through symbols, exploiting both the post-WWII Japanese fascination with Western modernity and traditional Shinto values of purity, simplicity, and continuity. Whereas in the 1960s only 5 percent of Japanese brides wore engagement rings, diamonds have been so seamlessly woven into Japan's gift-giving tradition that Japan is now the second-biggest diamond market after the United States.

Hypnotized by the slogan, each new generation of fiancées felt compelled to cop their own fresh batch of ice, keeping diamond prices stable no matter what the economic cycle. Now to death and taxes was added a third permanent phenomenon: newly bought diamond engagement rings. And the baby boom population explosion of the 1940s and 1950s kept rolling, perhaps thanks in part to the shine that flashed on the fingers of these young wives, now pliable, horny, and grateful to their factory worker and soldier hubbies out there getting paid.

In less than a generation, the old tradition of gifting diamond engagement ring heirlooms passed down from generation to generation was completely erased from the American memory. The "Diamonds Are Forever" slogan programmed the mass American psyche into a collective "diamond mind," as Edward Jay Epstein, author of *The Rise and Fall of Diamonds: The Shattering of a Brilliant Illusion*, states:

> Fellas bold enough to go old-school, and bequeath wifey with your grandma's engagement ring (the way it was done prior to the Ayers campaign), God bless you. Some girls might think it's cute and quaint, sure,

but many will quietly frown when you leave the room. They'll roll their eyes hard enough to kick up a small gust of wind, and think, "hmmmm . . . *hand-me-down*."

It didn't and doesn't matter that the stronger, more secure, and sensible gesture was and is the use of that money as a down payment for a house or as an interest-bearing investment. De Beers had blazed a new trail in mind control worthy of George Orwell's *1984* world, in which slavery was freedom and weakness was strength. One would expect this Jedi mind trick to be so transparent as to be insulting, until one considers similarly counterintuitive campaigns by the modern dairy and tobacco industries.

DIAMONDS, SEX, AND HIP-HOP: "MY CHAIN HANGS DOWN TO MY DICK"

As it regards the science of symbols and public demand for them, De Beers also innovated marketing practices that have landed current rap fashionistas like Russell Simmons, P. Diddy, and Jay-Z on the *Forbes* and *Fortune* radar: the concepts of product placement and marketing celebrity lifestyle. In the 1940s, 1950s, and 1960s, studios such as Paramount, MGM, and 20th Century Fox were loaned or given millions of dollars in diamonds to display on studio starlets like Grace Kelly, Marilyn Monroe, and Liz Taylor. Publicists and journalists were recruited to plant stories about diamonds in the press. The British royal family was even approached, given their vested interest in the industry that so enriched their empire—and they began publicly promoting the legendary diamonds in their crown jewels, which themselves were a symbol of British imperial power and mystiques. Even writer Ian Fleming, inspired by an MI-5 intelligence officer in Oppenheimer's employ, had his British superspy

James Bond get into the act with his *Diamonds Are Forever* novel and movie.

Currently, De Beers and celebrated jewelers like Sir Harry Winston are still hitting Hollywood with loaned ice for major public appearances at award shows and the like, but younger upstarts like Jacob the Jeweler and Chris Aire are eating well off—better yet, *feasting* on—the ignorance of the hip-hop generation. Whereas old-guard celebs were loaned or given jewels to promote the diamond trade, many of our rap stars (and those they hire, hang with, or inspire) are generally persuaded to spend millions *out of their own pockets* to ostensibly promote themselves while simultaneously churning that insatiable American demand for the ice.

This glaring lack of understanding stems from the often outdated, outmoded minority approach to wealth and consumption in America, but in a sense, it follows the historical American pattern: it's only fair to note that those now considered old money once splurged on the stones in the same manner. Diamonds represent financial elitism, confidence, and independence—after all, if you're ballin' in the seven or eight figures, $100,000 worth of diamond jewelry represents only between 1 and 10 percent of your income. And for the newly minted Big Tymer, diamonds are the trump element, the ultimate rock in the rock-paper-scissors game. They cut and break everything, but nothing cuts or breaks them.

Symbolically, this especially appeals to hip-hop culture. Since its birth, hip-hop has struggled to deal with the trauma it has inherited from the violent jack moves and pimp slaps of slavery and colonialism. Its psychological response has been a classic one of overcompensation through bravado and machismo, displayed as loudly and gaudily as possible.

With this type of show, the hip-hop celebrity, true to the culture's strength of remixing and redefining style and aesthetic, has also managed to swing the symbolic pendulum back to the ancient traditions in which diamonds represented masculinity, privilege, and power. The use of a diamond as a phallic image, dating back to ancient India and medieval Europe, is resurrected, for example, by rapper Prodigy's boast, "My chain hangs down to my dick." The irony is that for most of the twentieth century, the modern marketing campaign for diamonds worshipped the cult of the female head of household. It was she who inspired the "Diamonds Are Forever" and "Diamonds Are a Girl's Best Friend" dictates. But the "bling bling" movement turned the assumption on its head that it was the woman's desire that compelled the man to buy the diamond. The current diamond craze among hip-hop thugs, stars, and ballers has more in common with European lords competing with each other's royal treasure than it does with the hardworking union man bringing home a sparkler to please his wife.

There is another timeless, undeniable connection between the hip-hop and diamond industries: the power of a good story. The modern music industry persists in selling rap acts from 50 Cent to J-Kwon by using some kind of fall from grace—homelessness, a criminal rap sheet, or a near-death experience—to drive sales in a nation known for its rags-to-riches obsession; likewise, it's common knowledge in the diamond trade that a good story raises the demand for a stone. Names like the Cullinian, the Hope, the Koh-i-Noor, the Golden Jubilee, the Deal Sweetener, and the Millennium Star speed up the heartbeats of rich bidders and drive up the price. That sort of rudimentary word-of-mouth buzz building was the game's standard for years, and it's still effective even today.

The immobile eight hundred–pound gorilla in hip-hop for nearly the last decade, Roc-A-Fella Records, successfully vaulted from underground to mainstream with a classic

American story as well. Echoing American new money traditions, Jay-Z and his Harlem-bred partner Dame Dash borrowed the name and swagger of one of De Beers's most favored customers, John D. Rockefeller, with dynastic ambitions. Fittingly, both men began folding their rock-studded hands at 45-degree angles and pairing them high over their heads like halos to form a sign of dynastic dominance: a diamond. Roc-A-Fella would never lose, never fall off, never end, they promised. Even in the wake of Dash and Jay's split, Grammy winner Kanye West, the current driving force at the label, released a hit single, "Diamonds Are Forever," swearing to uphold this vow "as long as [he's] alive."

Interestingly enough, in the summer of 2005, Kanye released a remix featuring Jay-Z that questioned hip-hop's hunger for diamonds in light of the poverty and devastation the gems have produced globally. The criticism is long overdue: diamonds have been implicated in devastating civil wars in Angola, Sierra Leone, Lebanon, and the Congo; the robbery of indigenous lands in Australia and Brazil; and even in money-laundering activities for terrorist groups like al-Qaeda and Hezbollah. Will Kanye's new social critique shift the obsession away from diamonds as successfully as his mentor Jay helped create it? Call me optimistic, but for the sake of millions of young 'Zooses, from New York to Houston, Washington, D.C., to Los Angeles, Atlanta to Tampa, we damn well had better pray it does.

HEATHER HUNTER

THE INTERVIEW 2005

With on-wax shout-outs by artists from Lil' Kim to LL Cool J, Heather Hunter's raw erotic persona was the benchmark for X-rated hip-hop fantasies. Dubbed Double H, she was the first black porn star to crack into mainstream erotica and the only black woman inducted into the Adult Film Hall of Fame. Back in the day, she was an aspiring R&B starlet, but her film life began in 1988 on her eighteenth birthday when an audition for a burlesque show landed her a starring role in an adult flick. Although she retired four years later to pursue more artistic interests, she's forever shadowed by her porn queen status, forever shadowed by her work (both literal and figurative) in stilettos.

I've been proving myself to other people who really don't know who Heather Hunter really is. I think the misconception in the adult industry, even though I've been out of the business for twelve years, is that you lie on your back because you have no other choice. So when you transition yourself into the mainstream they still want to keep you in the genre of the adult business. I know a lot of girls in the adult business who've tried to break through, and they've really struggled. So it's really hard to have another career.

I think I'll be branded for the rest of my life because of something that's considered taboo. So I gave my whole life to make people more comfortable with their sexuality. Now with this new generation it's glorified. And that's a double-edged sword because I didn't expect it to get so out of control. There should be other solutions for making money while still keeping your clothes on. You don't have to always do the nasty. You can just talk the nasty and still make your money. For me to see the world as it is now, I'm all for the fact that the sexual revolution has taken over in the 2000s, because it opened the doors for me. But at the same time it bothers me. When it comes to the young generation, I think they should have more knowledge about the sex industry, because it's not always glitz and glamour. I've been through dark paths to get to where I am now. I survived while a lot of the girls didn't.

I got in the business when I was eighteen. I got out when I was twenty-two and then I came back and gave them a few more movies. But I realize that I should've never gone back. I was growing into a woman. I was realizing that I needed to go on into something else, into my future. But the business is very addictive. The lifestyle is very addictive, so it was hard to be out of it on my own. But when HIV came to lives across the nation, that got me out a little quicker. I finished out my contract and that was it. I had other talents I wanted to get into, from my writing, to my art, to music.

My passion to do a hip-hop album was for it to be a tribute to hip-hop, and I can't say that I'm bringing anything new into the game because I've been collaborating sex with hip-hop from day one. I'm just being Heather Hunter. I'll always be the queen of that sex and that hip-hop. I'm shocking people that I'm up to par, though.

When you progress in the studio you get better beats and better producers. They have faith in you. And I got to the point where I was able to work with Scott Storch, Timbaland, Noreaga, Kool Keith, and so many others who came along as I got better. I don't want to put out anything that would be considered a gimmick. I'm very proud of what I've done.

I like Queen Latifah because I like the whole package of what she brought into the rhyme game. I love MC Lyte. Missy is amazing. I think she's a triple threat [as a rapper, singer, and producer]. Babs has a wonderful future. Lil' Kim, Foxy Brown. I have so much respect for female MCs because it's such a hard game. It's such a hard hustle because the rap game is really a man's world. A woman has to have so much strength and confidence to be with the big boys. I've been in hip-hop culture for a long time, but actually trying to put out a product is hard. I've been rhyming for like seven or eight years now. And I can truly say that I've mastered the craft. It's definitely a budget cut from the porn business, though.

I think sexism exists because there's no equality in this world. If the world was balanced in all ways, then we wouldn't have it. If there are rappers that wanna do porn, then there's no reason why porn stars shouldn't get into the rap game. There's plenty of equal opportunities for everyone. I'd love for all of us in the world to get together and ask questions about the states of things and find solutions so these [inequalities] don't exist.

THE STILETTOS

Tie them tight around the ankles. Get that cleavage right and in line. Twist those hips from left to right, a whirling dervish to a laced-up track. Too bad the viewers see her as nothing but that. Body without substance. A garnish for the given rhyme.

ON SOLACE

BY MARIAHDESSA EKERE TALLIE

-1-

When I was about nineteen, my best friend, Kyle, and I were hanging out enjoying the Village on one of those gorgeous summer days when the Village was still a place for dreamers. A video scout stopped us on the street and asked if I was interested in being in a music video.

I had spent most of my teenage years wishing that I could be pretty. I would see guys try to talk to girls in the street and think that those girls were lucky because someone thought they were pretty. I knew I was smart. I knew I had personality to boot. But I was skinny, wore thick glasses, and could never get my mother to buy me the latest styles. Besides that, in my world, pretty meant lighter skin and straighter, longer hair. So pretty could not mean me.

My late teens were when conscious hip-hop was the dominant force in the music. Brown skin was becoming beautiful again. Kinky hair was a sensual site of resistance, taking the form of braids, cornrows, and various twists. I read *The Autobiography of Malcolm X,* in which he praised our African features and encouraged us to be proud of them. With this consciousness came confidence. Then at eighteen, I experienced a miracle: contact lenses! After that, life was never the same.

"Come to the address on this flyer. There will be a screen test tomorrow," said the video scout.

"Okay," I said excitedly, reading the piece of paper she'd handed me.

"Take a bathing suit," she added. "There's supposed to be a scene by a pool."

Now, mind you, this was 1992 and hip-hop videos had not reached the sleaze level they have today, but they were clearly heading in that direction. Think BBD's "Do Me." A bathing suit. My heart sank. This was a time when I was developing ideas about gender that made me reexamine just about every aspect of my life: my ideologies, male-dominated race theory, religion, relationships, music, and music videos. So when the video scout approached me, I was flattered at finally getting the attention I had longed for for what seemed like forever, but I needed to make a decision that I could be proud of. I needed to make sure that I didn't do anything to compromise my integrity as an activist, a writer, a daughter, or an aunt of eight. I didn't want folks in my home or my community to be ashamed of me. I didn't want to shame myself. Yet I did want to be in the video.

"I'll go to the test," I said, "but I'm not going to wear a bathing suit."

"Okay," she said.

So a few days later Kyle and I went to the audition. I don't remember much of what happened. Kyle says that I was angry afterward, but neither of us can remember why. I do remember that when it was all over, he said, "You were the chocolate center of a caramel candy."

All the girls were light-skinned and had long hair. They were all more than anxious to change out of their clothes, get into their bathing suits, and strike sexy poses for a group that as far as I know never even came out with a single.

I remember wanting to connect with the other girls but not knowing how. I walked around in my baby-doll dress, watching from a distance inside myself, knowing that I would not be getting a call back.

-2-

Let's get this straight. I mean, really, let's just get it out of the way so we can move on to the subject at hand. Being a conscious woman and/or a feminist does not mean wearing tents, sweatshirts, or other shapeless frocks that land around the ankles. It does not mean eschewing lipstick, eyeliner, or the kind of perfume that brings your image to mind whenever or wherever a lover (or ex-lover) catches a whiff of it. Let's clear up the myth that anyone who takes issue with hip-hop lyrics or the way women are represented in hip-hop videos has a problem with men, sex, sexiness, or sensuality.

After all, sensuality is a gift, a blessing, a weapon even— if it's wielded right. There is great value in embracing one's own sexiness and beauty. But it's a dangerous move to show your physical assets while excluding all other aspects of yourself.

-3-

Men in hip-hop videos are usually dressed. And with their clothes on they still manage to exude power, intelligence, sexiness, and humor. Even the star's entourage, who usually don't have any lines in the song or the video, appear to belong on screen. Whether they are popping another bottle of champagne, sliding their arms around a woman's waist, or staring icily into the camera, these men look in charge. They look powerful. Sometimes they look like stereotypes, sometimes they look as dangerous as the world believes all black people are, but they rarely look like folk to be disrespected or dismissed on a whim. These men appear to have a place in and of themselves.

Some of these brothers even prove that one does not have to take off a stitch of clothes to be sexy. (Much to my dismay, I haven't seen Nas half-naked in a video.) I mean, really, we ladies are lucky if we even get to see our favorite rappers' necks. It is always impetus for me to change the station when I see a man in a rap video wearing enough clothes to survive New York in January standing next to a woman wearing something comparable to a loincloth. Were these people on the same set? Did they get different scripts? Something doesn't add up. Brothers in those videos are cool—so cool that if they take off their hats they'll start to shiver. But the ladies, they are hot. And we know they're hot because at least half of these songs provide the listener with graphic descriptions of what these women can, will, and should do in bed.

Remember the Native Tongues' "Buddy"? The whole thing was a clever ode to sex. De La Soul, A Tribe Called Quest, the Jungle Brothers, Monie Love, and Queen Latifah all vibed on sex, pleasure, and the never-ending pursuit of sexual pleasure. The song was funny, tasteful, and catchy. Even with the topic being sex, women didn't show their ass cheeks or pull up their shirts in the video. Imagine the 2004 "Buddy" remake. It wouldn't be able to be played on radio and the video would be available only on DVD.

In her essay "Narratives of Struggle," writer and professor bell hooks paraphrases Ivan Van Sertima: "It is not just our minds that have been colonized, but our imaginations." One look at an hour of popular rap videos illustrates this pretty clearly.

We all know that when a song comes out and espouses a clothing label or a drink or a car, folk will run to the store to get their hands on whatever it is. Music can move people to action; it can educate, uplift, inspire. Unfortunately, we are using music not to promote the cultural or the spiritual but to inspire consumerism. We say our music simply reflects reality. Are our imaginations so shackled that we can't see our part in creating that reality or changing it?

-4-

During a much-needed vacation in Charleston, South Carolina, in between marveling over magnolias and basking in the sun, I decided to visit a former slave market. It was a humbling, emotional experience. I also spent a great deal of time with members of the Gullah/Geechee Nation who maintain much of the African culture that was lost with the Middle Passage.

I bought a sign dated 1848: NEGROES FOR SALE. When I look at this sign, I am saddened, strengthened, angered, and absolutely amazed, awed by the will of our ancestors to survive the atrocities heaped on them during slavery. Our ancestors fought hard to get us off the auction block. Looking back at their plight, I am stunned that they chose to live. They must have thought about us, the generations they could feel but not see; they must have planned to leave us a beautiful legacy of dignity and resistance.

I sometimes wonder if those same enslaved people were to find themselves listening to the radio, watching television, or walking our streets in the twenty-first century, would they marvel at the signs that some Negroes are clearly still for sale?

-5-

I once read that when Picasso fell in love with a woman he would draw and paint the most alluring portraits of her, but as he fell out of love he would use his charcoal and brush to distort that same woman's features until she was beyond recognition. When I see hip-hop videos, I don't recognize myself. Are our brothers using music the way Picasso used his paints? Have they bought into the mentality of the slave master? When you watch hip-hop videos, do you recognize yourself?

-6-

I used to be a hip-hop fanatic. There is a legion of folk who can testify that back in the day I frequented a hole-in-the-wall hip-hop club in Atlanta's West End. My girls and I would get there soon after the club opened and we wouldn't leave until six A.M. when it closed. I danced so hard, I'd be sore well into the next week.

I loved hip-hop and hip-hop loved me. Our musical romance used to send me to encyclopedias and dictionaries and to the depths within myself in search of truth. KRS-One told me about the problem with America's red meat supply. De La Soul told me to be "Me, Myself and I." The first time I heard reference made to Elegba, the guardian of the cross-roads in West African Yoruba culture, it was coming from an X-Clan record. I marveled at the finesse with which a sincere man could seduce a woman whenever I heard "Bonita Applebum." Salt-N-Pepa (pre "Shoop" and "Whatta Man") proved that women could be strong without sacrificing style or femininity. And MC Lyte and Queen Latifah made me intensely proud with their savvy, uncompromising lyrics. Back then, Big Daddy Kane could be a pimp, Slick Rick could say, "Treat Her Like a Prostitute," and I could laugh because there was balance. I didn't have to listen to anyone call me a bitch twenty-four times on one record or hear about some guy's gun every five minutes. And I certainly didn't have to look at some woman's behind in almost every video that came on. The hip-hop I heard then was a music that represented us in our entirety. Some of us were righteous, some of us were exploring love, some of us were proud of our heritage, some of us were storytellers. Some of us were toting guns, some of us were selling drugs, some of us were talking about day-to-day life in dangerous places, and some of us were just bragging, talking trash, or playing verbal trickster. We weren't all pimps, hos, and killers. We were real people: ordinary, flawed, questioning, feeling, and brilliant in all that varied creativity.

-7-

In our fame-fixated culture, most people entertain dreams of stardom at some point in their lives. I think it has something to do with a need for acceptance. Being in the spotlight is an affirmation. Fame means we are beautiful. Even if we are only famous for a few frames. But fame is hocus-pocus, a momentary illusion.

I propose that we make our own magic. A real magic. Not the sleight of hand that happens when a camera captures wiggling thighs, but a magic that won't fade as our laugh lines deepen or our hair turns a celestial silver. I propose a magic based on an unshakeable love of self and community.

-8-

I marvel at how women with multiplatinum albums, steady fan bases, and careers that span years, parade around in their own videos looking like they were discovered in a strip club and asked to come on set. See Janet strip. See Lil' Kim crawl. See Trina bounce. These women all know that sex sells.

But there are other ways. Remember the smoldering sensuality of Sade? On stages she can give us an entire night's worth of pleasure without revealing much more than her midriff. Remember when Janet worked the hell out of her tight black jeans and loose T-shirt in "The Pleasure Principle"? Remember how so many men lost their heads over

Lauryn Hill (pre Fugees reunion) and Erykah Badu with their mysterious beauty and tasteful sexiness? The ladies in the music business do have a choice. The question is, which road will they choose?

-9-

Sara Baartman didn't have a choice. She didn't choose to be taken from South Africa by Europeans, renamed the Hottentot Venus, stripped, prodded, put in cages, and controlled by animal trainers. She didn't choose to have her genitals measured, to play a part in the creation of theories about black inferiority, or to be cut up and put on display because of her "abnormally large buttocks." I'm sure she never wanted to be turned into a sideshow. But Jennifer Lopez doesn't seem to mind.

-10-

Remember when black politicians had a press conference about a record Eminem made before he hit the big time? There was a big uproar by the *Source* and black politicians because he said some nasty things about black women. When my friend Bruce called to tell me about all this, I guess my reaction was unexpected.

"Oh, so it's bad when Eminem does it (even if he was nineteen at the time) because he's white, but it's fine when black men well into their thirties insult us in their videos and call us hos and bitches."

"You got a point there, Ekere," Bruce said.

Eminem says racist, sexist things ten years ago and that is reason to riot but we don't take our brothers to task when they commit real-life crimes? I'm still pissed about that "welcome home" rally for Mike Tyson back in the day, and I'm at a total loss about why R. Kelly is still selling records in droves. The situation showed me the dire need for black leadership in this country and proved that hypocrisy has found a nice cozy bed in our community. Eminem was an easy target for our so-called leaders. If our "leadership" was to deal with the reality of our community—that the divorce rate is over 70 percent, that a majority of our households are being headed by single mothers, that we are uninsured and unemployed at alarming rates—they wouldn't even have time to think about Eminem.

-11-

"Hell, this is a sexist society, so of course we're gonna be sexist." Yes, I've heard this more than once when discussions about men and women in videos and music take place. Point well taken, but let's not pretend that we are completely invested in this society's ideas. One of the things I find so incredible about black folks is that we are masters at creating our own parallel universes. We have our own magazines. We have created our own standard of what makes a body beautiful. Hey, some of us have made crime something to put on a résumé. Some folks have turned the word *nigger* into a term of affection. We've transformed every language we've wrapped our mouths around into something swinging. We hid Yemaya behind the Virgin Mary and spoke to Chango through Santa Barbara. We've turned poetry into an empowering art and smashed the notion of the "ivory tower." We have survived. If we can do these things, anything else is possible.

The world watches us. We set the trends in so many ways. We know that the world imitates our speech, our culture, our music, and our style. People around the globe created their own movements inspired by our struggles for civil and human rights. We could once again set the example and begin to dismantle sexism in our communities, but we've got to love ourselves first. We've got to love each other first.

We've got to love each other more than dollars, bracelets, champagne, or record deals. We've got to love each other more than a "good beat." We've got to turn the music down so we can hear each other.

One evening, in a club much bigger than that hole-in-the-wall I spoke of earlier, I stopped dancing to hip-hop. In that club, women looked at each other with more malice than sisterhood, the dance floor was dark, a hint of cigarette smoke hung lazily in the air, and there was barely enough room to turn around without touching a stranger and drawing an angry glance. Right there, in the middle of the floor, I just stopped dancing. Biggie had come on and called me a bitch or three and then Snoop backed him up with a few *hos* thrown in for good measure. I'd ignored it before. I had traded my serious nationalist behavior for an I-don't-give-a-%^$& attitude, or so I thought. Hell, I'd even played my boy's copy of *Doggystyle*. But I couldn't do it anymore. I couldn't pretend something didn't bother me when it did. All those words, for someone who comforted herself with words, gnawed on me. They hurt me in some way I could no longer ignore. So I walked off the floor and my unconditional love affair with hip-hop ended.

-12-

We can't live this way. We can't continue portraying ourselves as stereotypes of what it is to be hip-hop. Sure, some of us are making a nice living reducing our generation to pimps and hos. But the unfortunate truth is, the men surrounded by the hired honeys are the biggest hos of all. Just ask the heads of their record labels.

-13-

We discourage tears in our brown boy babies. We giggle and say, "He's going to be a heartbreaker" or "He's so bad!" In some circles, manhood means being hard, getting as much ass as possible, and never being uncertain. To survive slavery, we needed to be strong. In fact, we needed to be invincible, but now we treat each other like enemies. Vulnerabilty—even behind closed doors—is frowned upon. We are dealing with men who are uncomfortable saying "I don't know" or "I need help." We have been passing our ideas about manhood down for generations. "Be strong, don't cry, don't break, don't buckle, don't even sweat, man up." It seems to me that men are keeping a whole lot of emotions inside and it's acceptable for those emotions to come out only as sexual prowess, bravado, or rage.

Even a smile is dangerous. I've noticed how so many of our men have jagged, guarded laughs. It's as though even as they try to express joy, they are looking over their shoulders. If a man can't really show emotion, then the deepest and most profound of all emotions, love, is off-limits.

I have worked with teenagers in different parts of the United States and England, and most of these kids are very aware that there are forces at work against them. Only some of them feel strong enough to go up against those forces or to create new models of being for themselves. I've had seventeen-year-olds tell me, "We can't say we don't know because we don't want to look stupid. Especially not in front of our boys." That "looking stupid" can extend to questioning anything that challenges life as we know it.

Who is willing to look stupid momentarily in order to get the ball of respect rolling again in our community?

A man who is working toward wholeness has to be a strong man because he is swimming against a strong current. He is building a safe space to ask himself difficult questions. He is looking beneath the anger he feels and moving toward hope. He is chipping away at the shackles of racism and sexism and homophobia. A man working toward wholeness might love the feel of his hand on the small of a woman's back, cherish the sound of her voice, and value her words. A man working toward wholeness appreciates the survivor in a black woman. A man working toward wholeness can love lingerie and long talks. I know men like this. I thank God/dess for them. It is easy to be a woman around such men. A woman—not a pinup, not remote-control flesh, not a nameless, faceless hole—a thinking, breathing, living, complex being. There is a grace to true manhood.

-14-

There are no easy answers. We want the American dream. We are a people in survival mode and survival is only about today. So beautiful women who have reduced their worth to their measurements will dance, barely clothed, for that dollar. Men will say whatever they have to say in order to get paid. We are building a shaky structure on an even shakier foundation. We are using music to travel from financial poverty to spiritual bankruptcy. We want the dollars. But our wealth hasn't always been based on a bank account. When we had lashes on our backs, a stump for a foot, and children being sold away by the slave master, we could at least turn to each other for some type of solace. When I see the same cold stares exchanged between men and women in videos happening on the street and hear the same venomous words that forced me off the dance floor being thrown around in subways and stores, I realize that our solace is quickly slipping away.

MIRI BEN-ARI

THE INTERVIEW 2004

Who yearns for the banging strings of the violin in hip-hop? You never heard those words until Miri Ben-Ari came along. The Israeli-born violinist rocked break beats on her electric violin at the Apollo one night and shattered misconceptions about instrumentation and rap. Playing for Kanye, Jay-Z, Alicia Keys, and more, Ari proved to kids in music class that the violin can freak hip-hop, too. Forging a new twist on street-born creativity, she is a reminder that anyone with crazy skills and a fierce love for the craft can find a home in the music of urban wordspeak.

The journey started in Israel. I didn't know I was going to become "the hip-hop violinist." I was just playing the violin like other kids in Israel. But I won competitions, so they sent me to the United States. That's how I came here for the first time as a teenager. And I wasn't even hip to other kinds of music [then]. Thanks to my parents I was in a classical bubble. And thank God for that, because it made me practice the instrument the way you're supposed to practice it.

[But then] I fell in love with Charlie Parker, Bird. I got a

CD of his. I didn't even know who he was. It was like Bach, but groovy in a different kind of way. I was so taken by the music that I said to myself, "I'm only going to do what he does." I started getting gigs. I played with really famous jazz musicians: Benny Carter, Wynton Marsalis. Then this industry executive dropped by one of my jazz gigs and sent me to the Hit Factory to meet Wyclef. That was my first experience with hip-hop.

The first time I met Clef he played a beat and asked me to play to it. People around him really, really liked me. With me hanging out at the Hit Factory, I got to meet other hip-hop producers. I started jamming along with everything. If you played a beat in the studio, I'd be in the hallway trying to freak it and really listening to the vocalist in the studio at the time. One of those vocalists was Alicia Keys and she was recording "Fallin' " at the time. There was word going around that there was this crazy violinist playing beats in the studio and doing nice stuff. And she asked me to come and play on the album.

The Apollo was a turning point in my career [though]. It was the point when I decided this is what I want to do, it felt right. Rap music includes all of the elements. If you listen to producers like Dr. Dre, he's all Bach, taking classical elements and making them sound like grooves. It's so unique the way he does it. A lot of rap music includes classical samples. There are a lot of producers who like classical. They like the sonic sound, like Kanye West.

When you hear good music it brings you to tears and you get the goose bumps. I think about the first time I heard "One More Chance." It was the most beautiful thing I'd ever heard. I was totally feeling of course the lyrics, and of course the beats. The thing I like about hip-hop that really represents me is, the hip-hop mentality is "You do you." It's not about trying to please anybody. It's not about selling out. It's not about trying to do something that's politically correct. That's the way I am, that's my personality. If I feel like I want to do hip-hop, if I want to freak a beat, go crazy on the violin, that's what I'm going to do. I don't really need to consider what other people think I should be doing as a violinist. I like hip-hop because it's for everyone. It's not like exclusive music for people who are rich, or white people or Asian people. It is for everyone. I love that—it humbles me.

THE TAG

Lines of paint on other people's property. 30 seconds of fame on a Bronx-bound train. Watch out for that third rail 'cuz Ramo didn't. Watch out for the cops 'cuz no one else will.

THE TAG

BY CHINO, LEGENDARY GRAFFITI ARTIST,
AS TOLD TO YTASHA L. WOMACK

I'm thirty-six now. When I grew up in N.Y.C., graffiti was a part of my landscape. It was on subways and buses. It was everywhere I went. The energy, the color, was exciting. Every graffiti artist had a cool name. Stay High 159, Super Strut, Futura 2000, Revolt, and Crash. Tons of names. Everyone had such a unique signature. Some of the artists used superheroes from comic strips. Graffiti artists used the best of the spaces they were provided with.

The first tag I remember was this guy from the 7 train named Conan. I was five or six. I knew Conan from the comic books. I didn't know how this stuff got on the trains back then. I figured they did it on a crowded train or something. I didn't know they made graffiti at night. I didn't know they did it in train yards. I didn't realize it was done illegally.

I remember a piece (*piece* is short for *masterpiece*, a word used to describe large painted graffiti letters) on the 7 train that used the *Spy vs. Spy* characters. Those were the first ones that stood out as art to me. Keith Haring, he wasn't a graffiti artist, but his chalk drawings were all over the city. His drawings were at every station before I got there. There was BT2 (Bad Tek 2, a.k.a. SIKO) and his partner, Kik. They had lots of tags on the buses. This guy named G-man was big, too. When someone becomes prolific they say he's "all city." He was everywhere I went.

I was probably in the sixth grade when I started. I was mimicking stuff I saw, doing it in staircases and on the rear seats of buses. A classmate of mine, I saw him on the weekend. He was with some older guys. They were smoking a joint and writing on walls in the schoolyard of Brooklyn Tech High School. They passed me a joint; I didn't want one. Then they passed me a marker and I took it. One of them called me a toy, a term for an inexperienced graffiti artist.

From the time I took my first tag to when I started writing on subways in 1982, I was learning. Probably my freshman year of high school was when I got prolific. I was around other more established graffiti artists at school. It wasn't uncommon to have a mentor. They showed you where to go, where not to go, how to get inside trains, how to turn the lights on or off, and most important, where the escape hatches were in the tunnel in case you needed to get away from the cops.

Most writers had their particular area of expertise. I was most famous for being a bomber, someone who got their name up by way of taking lots of tags on the insides of subways and on the streets.

I wrote on my first train in 1982 and by the mid eighties I had achieved king status.

By 1985, I was bombing with a certain sense of confidence. My tags became bigger, drippier, and I was saturating trains more effectively. My goal was to claim the car, the train it was attached to, the line it ran on . . .

We'd go to Brooklyn and hit "layups," places where they'd lay up trains overnight or on weekends. It's where track workers (or as we call them, "work bums") prep the trains there for rush hour, too. A layup would pull up on a

Friday and would be there until Monday. The only problem with a layup is you can only hit three, four, five trains. The 175th Street layup in Washington Heights may have thirteen or fourteen, which is a lot. But that was rare. In a train yard, on the other hand, you could hit fifty. Eventually, we graduated to yards. In a train yard, provided you have enough time, enough supplies, and you didn't get spotted, you might hit twenty, thirty, forty trains.

The Coney Island yard, also known as the Dewey yard (because it's only a few feet away from John Dewey High School), was pretty big. Over there we went from doing five or six trains in a weekend to doing twenty trains in one night.

There were plenty of dangers. Arrest was always a concern. You could step on a live rail to get to a train and be killed. You crawl under a train, and you don't know when that train might pull off.

But the worst and probably our greatest fear was getting caught by more experienced artists who were often older, bigger, and stronger. Lots of them rolled with their crews for protection. When the movie *Aliens* was out, the line was "In deep space no one can hear you scream." You're in an enormous space like the train yards, it's the same thing.

Anything could happen. You couldn't report it because you're not supposed to be there in the first place. Plenty of artists have been stabbed or beat up. It wasn't a user-friendly culture. Getting beat down was more feared than the police. You name an area of Brooklyn, Manhattan, the Bronx, and I can name a writer or crews who'd beat you up. To get to Coney Island yard, you had to get through Marlborough projects. The Bronx was always trouble for me. One-seventy-fifth was an all-Dominican neighborhood, which at the time was inundated with drugs, guns, and crime.

If you left the layup to get a soda, you might not make it back into the tunnel. You'd go up, then get beat up and robbed. No one cared. This was early to mid eighties. Back then, the neighborhoods were more divided. There were cut-off lines in most communities: the Italian, Puerto Rican, Hassidic, Caribbean, and Slavic areas. Lots of neighborhoods weren't very welcoming to outside visitors.

I'm Latino Philippino. But I'm always black when I get pulled over by police. But there were certain communities I couldn't go into. Lots of black and Latino writers I know feared going into Italian communities.

No one wanted to get beat up on the way to the train yard. The Howard Beach attack in 1986 and tragic murder of Yusuf Hawkins in 1989 all but confirmed many of our worst fears.

Things have changed considerably since then; at least, at the surface, it appears that way. I don't want to come off like one of these old guys, like "When I was young I had to walk thirty miles to buy a can of spray paint," but things are different. Very different, and the thrill of illegal graffiti is gone.

True champions shine best under pressure. Nowadays, we have all the time in the world to finish a mural. People take four or five days to do a mural. There are German companies like Montana Cans and Belton Molotow that manufacture spray paint specifically designed with the aerosol artist in mind. Back then we were using industrialized spray they used to paint a wagon. Our weight was supported by a dilapidated wooden plank that ran above a live third rail and that was the only thing between life and being electrocuted. If you can paint in the dark illegally and still be creative under those conditions, you should be able to take your talents anywhere.

I've noticed how the culture, its mediums, and the rules have changed over the years. When I grew up, if you wanted to learn graffiti art you had to go on the subways. There was an apparent hierarchy and new writers got their heart tested all the time.

What I saw written on the subways is what taught me my craft. Now you can go on the Internet. Subway graffiti was never meant to stay still. You had thirty seconds to a minute to scrutinize an image. Once you painted your name on the side of that train, it was going on until someone painted over it. You're in a dark tunnel, you don't know what you're painting. Now you can buy a book and scrutinize pieces from that, or watch videos and learn how.

September 11 has made some of those things almost impossible. When I grew up ten people could jump on the train tracks with bags in their hands and hoods on their heads and no one would think anything. Nowadays they would think you were a terrorist. This is the home of Ground Zero. The risk clearly outweighs the reward. I know graffiti writers who have been approached by the feds. New York City has a list of the Top 100 graffiti artists who the police are looking for. They have alarms in the tunnels. Guards in certain train yards. There is no longer an active subway graffiti scene in N.Y.C. So you run an enormous risk of being arrested and being the only one caught that day, week, or month. When you're the only one caught, you're a scapegoat. That didn't exist when I grew up. Everyone was caught at some point. You didn't have to worry about your name and address being the next blurb on New York 1 or 1010 Wins News, or a sidebar on *A Current Affair*.

I do like the new stuff. It's more conceptual now than it was when I was growing up. The geography has changed. It's moved from subways to wall spaces. I guess the order of the day is large-scale murals.

What I'm about to say comes from talking to people who were part of the inception of graffiti [people like Blade TC5,

Tracy 168, Cornbread from Philadelphia, and Taki 183 from New York]. Cornbread is the first graffiti artist and his partner was Cool Earl. (The movie *Cornbread, Earl and Me* was supposed to be about their life as graffiti artists but ended up being about basketball.) I had the pleasure of meeting Cornbread a few years ago. He is believed to have started writing in the late 1960s. Point being, there was no hip-hop around then. There wasn't break dancing or rap. Graffiti's roots weren't in hip-hop.

The early guys I was talking to say they were listening to Hendrix, The Who, Led Zeppelin, and funk. As it relates to hip-hop, graffiti was the first aspect of hip-hop culture. Before the first vinyl was cut. Before there was breaking, there was graffiti.

You can't knock that thought of the DJs, dancers, and graffiti artists all running together. In early films like *Beat Street* and *Breakin'* it appears as if it's all going on side by side, simultaneously. Some people discovered graffiti artists, the DJs, and the dancers all at the same time. I guess it makes sense. Rap, breaking, and graffiti all flourished during the same years, during the early to mid eighties. It all comes from the streets. MCs were rapping, people were battling. In all fronts people were competing. They were competing on the subways, competing on the mic, competing on the floor. So I understand the argument when people lump graffiti in with hip-hop. But graffiti predates the other forms.

In the early years there were tons of political messages. You had people like MICO, who had the Puerto Rican flag and a noose that said "Hang Nixon." Graffiti legend Lee from Fabulous Five's work often contained messages like "Stop the Bomb," "Merry Christmas" . . . Whether these messages read "Free Lolita Lebron," "Dump Koch," or "Disco

Sucks," lots of people who were painting had some sort of message they were trying to communicate.

There were tons of rappers who were involved in graffiti. Peso 131 who was also the Great Peso of the Fearless Four, Blas TDZ was also Fresco. Fresco won the New Music Seminar MC battle back in the eighties; he had a few singles out with his partner, Miz. The Drama King, DJ Kay Slay, was a subway legend before he was a mixtape king. He was known as Dez from TFA. In the documentary *Style Wars*, DJ Kay Slay admitted he had to figure out how to make a living. Graffiti wasn't doing it.

Hip-hop is this big business nowadays. Not everybody wanted to be a rapper back then. Everyone knew they couldn't do it. Now everyone feels there's a space for him or her in hip-hop. It's an enormous industry. I've been all around the world as a result of graffiti and there hasn't been a corner of the globe that hasn't been affected by hip-hop or graffiti for that matter.

As defined in *Style Wars*, graffiti has always been a subculture within a subculture, which was hip-hop.

You had to look at a moving train to see what the people in the Bronx were saying, or looking at who was cool with who, who had a battle with who. It was always there, but it was on the wall. It's decorative. It's a backdrop for the rapper or the dancer, but it was never center stage. The guy who painted ten thousand trains isn't as famous as a rapper with one hit single.

Today's hip-hop crowd doesn't always embrace graffiti. It's been underground. It's not as lucrative as other aspects of hip-hop. I know tons of graffiti artists who have become rich, or comfortable, because of their craft, though.

Now every MC I meet wants to sign with Roc-A-Fella or get a deal of some sort. Some people are more driven by dollar signs. But not many people enjoy it for the sheer passion of it. Not many people can go and spit for the sheer joy of it. There's never been an equivalent of a record deal for the graffiti writer, so we've always had to do it for the passion.

For the past twelve years I have edited "Graf Flix" for the *Source*. I resigned in August 2005. Up until I left it was one of the most popular sections for those under twenty-one and the most popular for those not in our demographic. The pioneering graffiti community, the forty-five to fifty-five age group, was purchasing the mag. I've met backpackers, skaters, rave, goth, skinhead types . . . people who do not like rap, people who couldn't care less about who is on our cover. But they purchase the magazine because it's usually the only publication available at their local Blockbuster Video in West Bubblef@#k where they can learn about graffiti.

Former New York mayor John V. Lindsay, who served from 1966 to 1973, was the first person to make graffiti a

"quality of life offense." In 1994, Mayor Giuliani became the first mayor to aggressively enforce these laws. Back in the eighties when I got caught, law enforcement was pretty relaxed. When I got caught none of that was on my record. I was able to be part of illegal graffiti and it didn't ruin me as an adult. The majority of those arrests were what they were. Thankfully, I have nothing on my record. When I fill out a job application, I don't have to mark that box for criminal offense. Today graffiti comes with a felony charge. The risk and reward are very little. I tell kids to do legal murals. It's in no one's best interest to do what I did coming up.

PETE ROCK

THE INTERVIEW 2004

The producer half of the enigmatic duo Pete Rock
and CL Smooth, Rock helped usher in the alternative
melodic hip-hop sound of the early nineties with his
distinct jazz-infused productions with trumpet snip-
pets and bebop loops. Originally a radio DJ with
Marley Marl in New York, Pete leveraged local popularity into producer gigs. Here, the "Chocolate Wonder" reminisces.

I have a passion for music. A typical day for me: I wake up
early in the morning, eat breakfast, maybe go out to run a
few errands during the day. I come down here and do interviews like this one. Go back home and make beats or tap up
a few stores to see if I can find anything that arouses me. I
love the way orchestrated samples sound. I love making
drums. All of that stuff is fun to me.

I wouldn't change anything about the beats I've done.
Back then I was ahead of my time. Listening back to it now I
think I could make a few changes. I wouldn't use some of
the drumbeats I used over and over like "Long Red," which

I used three of four times. Maybe I would've chopped that down to one and a half.

Yeah, Puff kinda stole my shine [when it came to pioneering the art of talking on records]. But who cares? I don't give a damn about that. It's all good. When I do things it inspires people and that's great.

The most startling change I've seen in the music is actually seeing death with Tupac and Biggie. I've seen people I've known die. I've seen people I've met before (Big L, Trouble T-Roy) die. You're seeing them and talking to them and the next thing you know they're dead.

There's no soul in today's hip-hop music. You can tell that it's just slapped together. It's basically wack and it got that way because of money and control. Someone being greedy. Someone wanting to take the music and do more extra things that's not kosher to it. I used to turn on the radio and hear "The Creator" every day on mainstream radio. I used to hear Big Daddy Kane, Biz Markie. It's these new kids, these clown A&Rs that's putting on their wack-ass man. They're young and don't know shit about music. And then they get on the mic and pop all this shit about their money and their jewelry and this Jacob cat. They're gonna keep fuckin' with him and he's gonna fake y'all out one of these days.

James Brown, Isaac Hayes, and Barry White are my three choices for the greatest producer of all time. If you say hip-hop producers I have to say Howie Tee, Marley Marl, and Teddy Riley, Larry Smith, Rick Rubin, and all those guys back in the eighties. And it's not because they were some of the first—it's because they really did good work. It was an art for them. I enjoyed that. Them being the first, that's just the way it is.

———

I have some regrets about my career. There's a lot of contracts I wish I hadn't signed, but it was a learning experience and I've moved on. Being on top of your business is very, very important.

I accomplished a lot in the game, and it was very good to me. It gave me a chance to learn. It gave me a chance to see how people are and how far they will go. And I learned that you can be a big inspiration to a whole generation.

THE TURNTABLE

Scratch. Mix. Cut. Cut. Cut. Exclusives. Transforming tricks. DATs ain't got nuthin' on the real thing, even if the kids today barely know the difference. Any time is the turntable's time.

THE TURNTABLE

BY IMANI DAWSON

DJing is the cornerstone of this culture we call hip-hop. Before MC meant "move the crowd," DJs kept the people and the party hype. In the guilt-covered commercialism that currently passes for rap music, DJing's hallowed position has become obscured. The method of playing extended break beats, pioneered by Jamaican import Kool DJ Herc, is the very foundation of all of hip-hop's other elements: graffiti, rapping, and break dancing. But in the minds of most listeners, the men and women behind the turntables are merely supporting players overshadowed by the stellar brilliance of the MC. But if we go back to the ether, the birthplace of hip-hop on the desolate streets of 1970s South Bronx, where the neighborhood's black and Latino youth had poverty and restlessness as their constant companions, the DJ had the power to save souls.

On sultry nights, with heat-filled smog hanging thick and swollen in the air, those kids could ignore the bleak uncertainty of the future stretched dismally out before them and dance their troubles away when Kool Herc, using the model of mobile sound systems from his homeland, plugged his set up to the streetlights and played the best parts of records like "Apache" and "Impeach the President."

Rhyming over the beat, the irresistible urge to move to the pounding bass line, and scribbling tags over walls all emerged as ways to pay homage to the DJ's magic. Under Herc's nimble fingers, turntables, designed simply to play records, became the canvas of an artist.

Other spinners built upon Herc's robust foundation. Legend has it that Grand Wizard Theodore discovered the scratch by holding a record in place while his mom entered his room to scold him. When his hand accidentally slipped, he created the sound that would become the DJ's universal language. Variations on the powerful new scratch emerged, like the transform scratch, a laserlike slice of a sound invented by DJ Spinbad and Baby DST and immortalized on wax by DJ Jazzy Jeff of Fresh Prince fame.

As rapping emerged as hip-hop's most commercially viable product, the DJ was initially considered the preeminent part of the crew (note that "Grandmaster Flash" always came before "The Furious Five"). Songs showcasing DJ skills like "Mr. Cee's Master Plan" on Big Daddy Kane's debut *Long Live the Kane* were frequently included on albums. Rappers Joseph "Run" Simmons and Darryl "D.M.C." McDaniels of Run-D.M.C., the first rap group to garner mainstream love, wrote rhymes praising their DJ, Jason Mizell, better known as the late Jam Master Jay. And rightfully so, according to Connie Mizell-Perry, Jay's mother: the childhood friends would spend painstaking hours practicing at her crib when they couldn't find anywhere else to go.

In those days, the DJ's moniker was known and respected by the crowd and groups like Eric B and Rakim or Rob Base and DJ E-Z Rock gave the DJ billing alongside the MC. Even solo artists bowed before the majestic thrones of their turntable kings. Big Daddy Kane's early albums are laced with shout-outs to Mr. Cee, who discovered the martyred Brooklyn rapper The Notorious B.I.G. And what would the brash rhymes of a young LL Cool J have sounded like without Cut Creator supporting them with his full-bodied mixes? When the public's unquenchable thirst for celebrity thrust the DJ into the shadows, he began amassing other skills to preserve his value.

Many DJs became track masters, bridging the gap between manipulating records and morphing melodies into stand-alone tracks. Rakim is universally hailed as the god responsible for birthing modern rap's complex metaphor-filled lyrics, but the hypnotic melodies that provided the perfect complement to Rakim's thunderous vocals were created by his DJ, Eric B. As a child, Eric B played the trumpet and guitar but fell in love with the turntables in high school and eventually landed a prestigious gig spinning for New York radio station WBLS, where he met Rakim. *Paid in Full*, the first product of their partnership, was an undeniable classic, and Eric B essentially crafted the album's sounds. His beats for seminal singles "Eric B Is President" (a tribute to his DJ skills), "I Ain't No Joke," and "I Know You Got Soul" sent other beat makers scurrying to record crates to sample classic James Brown funk.

DJ Premier, perhaps one of the greatest producers in the history of hip-hop, began his career as Waxmaster C, a turntablist who studied computer science at Prairie View A&M and once managed a record store. His legacy began as a member of Gang Starr. Premier's smooth melding of hip-hop with jazz garnered the group critical acclaim and established him as a talented beatsmith, leading to work with other high-profile rappers like Lord Finesse and tracks on the classic debuts of heavyweights like Biggie, Nas, and Jay-Z. His trademark sound, replete with heavy scratching and multilayered loops, is even today highly requested, and his influence grows as he expands his professional repertoire. Others like Pete Rock, Just Blaze, and Tony Touch have distinguished themselves as producers, with bodies of work more renowned than their spinning skills.

Before DJs became prominent producers, a number of enterprising New Yorkers stacked chips by hawking mixtapes on the side. Mixtapes, initially called "party tapes" in the mid-1970s, rendered the ecstatic release of a DJ-led celebration made portable for the people, usually flashy drug dealers and hustlers who could afford to shell out twenty bucks or more. Old-timers like Grandmaster Flash and Kool Herc could charge one dollar per minute for the hottest street jams interspersed with personal shout-outs to tape purchasers. Because of the level of personalization and the still limited access to hip-hop in other outlets like the radio, tapes were rocked until they popped. By the late eighties, a new wave of DJs like Brucie B and Kid Capri had emerged, making mixtapes readily available to the masses. Hip-hop had been established as the official culture for the nation's discontented urban youth, expanding the mixtape market. As gigs at high-profile nightspots dried up, DJs turned increasingly to tapes as steady sources of income.

The early 1990s, widely hailed as hip-hop's golden era, brought the rise of the celebrity mixtape DJ. The mix masters began distinguishing themselves with trademark effects and styles. Perhaps most successful at brand building was Queens native DJ Clue. Shying away from the traditional turntable skills flaunted by most DJs on their cassettes, Clue carved his niche by offering hard-to-find freestyles and talented new artists, exclusive unreleased songs, and constant name checking to ensure that no one bit his material. Clue broke some of the most influential rap tracks, including Biggie's first big hit "Juicy" and Jay-Z's "Ain't No Nigga," and helped launch the careers of artists like DMX, Cam'ron, and Ma$e.

Mixtapes have become an invaluable component of marketing and promoting artists, and a select cadre of DJs have reaped the benefits. Though most don't earn much by churning out tapes, they're able to leverage name recognition to pursue other projects. Despite an almost wooden personality, Clue has become an MTV VJ, has dropped platinum major-label projects, and is co-CEO of Desert Storm records, home to platinum-selling artist Fabolous. Other DJs like Kay Slay and Envy have traded on mixtape credibility for radio shows, record contracts, and endorsement deals.

While some DJs abandon the art to pursue the more lucrative and respected avenues of producing and making mixtapes, the renegade purists remain faithful to the turntables. Drawing on the African American tradition of creating something from nothing, starting with only a trusty set of Technics SL-1200s and a mixer, these underground kings have created a phenomenon known as turntablism, revered everywhere in the world, except, sadly, the United States.

More than any other of the creative palettes available to the DJ, turntablism views its practitioners as bona fide musicians and the tables as the ultimate instruments. Scratches are the foundation notes, but these DJs also make music by blending songs and toggling between two records to create a new beat, also known as "beat juggling." Respect doesn't necessarily come from paper. Instead, tablists battle it out for their version of ultimate glory: the adoration of dedicated fans and praise from their peers for the creativity and innovation.

Though they thrive in contests like the DMC World DJ Championships and Kool Mixx Battles, and well-known and well-respected crews like the X-Ecutioners, the Allies, and the Beat Junkies manage to live off their craft by releasing instructional DVDs and break records, as well as touring places such as Australia and Japan where all of hip-hop's elements are viewed reverentially, most tablists just work for the love.

Grandmaster Roc Raida isn't a household name, but among turntablists he's an icon. Raised in a Harlem housing project, Raida began spinning at the age of ten, and joined turntablist crew the X-Men, the uptown rivals to the Brooklyn-based outfit the Supermen, led by DJ Clark Kent. Raida's X-Men became the X-Ecutioners for copyright reasons, and his reputation for mind-boggling beat juggles and gymnast rivaling body tricks grew as he won a host of impromptu and organized battles, culminating with his prestigious 1995 DMC World Championship victory. In 1999, DMC inducted the DJ into its hall of fame, and the following year he was granted the title "Grandmaster" by turntablism's most elite figure, DJ cipher.

Hip-hop may have turned its back on the tables, but DJs still thrive in genres like rock, house, and electronica. Step outside hip-hop's arena and spinners are seen as gods. Dance music, also derived from the rhythms of African people, relies on DJs to innovate the music, which is driven wholly by its pounding, insistent bass line. Pros like Carl Craig, Jeff Mills, and Kevin Saunderson, who've established themselves as turntable titans in the dance community, are paid thousands of dollars per night overseas to whip crowds into a trancelike frenzy. Chicago's deep house culture birthed DJs like Farley Jackmaster Funk, Steve "Silk" Hurley, Terry Hunter, and Maurice Joshua, whose names reverberate within European dance scenes. DJs also create the bulk of dance music's ubiquitous remixes, with in-demand cats earning upwards of thirty grand and even getting points (a piece of the royalties) for a fresh spin on a song.

Rock bands use turntable techniques like scratching and beat juggling liberally in their tunes and hybrids like über-successful Linkin Park feature DJs as group members.

Outside America, DJ culture thrives, particularly for dance music specialists. England's DJ Paul Oakenfold nabbed the *Guinness Book of World Records* title for most successful club DJ by selling more than one million records and earning around $400,000 in a single year. Germany is home to the techno maestros Swen Väth, Westbaum, and Paul van Dyk, and hosts the world's biggest music event, Berlin's Love Parade, a yearly festival that attracts more than one million music fans every July. In France, house music reigns and DJs like Daft Punk, Etienne de Crecy, and Cassius rule. Trip-hop, downtempo electronic music—characterized by break beats and recognizable samples—also commands a huge crowd, served by spinners that trace their origins to the Paris hip-hop scene, dominated by the timeless MC Solaar, Soon E MC, and Menelik. Japan is also a trip-hop mecca for DJs like Krush and Major Force Orchestra, and Towa Tei, former DJ for the groovy trio DeeeLite, was elevated to superstar status when the group disbanded.

When it comes to worldwide acclaim and recognition, few can top UK native Norman Cook. His deft combination of musical genres into an innovative sonic gumbo has earned him legions of fans. Though he's used many monikers, he's best known by the enigmatic name Fatboy Slim. Cook's stints as a bassist and producer inform his spinning sensibility, which is reported to leave audiences sweating and smiling after a two-hour set of dance floor anthems and old-school jams. The 1998 hit "The Rockafeller Skank" from his album *You've Come a Long Way, Baby* propelled him onto the world's stage and garnered awards and multiplatinum international sales.

Unlike the brightest rap stars, who are mostly black and

Latino men professing hard-luck childhoods and mile-long rap sheets, successful DJs come from all ethnic backgrounds. Whites and Asians are equally seduced by the allure of the ones and twos and often distinguish themselves as leaders. Multiculti crews like the Allies and 5th Platoon are among the most respected in the game, holding individual and group turntable championships. DJ Green Lantern, one of hip-hop's most celebrated tour and mixtape DJs (not to mention Slim Shady's official spinner), is said to be Spanish and Italian, but most people are so busy checking for his skills that his ethnicity isn't called into question. DJ Honda, a Japanese DJ and producer, has worked with and befriended various hip-hop legends, including Afrika Bambaataa of the Universal Zulu Nation, De La Soul, and KRS-One.

It's also worth noting that Filipinos have made significant contributions to this art of noise. The Bay Area, home to a thriving Filipino community, birthed a number of renowned Filipino American DJs, including Q-bert (one of the most venerated scratchers to ever get behind a turntable), Mixmaster Mike, and Apollo, all of Invisibl Skratch Piklz fame. Beginning in the early eighties, mobile DJ crews coalesced in the Frisco community, pooling resources to purchase equipment and performing together. Sporting names like Electric Sounds and Audio Technique, the groups rolled deep like gangs, inspiring a party scene and competing against one another in organized sound clashes. This collective DJ movement eventually spawned the huge Filipino presence in turntablism.

Though DJing was and still is perceived largely as a male domain and the steel wheels an extension of masculine power and virility, there are a few women who qualify as crowd controllers. Generally seen as a novelty or no-talent poseurs trading on looks, lady DJs sometimes struggle for acceptance in DJing's many realms. Despite the hardship, there are still women who manage to invade the DJs' all-boy network, such as DJ Kaori, who blessed turntables at chichi fetes for everyone from P. Diddy to Michael Jordan and is the only female in Funkmaster Flex's vaunted Big Dog Pitbulls clique. Others include turntabling bad-ass Kuttin Kandi and DJ Lazy K, an award-winning mixtape DJ and CEO of Murda Mamis, a largely Latina association of powerful women in the music industry.

Beverly Bond is one of most popular female DJs to step behind the ones and twos. A former model and lifelong record collector, she purchased a set of turntables on a whim and essentially taught herself how to spin, gleaning information from DJ friends. Blessed with industry connects, she quickly became the toast of New York's celebrity party circuit, spinning for celebs like Kimora Lee Simmons and D'Angelo and at major award shows.

For all the venues available to innovative DJs, party rocking, their traditional domain, might be the most fickle and treacherous. Parties are still hip-hop's main stress-relieving outlet: the young and increasingly the older members of the self-declared Hip-hop Generation consistently line up on Friday and Saturday nights, ignoring the vagaries of seasonal weather—blustery winds, hailstorms, sweltering heat—and plunk down ten or twenty hard-earned dollars to lose themselves in the beat. But in most cities, DJs are plentiful and easily replaceable, and flinty club owners exploit their advantageous buyer's market by overworking and underpaying them. Sure, there are the superstars, the DJ Enuffs and Funkmaster Flexes who can easily command more than five Gs to play a spot because their big names will draw people out in droves, but for every big name there are legions of unknowns with loads of talent, skills gathered from years of exacting practice, and unbounded drive, who are willing to schlep their tattered record cases cheaply or even for free to prove themselves and ascend to the next level.

Choosing to become a DJ requires a Herculean level of dedication and love. It's a difficult craft to master, and many with the desire lack the necessary manual dexterity to really measure up. As effortless as it may appear, even simple blending takes an innate sense of rhythmic timing and fingers agile enough to finesse a smooth transition. One false move and a DJ could wind up with a riotous, bloodthirsty crowd on his or her hands. Being a DJ means leading a complicated, art-driven life. Spending hours in dusty record stores, crate digging for obscure rare grooves from across genres and knowing that a six-hour search netting one Mar-Keys record is an unparalleled victory. Driving your family crazy by meticulously playing the same song or practicing the same beat juggle over and over again in order to perfect a routine. Watching battle tapes to learn about an opponent's style. Listening with a critic's ear to the late-night DJ spin shows. Begging, borrowing, or stealing the money to make record pool payments. Never having dough for dates because music is the ultimate mistress. Squeezing in a social life between spot dates, battles, and studio sessions. Infatuating the audience after each and every performance. Falling in love anew each time you're behind the turntables.

Hip-hop's attitude toward turntable kings and queens may be flippant, but the truth is that the culture couldn't exist without them. Record players were supposed to be used for just playing vinyl. But DJs made them outlets for musical genius, bridging the gap between old-school revelry and youthful rebellion. Since the beginning of time, music has been a vehicle for liberation. In all their incarnations, DJs create and nurture the melodies that keep us moving forward through stumbling blocks like ignorance, indigence, and racism. DJs are hip-hop's unacknowledged, invisible leaders. Past all the industry smoke screens and behind all the screw-faced, bling-happy rappers, DJs run this shit. The power to reach the people has always been and will always remain at their adroit fingertips. As it was in the beginning, so shall it be until the end: DJs capturing happiness, sorrow, power, suppression, displacement, and freedom, in the essence of a single scratch.

MOS DEF

In an industry that prefers flash to substance, Mos embraced the latter. Originally one in the Black Star Project, he with Talib Kweli continued the traditions of birthing consciousness in hip-hop. As a solo artist, he spews thought-provoking lyrics and spins social commentary, pulling from jazz, rock, and the blues as his backdrop. Not one to be confined by conventional standards, he scraped together black rock's unheralded greats to launch his band Black Jack Johnson, starred in *Top Dog, Underdog* on Broadway, for which he won an Obie, and was nominated for an Emmy for HBO's *Something the Lord Made.* His acting credits continue to mount.

T he first reaction to new things is always a little bit apprehensive. When Miles started including electronica and electronic elements in his music, people in the jazz community started looking at him with a jaundiced eye. When Bob Dylan went electric and stopped using an acoustic guitar, he'd go on stage and people would straight boo him. But it's those types of strides that have been important not just to music or just to their idioms but to art in general. Whoever's ready for it is gonna get on board. Whoever ain't ready for it, they not gonna get on board. And fortunately there's enough music and artists out for them to find what it is they're looking for. Personally, I think that people is ready. But I'm not doing it because I'm trying to curry favor with the in crowd or nothing like that. You know, I want Negroes in the ghetto to get it. I want the hood to get it. And I know there's cats in the hood that are gonna get it, and I know there's some folks that ain't gonna get it. I know some folks that's gonna have some very not nice things to say about it, black and . . . you know, the ghetto and the rock press. But that's cool, 'cause I believe in what I'm doing.

[You gotta] be you wherever you are. It's the only thing that will save you. If you like rock music and you live in the ghetto, like that shit. They think that black folks like the same shit. We all look alike, we all dress alike, all the same shit is important to us, niggas listening to the same thing, we live in the same house, all of that shit, and that's not the case. Fuckin' Amadou Diallo gets shot forty-one times and suddenly that's a black issue. How the fuck? I thought that he was a human being that didn't have a police record that got shot on his doorstep. So what the fuck is up with that? That's not a human rights issue? You gonna go save the fuckin' tigers in India and stop motherfuckers from poaching elephants. Meanwhile, motherfuckers in Sierra Leone is getting their hands cut off. A generation of people coming up with no limbs. That's not a human rights issue? I guess that's an African issue. I guess the AIDS epidemic in Africa is an African issue, it's not a human issue. Like I said, I'll stop saying it when it stops being true. I've done my part. I've raised the issue. But then y'all motherfuckers gotta stop making it be a issue and stop looking at me—to quote Flavor Flav, "I got a right to be hostile." Your ass is hostile against me. Your policies are hostile against me. Your media is hostile against me. Your whole shit is hostile against me. And to quote KRS, "Tell me, what the fuck am I supposed to do?" You wanna paint me into that fuckin' angry black man fuckin' corner, and you know, throw all that conspiracy theory shit, you know what? Say what you want, just spell it right, to quote Flavor Flav again, "I got a right to be hostile." And if the shoe was on the other motherfuckin' foot, y'all couldn't take it, 'cause you don't take it. So don't get on that whole, "It's on me." It's on y'all motherfuckers, man. Y'all want it to be better, make it better. Get off that bullshit, 'cause the world is waiting on y'all motherfuckers. The world. It's on them, man. You know, I be feeling crazy, man. I swear to God, I be feeling crazy. I be feeling like, why am I all burnt up about this shit? Because I get to see niggas, man. I still get them calls and them letters from upstate, man. Shit is not fun, it's not fresh. Yeah, I'm Mos Def, I'm still a nigga man. Still a nigga man. They don't give a fuck about that, not really.

I'll tell you a story, man. I go to the theater, right. I go to the theater to see John C. [Reilly] and Philip Hoffman, they doing a play. I'm there with a friend, right. Me and her the only two black people there, right. Only two black people. [Sighs.] Nobody recognizes me as Mos Def 'cause that theater shit is like [sighs], whatever. They in a whole other world. One white kid recognizes me. But for all of the other white patrons, they looking at me like, "What the fuck is he doing here? You're not in the play, and you're not a usher. So what are you doing here?" Right, Chris Rock walks in, right. The same motherfuckers that was looking at me like "What are you doing here?" was like, "Oh, it's Chris Rock!" And Chris Rock is just as black as me. Matter of fact, we come from the same fuckin' neighborhood. I'm from Bed-Stuy, he from Bed-Stuy. But [low voice] Chris Rock ain't a nigga no more. It's like that shit in *Do the Right Thing*. You like

Michael Jackson, you like Michael Jordan, but they're not niggas, okay. That's what I be living with. I know the same motherfuckers that shake my hand and be like, "I love your music," if I wasn't quote unquote Mos Def, if I hadn't been validated by their media agencies and the press and all of that shit, they might be nervous when they get on an elevator with me. They might cross the street, they might lock that door, and I'm the same motherfucker that I was.

THE SHELL CASING

Buck. Buck. Buck. Ratatattat. Grab your gat a.k.a. burner a.k.a. piece a.k.a. heat and squeeze. Hit or miss, you've got a better chance of losing for picking it up in the first place. But how you gonna put it down when the whole world has you in the crosshairs?

THE EVIDENCE OF CAPS
ONCE PEELED

BY KENJI JASPER

Pulling the trigger is easy—when you're aiming at a paper target, that is. I was maybe ten or eleven at the time, standing within the partitions of the firing lane my father and I had been given. The weapon was a single-action .22 pistol, a cowboy six-gun that splashed powder in my face with each and every round. I never hit the bull's-eye, but there were a few times that I came pretty darn close.

Within an hour, we'd emptied the fifty rounds my father had purchased. The empty casings kept a tally of shots fired until no lead was left. When we finished, I begged good ole Dad to let me keep that plastic rack of casings. And he agreed. The little plastic box stayed on my dresser for years, physical proof to support my schoolyard claims that I had fired a real gun, that I could lick lethal shots outside my vivid grade school imagination.

I was obsessed with firearms. But then again, most boys of the eighties were. From GI Joe to Transformers to *Battlestar Galactica* and *Buck Rogers in the 25th Century*, power and prestige came to the man with the gun in his hand. I'm sure it hadn't been too different for my father's or grandfather's generations, with Westerns, sci-fi serials, and war films.

I was in love with *The A-Team* and its weekly displays of explosives and the latest in automatic hardware. I studied the encyclopedia and books in the library to learn the names and calibers of the pistols and rifles I saw on screens big and small. Stallone and Governor Schwarzenegger made it look so easy. They hadn't buffed up for the hand-to-hand combat. They needed that bulk to support all the artillery their story lines required.

So as I said before, I was gun crazy. At every dime store and in every toy section of every supermarket and department store where I might have had duckets to spare, I always chose the gun. Squirt pistols, battery-operated water cannons, Han Solo blasters, the sawed-off ColecoVision target pistol, Lazer Tag, Laser Combat, contraptions that fired plunger darts both soft and hard, plastic balls, spinning discs, and even colored paint when Gotcha was the rage. When it came to imaginary shoot-outs in the neighborhood, I *was* the armory.

But at the end of the day, no matter what I did at playtime, no matter how many harmless shots I fired into the arms, chests, and backs of Butchie, Damon, Bobo, Marcus, and all of my other playmates, I knew, we all knew, that none of it was for real. Real stories only appeared on the news or the movie of the week. Our little replicas of real-life killing machines were only props to help us live out the make-believe fantasies executed by our favorite Hollywood heroes. And we even knew that those men were actors, people pretending to be what they really weren't just to make a dollar and get themselves on TV and in the movies.

I even have a few gun replicas now, which I cock and fire just as something to do with my hands. But I have not and will not pull a real trigger. Because I have always known what real bullets do.

Gary and Rocky were two of the many boys around our

way who had raised themselves more than their parents had, and saw the wrong ends of heated barrels over ego. I never knew the particulars of Gary's murder, but Rocky was stabbed to death at a go-go club over a prior beef. My childhood best friend, Butchie, caught a ten-year case for manslaughter. And Rick, the local thug who I always suspected broke into my Mom's and my crib in '89, is doing twenty-five years for murder.

Legions of others walked the narrow maze of prison cells and closed caskets. Even more stalked the corners, jacking and pushing weight with "four-pounders" packed in their boxers, expecting anything, and reducing encroaching foes to nothing, over nothing. Multiple murders and the night became bedfellows. Coroners' vans worked double shifts, and everyone in school knew someone who had something to do with the latest body to get dropped. Real murder and mayhem, acts we'd dramatized for years with toys, had shown up right at our generation's doorstep, and, in my case, at school.

I was hanging out on the rear field during lunchtime, just a few months before a shoot-out at nearby Dunbar High ended off-campus lunch for the entire school system. I was out there alone, perhaps writing, or thinking, or dreaming of what it might be like to be still sitting down in the cafeteria, locking eyes with one of the many girls who were reluctant to give my "trying too hard" adolescent ass the time of day. And that was when I saw it.

It was a brassy kind of color, a shiny cylinder caught in the wind, rolling back and forth on its side like a child playing in snow. I don't know how I noticed it among all the bottle tops and broken glass, the chipped paint and playground sand riddled with plastic straws and cellophane wrappers. But I did. So I stooped down and picked it up.

It seemed larger than the .22 casings I'd kept on my

dresser all of those years before, probably from a Baretta, or a Glock, a chrome-plated .380 or any other gat some kid might have grabbed from the local arsenal. I stood there and studied the thing, my young journalistic mind a glass filled with questions. It had once been a whole bullet. And had that bullet been one that had wounded or taken a life? Or was it merely the remainder of some prankster who only had the balls to shoot in the air beneath the silky covers of night?

Where was the shooter? Was he in hiding or in the clink? Did he feel guilty or had it been just another autopilot move to maintain his own survival? I didn't know, and there was no way for me to ever find out. There were no witnesses, no reports, no articles in the paper with info on the logistics. There was just the metal shell between my fingers. And it, on its own, had to be enough.

I found my manhood at the end of ugly years for our nation's capital: Marion Barry busted for crack possession after being caught in the act on video. University of Maryland basketball star Len Bias dead from an overdose before he ever made the big time. And most important, the city, my city, became known as the "murder capital" of the country.

But things weren't bad just around my way when it came to black-on-black violence. Between 1985 and 1993, homicides of black males aged fifteen to eighteen increased by 158 percent (Uniform Crime Reports, 1994). In 1991, guns were used in 75 percent of the murders of blacks aged sixteen to nineteen, and in 65 percent of those aged twelve to fifteen (U.S. Department of Justice). And a year later, in 1992, firearm homicide was the number one cause of death for black men ages fifteen to thirty-four and the second leading cause of death for all fifteen- to twenty-four-year-olds (National Center for Health Statistics, 1994).

Black America was blowing itself away, over drugs, over

jackets and shoes, and over its anger toward itself after several centuries in a POW camp. The only cash flowing freely came from crack. And those who'd cut corners for themselves had to protect their investments. So many of us could only bear witness as the play went into motion. Some of them wrote about it and then put it to music. Next thing you knew, hip-hop was mercury rising in America's cultural thermometer.

Artists are almost always products of their own environments, and as MCs evolved from the late seventies into the nineties, they saw black America in terms of what was right outside the window. Mostly concentrated in the inner city, they saw the world through the eyes of those that mattered to them, whether they be sisters, brothers, cousins, best friends. And when DJs brought in the beat, it was them, their compatriots, that they spoke to, compatriots whose views of the world were limited to the same ten-block radius that theirs were.

This was a good thing for us. We could relate and pump our fists to the harsh words of urban reality, to all that we knew within our multiblock radii of experience. We had all buried friends. We had all chosen to be or not to be a part of the runners and hustlers on our various avenues. We had all sought after the women and men and the boys and girls who were the flyest, treating them like royalty because they were often the only role models and figures we had outside of the pews and pulpits. Those men and women on the mic were telling our stories. And as such, we knew the beginnings, middles, and ends.

But as the music grew, so did its audience. And by the midnineties hip-hop had of course stretched far beyond the city limits and into the suburbs. White boys turned their caps to the back and started stomping each other out at Pleasantville High, mimicking the action they'd caught in that clip on *Yo! MTV Raps* the day before. Parents' rights groups, religious zealots, and everyone else with a banner to wave took to the streets. Hip-hop was pure violence, and it had to be stopped. Luther Campbell, Ice-T, C-Bo, and of course the late Tupac Shakur were several among the many who bore the public brunt of their crusades. Moms and dads of all colors and creeds found their babies being seduced by the siren songs of the ghetto, corrupted by the people and places from which the good Americans had fled or of which the good Americans had disavowed all knowledge.

And that was where all the money came in, long before Sean "Puffy" Combs turned my music into the new disco. All of the negative publicity and congressional panels and Bush Sr.–era right-wing family values took rhymes and beats to the bank. All the hoopla just gave Junior, Todd, and Blair more reason to keep pushing Play so that they could be just like those tough niggers on BET.

In less than a decade the music business, once a diverse marketplace of labels and tastes, turned into a battle of the hit factories. Conglomerated businesses dumped their money into street kids with notebooks full of dreams, stretching them into icons for as long as they could hold the pose. *Gold, platinum,* and *double platinum* became words of note not only to those in the media or industry, but to the listeners. All of a sudden record sales mattered to the average Joe who might've formerly been interested in what was good but now cared only for "the hot shit."

And "the hot shit" was a forced hybrid of everything: strategically packaged collaborations, "superproducers," and designer labels mentioned every other lyric, topped off with a healthy portion of straight gangsterism. The product is now a shamefully focused attempt to bring all that was once for streets to hip-hop's now international audience in a concise, formulaic, and homogenized manner. And as a result, ghetto life has become the yardstick for true African American existence. If you're not struggling, if you're making something for yourself beyond the walls of the crumbling inner city, then you are not truly black. If you are an MC who once came from the streets, you must continue to rhyme about the street, even if you haven't lived there for the better part of a decade.

Former murderers and drug dealers must continue their exploits. A woman is not truly down for her man unless she's willing to go to jail or hit the corner for him. The pimp is the true symbol of black male power, an elder statesman of respect to be revered in every way for churning cash out of coochie. And everyone still carries a gun, even though they have bodyguards and security experts who should be paid to do the carrying for them.

But no matter how hard they try, the men who push the buttons can't re-create what hip-hop once was, or the descriptive elegance that MCs once used to diatribe on the hassles and horrors of the day-to-day. But what they can do is give a whole new generation the wrong idea about who they are and who they need to be. The shadows of the underworld are something to emulate, something to dream of being a part of, even when one's parents have done everything possible for their children to escape it. The way of the gun is the only option. The gangster mentality is the only way to survive. And thus we return to my shell casing.

The bullet as an image came long before hip-hop. It was a fixture in American imagery before the photograph, a weapon in the battle for independence, a tool of intimidation against those who would not yield to its owner. The fields of the American dream were fertilized with the blood of the plundered and betrayed. Men gunned one another down in the streets of the Old West, just because everyone had a pistol on his hip and something to prove. Manifest Destiny and Theodore Roosevelt's "Big Stick" political ideas said that if America wanted it, then it had a right to take it. Our government has rested on the laurels of intimidation since the very beginning. And it continues to do so in ways covert and blindingly visible.

The gun is the most efficient means of murder: quick, impersonal, and activated at a moment's notice. Thus, it has become our weapon of choice. Writers and directors have morphed the burner into a tool evoking both sex and style, the size and caliber saying so much about the she or he who wields it. Eastwood's Dirty Harry was a step above all the other cops because he carried a .44 Magnum, the world's most powerful handgun. Bruce Willis's John McClaine packed a nine-millimeter Beretta identical to Martin Riggs's piece in the *Lethal Weapon* series. As they dove and slid, firing one-handed at a moment's notice, millions of boys were seduced by the action, drawn to the growing power those characters possessed as each round discharged, leaving countless casings as evidence of the act.

It looked so cool, so inviting, so manly to young boys who learned manhood from the big and small screens in the absence of fathers, who were elsewhere. It seemed so tough, so strong, and so American. No wonder it found its way into the halls of hip-hop. From EPMD's "So Whatcha Sayin?" to Shyheim's "On and On," 2Pac's "Holler If Ya Hear Me" to The Notorious B.I.G.'s "Warning," and every Ice Cube clip from his first three records, guns and bullets were just part of the imagery we all knew. Shell casings spilled onto the urban concrete, implying gunfire and murder without hesitation or mercy.

As I said in the beginning, artists are products of their environment. And the art they create is in the context of all that is around them. Hip-hop music was not born out of African culture, but out of America, and is thus reflective of all its strength and contradictions. The United States is where the world comes in search of freedom and opportunity, a fresh start on soil that does not persecute because of creed or religion. Everyone has an equal shot at being Daddy Warbucks, if they just try hard enough. We're a big, steaming melting pot of overwhelming joy. Right?

But in reality we're all jockeying for position, at home, at school, in offices filled with people younger, smarter, and more ambitious. Minorities battle it out based on census demographics and our government bullies its way into every other nation's affairs, brandishing its muscle like the biggest gun of all. The commander in chief is a puppet controlled by a cabinet, with conspirators sharpening their blades in case of his failure. And men like myself cling to the hope that Charlie Rangel and others like him don't get the draft reinstituted.

So it's not exactly a surprise that the gun is still a big deal down at Hip-Hop Central. Because the rules of red, white, and blue suggest that it and the explosive are the two greatest means of bringing about change. When Jadakiss of The L.O.X., once a college engineering student, points two fingers and a thumb at the camera, he's professing his own power, the power of his words to effect change, garner respect, and most likely kill all of the competition. The same goes for Hassan Johnson's portrayal of a man shooting his woman and her lover in the clip for the Roots' "Break You Off." Hip-hop is just acting out what it sees. And what the hip-hop nation sees of this world is the larger problem.

I kept that little brass casing for a long time. It sat on my dresser where that other rack of shells had been years before. My questions never ceased, but sooner or later all the clutter of combs, brushes, and everyday debris made it more and more and more translucent until it vanished, perhaps discarded accidentally with some loose wad of paper. I think there was some kind of a lesson to be learned in that.

Violence is and will always be. And hip-hop may die. The bullet may become antiquated. But there will always be aggression in the heart of humanity. And it will always express itself in ways that it cannot afford. The only thing we can change are our own perceptions—of our lives, of our community, and of the truth, which exist beyond the electronic screens that have become our idol gods, draining our souls of the divine within and leading what remains down the well-trod path to nowhere.

COMMON

A Chicago native, Common brought a homegrown, sensical verbiage that was neither West- nor East-flavored when he debuted in 1992. But he stuck to an everyman approach to hip-hop that would ultimately have audiences coming to him. Penning love tributes and odes to the block, Common usually laces his lyrics with metaphors of black icons, with references to revolution and social empowerment underscoring his work. He's experimented with jazz and neosoul, musically ranging from the jazz-inflected beats of No I.D. to the funk grooves of the Roots and eventually the golden eclectics of Kanye West. Often lending his name to social activism, he's helmed fund-raisers for former Black Panther Assata Shakur and to fight the AIDS crisis. Plus, he lets his pop freestyle on every album. Here, Common reflects on his origins.

For me hip-hop was like that expression of being able to be a star and be masculine and revolutionary. It was such a good expression for the youth that we attached ourselves to it. I hadn't taken any music lessons but [just by] being a fan of music I could participate in hip-hop. I could rap. I could break-dance. It was like I was born into it. Hip-hop was our way of saying, "This is us." We're the black and Latino cats being heard.

I get asked a lot about what I think about hip-hop now, and I can't be looking at it negatively because it's providing economics, jobs, and ways of expression for our people. My mother be sayin' all the time, "Ya'll generation is doing it. Y'all are spreadin' wealth and gettin' wealth, and giving other people opportunity." For that purpose in itself I love hip-hop. We're teaching our children that it's cool to be creative. You can paint. You can rap. You can sing. You can be a director. With me growing up there was nobody pushing me to be creative in life. It was more about getting a blue-collar job. So I can't even complain.

When we were children hip-hop was a child. It had that innocence to it. We ain't have no fears. Now hip-hop's got fears and so do we. I feel like I have to say something now, not just for my child but for children across the world who don't have parents, children who don't have no love from their homes and children who just don't have no guidance. If the Most High gave me the opportunity to get some information, to have people to show me love, then why can't I give love through the music and show our children and grown folks, too, ways to love themselves and ways to feel free about who they are if I can offer that? That's why I'm here.

I think the substance [side of hip-hop] is gonna see more light. People are tired of [hearing about] this booty over here or I got this dope over here. People are tired of hearing about "I've been on the block" or "I got a homie in jail" or "Holler at your boy." Niggas is tired of that to a certain extent. You can still be a real cat. You can still be amongst your people. You can still say the hip-hop phrases, but there's gotta be something beneath that's substance, that's strong, that's bigger than any material things you got.

Chicago is a hybrid of gangs, the middle class, drug sellers, soul, jazz. It's a mixture of culture. It's a hustle-city-country-type feel. In the same gang-bang areas, there's the black middle class. No matter where you are there's the street element 'cuz you among black people. I grew up around black people in a black middle-class area that had niggas sellin' dope and gangbangin' and people that was sendin' their kids to private school. My mother made sure I had my ass in school. She made sure I was in at a certain time. She gave me the discipline to come home no matter what I was introduced to out there. So I wasn't gonna go out there and do anything too wild because I had that structure and that love.

I got homies who had parents with money and everything and they still tried to do the servin' thing. They was tryin' to be hustlers when our mothers sent us to decent schools. Part of that was the choices we make as people. Some of it is the way we was brought up.

THE BLOCK

No matter how much loot you get you're staying in the projects. No matter how far you go you'll never turn your back on the hood. No matter how much you grow, the hood will grow with you. Or will it?

THE BLOCK

BY SCOOP JACKSON

Inhale. Do not breathe out. Not yet. But it's not the air. It's the concrete. It's the bricks that house the cribs, apartments, and PJs that make up the hood you're in. The steel gates suffocate each balcony. The iron rims dangle from lonely backboards in empty parks. Ambition, if there, has a certain fragrance. Smell me?

Now . . . exhale. Open eyes, ears, and minds. Reminisce, reflect, run. Return. No other neighborhoods inside or across America carry this scent. No others hold this history. Without these blocks, without these Section Eights and four-corner hustlers, without mental poverty meeting financial brilliance, life would be without character, without depth, a void of emotion minus a soul. This is why we bless it, bless where we live. We have no choice. Inhale again . . . now exhale. The concrete is a muthafucka, ain't it?

America too often has a problem with the Block—its cause, creed, and color. They desperately try not to understand or embrace anything that comes from the corners. Uncivilized is what they've called the people that come from there: truculent, threatening, tasteless, ill bred, and belligerent. But it is America that built these blocks for us to live within, to separate us from them. If any other word could be used by this country to describe the place we call the Block that word would be *Un-America*.

Un-America is a reminder of all that's gone wrong. It is a system set up to suppress, to manifest failure. Yet success stories have emerged. Another nigger has escaped. Onto the cover of *Time*, into a Nobel Prize nomination, to the MVPs and Angel networks. Some of us do make it from ashy to classy. A few crabs do survive the barrel.

In 1903, W.E.B. DuBois claimed that the duality of living in America and being black would be the most important issue facing the Block; the duality of getting mentally and physically off the Block and still being We, still being sure and true to self without selling our souls. One hundred years later we're still dealing with that issue. America perpetuates life away from the Block—through all forms of media (print, TV, advertising; overt and covert, subliminal and straightforward) we're told to escape the life the Block offers us. Ever seen a soap opera or reality show that used the Block as even a backdrop? Ever seen or heard of anyone coming from the Block who made it who wasn't at first poor or disadvantaged? Yet we struggle to find pride in it, on it, even though we are psychologically driven away from it.

As a young brotha on a block in southeast D.C. once said, "The Block is all I got. Not only my family but all my peoples live here. This all we got, this all we know." Asked what he wanted to do for a living, the dude said, "an actor, a lawyer, and I want to work on cars." He was twenty-two at the time. Never read a script, never auditioned for a play. Didn't know what *litigation* meant. Could replace a transmission in less than four hours. Rip and replace the rims in one. Graduated high school four years ago. Had partial scholarships to go away to school. Didn't want to leave the Block. Still here. Confused, but also gotta chance. Hold, fold? Escape, remain? He doesn't even know. He wants a better life, but he won't leave the one he loves. DuBois's du-ality. Reality. And we wonder why the price of dime bags continues to go up daily.

Love it we must, but the Block got issues. Self-esteem is-sues that go beyond feeling inferior to other areas of Ameri-can society that tell us that the grass is always greener, water always wetter, on the other side of the white picket fence. It's become a badge of honor, a source of pride. Symbolic of everything else we've had to deal with as African Ameri-cans, we've been forced to unconditionally love what we are and where we're at. As written in the *Agenda* magazine more than ten years ago: if you want to visit the most beautifulest place in the world, don't visit Paris, visit Harlem.

It's 78 degrees on this day in May. Chicago rarely gets this warm this early. People rush the street like water. Up and down Seventy-first, down and up Martin Luther King Drive. It's a weekday, but you can't tell. All the unemployed and those who called in sick are out. Front porchin' and back yardin' it. Tags on Girbaud and South Pole clothes get-ting popped, joes and girls too fresh too clean to brush off any shoulder dirt. Cash money rotates. The Block is hot like Lil Weezy. Another Lil Jon classic comes out of the alley in back of the house where Mr. Johnson's daughter—with her fine ass—is the only one not outside. The smell of BBQ is omni. Present are the hypes, the neighborhood crack vic-tims. Those who when they aren't fiending, begging for dollars, are the most generous, gracious, friendly, and lov-ing folks on the Block. Some believe that without them, the Block would not be so sacred. It would just be a rest haven for black folks who are looking for life in more affluent zip codes.

A niggggggaaaaa pleeeezzzzze! floats from across a street, followed by the heavy laughter of five grown-ass men who are sitting around a closed newsstand on the corner. The bar two doors down will open officially at five—unofficially in five minutes—and instantly become their home for the night.

"Come here, young fellas," one of the old cats says to the young gun with Rocawear hangin' low. You can see the kid's eyes roll as he breaks stride, changing direction toward the old man as if this were his father he was obeyin'. His boys follow him, knowing they're about to hear the same story they've all heard the last ten years of their eighteen-year existence. But outta respect to the old man and where he came from, outta respect for what he stands for in the neighborhood, outta respect to the Block, the one kid turns from hoodlum to heaven-sent. Puts his arm on the ole G's shoulder and listens.

A few blocks away . . .

Their names are Kevin Taylor, Chris Murphy, Joel Garland, and Olawale Odukoya. They rep they Block. Their crew runs about eight, sometimes nine deep. The other half can't be found right now, but Joel confirms, "They on they way." Cru thik. That's what we call the new under-middle class of black America. They ain't poverty, but they closer to it than finding economic comfort. They're all between the ages of nineteen and twenty-two. Michael Vick jerseys, fresh blanco-on-blanco AF1's with jean legs tucked under the shoe tongues. Smoking squares, sipping Henn and Hein, hiding it from the mother whose porch they on.

It's three o'clock in the afternoon. The unemployment rate in this country hovers around the 12 percent rule. The Block is hiring no one. Many have been raised on and by concrete. I am one—that's why I feel these four. In them I see exactly where my life was twenty years ago; they see in me where their life is headed. The saying "You can take the person out of the hood, but can't take the hood out of him" never applied to me, because I've never left these four corners. And probably never will.

Wale and Joel have their domes tightly rowed in Sprewellian designs. Kevin's waves are Navy, like Steve Harvey's. Chris, he has the baby Ben Wallace. All shades of brown cover their faces, arms, and hands. Together they look like the cover of the *Essence* annual men's issue, if *Essence* were owned by Benzino.

Four regular black men of the same mind, unblind, but Stevie Wondering not just what this thing called life is all about, but how long it's going to last. There is no ribbon in the sky on the block. Superstitions ride shotgun every day. Young brothas stand around with the perfect balance of pride and paranoia. Along with their boys Yani, Lawrence, and Deon, they make up the classic diversity found in un-named, un-gang-related jiggas-for-life crews that populate most black communities. In essence, they make up the Block.

Like them, I inherited this Block. It was handed down to me by my father, and I in turn will hand it down to my sons and nieces. I will teach them everything my father taught me about the Block: the difference between living and surviving, the difference between playing and getting played, the difference between being the Block and the Block being you. Now don't get me wrong, my moms had a larger hand in my indoctrination to the Block. It was she who let me learn the Block on my own: develop friendships on the Block that last thirty years later; play the ball on the Block that allowed me to gain a deeper appreciation for Julius Erving when all I was being taught in basketball camps was John Havlicek; allowed me to discover early that Kool-Aid was not just for regular consumption in the summer, that, more important, it tasted better when mixed with white port; and did not shelter me from the sounds that were coming out of the speakers connected to the lightposts or the words that Melle Mel and Duke Booty spit. "It's like a jungle sometimes?" she used to say to my brother and me. "Lemme tell you, it's a jungle all of the time."

It's post–high school for the crew. Of the eight, only Wale experienced college. He's the youngest of the set, having just finished his first year at Rust College in Mississippi. Truth told, they all had the opportunity, but to the Man, they'll be the first to tell anyone, the Block is why they are where they are and why they're going to be what they're about to be. "Never let school get in the way of you getting an education" seems to be the creed. The education learned inside the classroom does nothing for them out here. They are the kids Bill Cosby is so worried about. Black America's father was speaking to and about them when he said, "People marched and were hit in the face with rocks to get an education, and now we've got these knuckleheads walking around. The lower economic people are not holding up their end of the deal. They're buying these kids five-hundred-dollar sneakers and won't spend two hundred dollars on Hooked on Phonics."

The cru talk about the Block with a sense of reverence only held for immediate family members: "It's the love," Joel says. "It's the love that keeps me here and brings me back." Kevin, who has since moved to Detroit, shakes his head in agreement. Wale and Chris do the same. The word *love* continues to come from their mouths and hearts. "The love that we get, the love because everyone knows us, the kinda love that makes us feel comfortable because we know everyone around here looks out for us, the love from the attention I [Kevin] get every time I come back."

The other noun that emerges, with oxymoron characteristics, is *safety*. All four claim they feel safe on the Block. And although they know every block is different yet the same, it's the safety of their particular block—even as gunshots, beat downs, and break-ins surround them—that, for lack of a better word, embraces them.

"Even when your boys ain't around, you feel it," Kevin says of the sense of strange security they all share. "It's something that I can't really explain . . . it's just probably because we know everybody on the block. I think that's it. We feel safe here because . . . because . . . man, I can't explain it. You just always feel safe here, if you're from here."

This is why Treach's lyric from "Daddy Was a Street Corner" "peace to the Block, my pops," has so much meaning. For many of us the Block was our second or third parent. The one that we listened to when Moms' and Pops' (if there were any) rules weren't making it. Which is why I so understand the love of which Kev, Wal, Jo, and Chris speak. From a very early age it is understood that the Block is going to have a hand in building your character because that's what it does. Build character.

It's a kind of character that can either be seen or is nonexistent. Seen in kids at parks, games, picnics, and family outings; in schools, churches, and holding cells. You could often tell who was about the Block and who wasn't. And it never came in the form of what type of clothes they wore or if they were bad-ass or good kids; it was in the way they carried themselves. Everything from their walk, the way they interacted with others, how they could nonverbally make their presence felt. And if you're about the Block, those were the kids you connected with—and if they were older, you knew those were the ones you wanted to be like.

The Block has its own crime rate and its own economy, with plenty of Fortune $100k businesses. It has its own schools with antiquated computers, its own banks with broken-down branches and alcoholic tellers, its own politics without budget-driven campaigns and uncorrupted elections.

Outsiders, those that have never spent any time on the Block, don't understand the way life is there—they don't understand brothas like Kevin, Chris, Joel, and Wale. They look at them and sense something other than comfort. They wonder why they stay and don't get out. They think the Block always needs escaping.

A tricked-out Chrysler 3000 rolls by. Jadakiss and Nate Dogg's "Time's Up" blasts through tinted glass. Arms fly up, lyrics get recited. "That's my shit!" one of 'em says. It only takes one song, one anthem to set off a mini-Block party. For these four, this song is it.

Already knowing the answer but wanting to see if there's a generational divide in their response and my knowledge, I ask why hip-hop is so enamored, so embraced by the Block. Their answer: "Where do you think the material comes from?"

With "The Ave.," the legendary Joseph Simmons (a.k.a. Run of Run-D.M.C.) released one of the greatest lyrical descriptions of what pops off on the Block: "You go to jail or get a bullet in your brain . . . That's how we living on the Ave."

To many, that lyrical image is grim. But we who live on the Ave. reap the benefits of the beauty that lies inside. And even though every block, every ave., every corner on which we—black men—stand is not the same, there is something that is universal. And for that universe, hip-hop music is the soundtrack.

"Look, man, I'm not from this block," Chris spits through a midwestern drawl. "But the block in Detroit, where I'm from, isn't like this one. It's the same, you know, same type of hood, but if I had to choose, I'd choose this one." A slight hidden smile escapes Wale's face. "This block's real."

"That's why I get an adrenaline rush every time I come home," Kevin says, reacting to his boy's acknowledgment of his hood's richness. "I can do the outta-town thing, but I gotta come back."

Wale chimes in with something extra. "I learned everything I know here," he says. "It's like forgetting one of your teachers. How are you going to forget the people that taught you?"

"Fuck this block!" yells an unknown friend, having been privy to the conversation from the curb.

"Don't pay him any attention," says a girl in a tight tank-top exposing her Damita Jos. "He got his ass beat on this block a couple of years ago." A few of the other girls around her start laughing, as if they were there. According to their beliefs, "He hatin'."

Kevin pulls on the Newport he and Joel share. Hand over ash, he makes light of the impact his block has had on and in his life. "Even if I had dough, I'd still come back." Joel, Wale, and Chris look at him strangely, as if his white shirt needs a white jacket to match. "Serious," Kev says before he walks away, heeding another one of the Block's calls. "I couldn't just pick up an' never look back. I can't do that. It, this block here, it will remember me for one thing," he says, "as being real."

> Basically I'm just reality
> loaded with vast stories
> of lust, greed and contempt
> no street is exempt
>
> —Nas, "Every Ghetto"

No *USA Today* dispensers or FedEx drop boxes. No Starbuckses, Home Depots, or Loews theaters. Instead, storefront churches with congregations of fewer than twenty preach faith without hope or charity. Church's chicken over-fries birds of prey that we pray ain't injected with some genocidal substance, yet we still buy.

"They spinnin', nigga, they spinnin'!" drowns out all sounds as the hood screams at the one-car parade that endlessly circles each Block. Shopping carts filled with thirty-gallon trash bags of necessities serve as homes to the homeless and whips to the whipless.

Couches and rusted folding chairs hold down front porches. Jordans hang from street lights. College-age women, four babies deep, walk to the Duane Reade, wondering if they're going to still be single by fifty. White folks sprinkle themselves throughout. From city to city, state to state, more sprinkle in. Find comfort. It's reverse integration. The Block allows this to happen.

Young mothers dress baby sons like pimps and young fathers ice out their two-year-old daughters. Then those same parents take the bus to work. Property value goes up. Self-worth goes down. Cost of living, up; chances of living, down. Stolen bikes that never find their original owners remain in the same 300-foot radius of where they once parked. Skullcaps and hoodies cover heads in 90-degree heat.

Corners get bent. Crenshaw. Pico. La Cienega. Caps get peeled. Georgia Ave. Frederick Douglass Boulevard. Delancey Street. All drama happens outside. The smell of ribs on a Weber never leaves—winter, summer, spring, or fall. Cinder blocks and manhole covers are used on opposite ends of a bar for brothas and Ese's to bench press. The bootleg man's got *Spiderman 3*, and the kids can't wait.

Dimes walk around with bags of Gucci, Fendi, and Coach,

but the letters face the wrong direction. Ten-cent crack valves and .45 shells line asphalt lawns. Meat market mascots are the closest most of the kids will ever get to meeting Mickey Mouse in person. Vacant lots are concrete football fields. Kids attend historically black schools without any knowledge of the person they're named after. There's—always—one house owned by people who smoke the mortgage payment, and another lost to the courts by some grandma who turned it over to bail out a guilty grandson. People either believe or be leavin'.

DR. ROBIN KELLEY

THE INTERVIEW 2004

An author and a former hip-hop fanatic, Dr. Robin
Kelley is a leading scholar in African American studies at New York's Columbia University. Heralded as
one of the brightest young historians in the country,
he's the scribe behind five works, including *Freedom
Dreams: The Black Radical Imagination,* and he
coedited *To Make Our World Anew: A History of
African Americans.* He's also consulted on major music documentaries. One of the few historians to
emerge from the hip-hop generation, Kelley isn't at
peace with the music of his childhood. In this interview, he tells us why.

For us, at least for those of us in L.A. and Southern California in the late seventies and early eighties, hip-hop
was just part of the whole dance music scene. It was also
something that was live. You had DJs that also doubled as
MCs. A lot of the party chants—"Throw your hands in the
air/Wave 'em like you just don't care . . ."—were a big part
of the culture. Hip-hop live is not the same as recorded hip-
hop. It's two different things. The community building that

goes on in a club setting or an outdoor park is something you don't get in a Walkman.

In terms of hip-hop now, my opinion changes depending on what day you ask me. It's so frustrating because it seems so bankrupt. We get what's presented to us commercially, whether it's Lil Jon or some of the worst aspects of 50 Cent. So much of it is about crass commercialism and materialism. The misogyny was always there, but I think it's much more intense now. The embrace of a capitalist culture, of ownership and prestige items, is not the hip-hop I knew when I was growing up. To me hip-hop was party music, music with a social conscience.

When I'm struggling with my thirteen-year-old daughter and what she's listening to I think that's the extent of the music now. But then you step out and you actually realize that hip-hop is a vast, vast world with all kinds of traditions and practices. There are extremely sophisticated and powerful narratives, an activism that is unlike any other kind of music. We have people who call themselves hip-hop activists. You've got political motion and feminism, a consistent radical multiculturalism. All of this is there but it's not the kind of thing that's at the top of the pyramid. It's under the surface.

I think of the current generation as being in two groups. There's a very, very young generation that comes to hip-hop through commercial radio. And they're really young, from ten to maybe fourteen years old. And then there's the late teens/early twenties generation whose palette is wider, who can seek out alternative music and actually get out of the house.

This younger generation is very impressionable. Many of these kids mimic the worst aspects of the culture. My daughter recently goes to a predominantly white school and they decided that they were going to have a "gangster" party or a "ghetto" party. We didn't know this until we showed up. My daughter's the only black child in the room. We go to pick her up and we walk in and you've got all these white and Jewish kids in bandannas and doo-rags and white T-shirts. I was disgusted. My wife and I were both shocked that the parents didn't think anything of it. They just thought it was cute. The kids are talking about "fo-shizzle" this and "fo-shizzle" that.

I had to sit down with my daughter and one of her friends and basically lecture her and say that there are people on college campuses right now organizing against ghetto parties because that's racist. If you want to have a party that celebrates black culture then have a black history party. Dress as Sojourner Truth or Ella Baker. Why come as some "ghetto" character invented from a video? What is "ghetto," anyway? The communities that they call ghettos that I live in have people who work for a living, a full range of people who really struggle. That's the thing that's problematic about commercial radio and the way certain aspects have shaped this younger generation.

This older generation, I think, has had hip-hop affect them positively. There are young people on college campuses who are trying to change the world, who don't want to go to war, who don't want to see people fall by the wayside. Hip-hop is a way of answering certain questions, and raising certain questions. So like Charles Dickens says: it's both the best of times and the worst of times.

THE FLOOR

The two-step. The bankhead bounce. The smurf. The wop.
Electric-sliding with happy feet while the running man does the
Kid 'n Play kick step as his partner does the Tootsie Roll,
screaming "Whoot, there it is!" Dancing people never stop
dancing, even when the music tells them not to.

THE FLOOR

BY BOB MEADOWS

Flat top? Check. Mustard yellow pants tapered at the bottom? Check. Shiny black shoes with metal band across the top? Double check. Weirdly patterned shirt with lapels that cross each other? Hell, yeah. Black, red, and green Africa medallion? You know a brother can't hit the club without it.

You ain't seen nothing 'til you seen me on the dance floor. Let me paint the picture for you.

Time: 1988 to 1991
Place: State Theater in downtown Motown
Event: Soul Night
Starring: Big Bad Bob and a cast of thousands

You can hear the bass, can't you? It's low to start, but rises smoothly. Your neck starts popping first. The rest of your body follows. It's Ralphi Rosario and Xavier Gold's "You Used to Hold Me." Then it's Crystal Waters on "Gypsy Woman." Groove is in da house. *Everybody* is dancing. *Everybody*. Public Enemy has dancers. Oh, hell, no, I don't mean Rosie Perez. I don't mean hoochie mamas flashing "I can see pubes" skirts. I mean *PE* is busting moves. Go, Flava! Go, Flava! Go! You can see it, right? Professor Griff leading his troops through paramilitary drills? That shit is *dancing*, dog. Dancing. Just tightened up. Looked hard. Niggas was gettin' down.

You wanna make music? You wanna just be heard? You want brothers and sisters to just enjoy the flow, nod their heads with your flow-rific tales? That shit is so new millennium. It ain't the "then." Hell, no. Brothers and sisters wanted to know one thing: Can you dance to it? Can you do the running man to it? Roger Rabbit? Snake? Listen to the man with the greatest flow ever. Are you listening? You hear Rakim, right? "Follow the Leader." "Paid in Full." You know what I'm talking about. And what's that playing behind him? A funky-ass beat you can dance to. Of course you can. It's James Brown, fool. Movin', groovin', feelin' good—J.B. is in the house! He wasn't dancing, but you sure as hell could.

Damn. Why don't I dance anymore? Why doesn't Jay-Z dance? Why does 50 Cent, "Fitty" to his friends, just stand there? You can't blame Eminem's non-dancing self on his lack of melanin. MC Serch from 3rd Bass and Vanilla Ice used to throw with anybody. And they were whiter than Marshall.

What happened?

I think I know.

Let me paint a picture for you.

Nah, wait. I ain't gonna tell you yet. Why give up the punch line without the setup? First, I'm gonna tell you how it went down, and really, you got to start with this: The seventies didn't prepare us for what was coming.

The decade tried. Man, growing up in Detroit, I wanted to throw down just like Shabba-Doo. He and his group, the Lockers, were always on *The Carol Burnett Show* or *Sonny and Cher* doing their acrobatic pop locking. Hell, when the fat Locker, Rerun, went on to star in *What's Happening*, I watched as much for the chance to see him dance as for the comedy.

Michael Jackson did his best to get me ready. Think he started dancing when he revived the moonwalk on *Motown 25*? Hell, no. You shoulda seen the nigga when he was an unmistakable nigga, back when he was sixteen, breaking out on "Dancing Machine" with a robot that looked like a *real* robot.

But that was about it. The decade couldn't know what was coming; it couldn't give any warning, so that's why I was so unprepared for a moment in October 1979. I'll tell you how monumental the moment was. I remember where I was when I heard a plane had crashed into the World Trade Center (just stepping into the shower). I remember where I was when I heard the *Challenger* space shuttle had exploded (history class in college). And I remember—hell, I can still feel what I felt—the first time I heard "Rapper's Delight."

It was real late, or real early, actually, on a Saturday morning. Me and my best friend Darrell James, both of us twelve, were at his house, listening to the radio and talking about girls. For some reason, we had a moment of quiet, and then this song came on. I recognized it immediately: "Good Times," which was kind of the jam at the time. But then something strange happened. It was the "Good Times" beat, but not the words. *I said a hip, hop . . .*

My boy and I stared at the radio in awe. What's this? This is something new. Not like a new song, but *something new.* I couldn't believe what I was hearing. Neither could my best friend. We stayed silent for the whole song, then just looked at each other. In the next days we raved about "that talking song" and couldn't wait to hear it again and again and again. A month or so later, this all-girl group, Sequence, dropped "We're Gonna Funk You Up." At Christmas, Kurtis Blow came out with "Christmas Rapping." And then the next summer, a year before MTV debuted, Kurtis released "The Breaks."

Clap your hands, everybody, if you've got what it takes. 'Cuz I'm Kurtis Blow and I want you to know that these are the breaks . . .

It was the jam. And we linked the music to a dance move, the one Michael made famous. In early 1980, my friends and I were watching a dance show in Detroit called *The Scene*. They showed a clip of this group, Shalamar, and one of their members, Jeffrey Daniels, started moonwalking. The next day at school, we were trying to do what we called "that walking backward dance." By the fall, you weren't on the dance floor unless you could do it.

That's who I am. That's my musical youth. (Musical interlude: *Pass the dutchie on the left-hand side . . .*) I don't know when "that talking song" became "rap" or when "that walking backward dance" became "the moonwalk." But I do know when I first heard and saw both. They were both the coolest thing that ever happened.

Growing up in the all-black Motor City, we listened to all kinds of music. It wasn't necessarily by choice. It's just that the most popular DJ in the city, this cat called The Electrifying Mojo, played whatever he felt like on a given day. He had a real strong relationship with Prince—Mojo was playing cuts off *Purple Rain* a year before the movie came out. (Someday check out the real small type on the album and you'll see that most of the recordings were done in 1983.) So he might play all Prince, uncut, all night long. He might do battles—Earth, Wind, and Fire against the Gap Band. Or he might play electronica or European or all white people. Listening to him was where I was introduced to the Art of Noise and Frankie Goes to Hollywood.

Did I know they were white? Yeah. Thomas Dolby was whiter than 3rd Bass, but it never occurred to me that "She Blinded Me with Science" was white music because Mojo played that song all the time. Mojo would throw down

Devo—and I don't mean "Whip It." I mean the decidedly less well known "Speed Racer." I thought Kraftwerk was as black as Afrika Bambaataa; alas, I was wrong. I was shocked when I moved to New York and black people hadn't heard of Kraftwerk. Was there ever a song better than "Numbers"?

In 1983, two things had emerged. The first was break dancing. Maybe if Jennifer Beals had stripped naked she would have emerged as the conversation piece from *Flashdance*. But it didn't happen in my hood. My sister came home exclaiming that I had to see the movie because of the breakers. Soon after, break dancers were spinning on their backs everywhere, even in a Gladys Knight video, I remember. Faster than you could exclaim "Turbo is dancing with a broom!" (*Breakin'* reference, for those not in the know), corny white folks like Jim Belushi and Alex Karras were doing "White Guy Rap" and trying to pop-lock on *Saturday Night Live*. The Keebler Elves got into it. So did Fred Flintstone and Barney Rubble, hawking Fruity Pebbles. Rap and dancing. Dancing and rap. Linked tighter than Lisa Lisa and Cult Jam.

But after a while, breaking waned. So did the litany of dances that followed: the smurf, the German smurf, the strut, the sperm, the schoolcraft, the cabbage patch, the wop. Each time something new would replace them. The German smurf was the coolest dance I had ever seen in 1983. But damn, don't be caught doing it in 1984.

So why did PE dance, but Snoop Doggy Dogg didn't? Why would 1989 Tupac Shakur be a dancer for Digital Underground, but 1992 Pac do little more than bop his head and give us all the finger?

It can be summed up in three words:

Stop. Hammer Time.

Hear me out. *Let's Get It Started* was, at the time, one of my favorite albums. Sure, MC Hammer was no Rakim (who was?), but he didn't pretend to be. He was just trying to get people on the floor:

When it comes to straight out rockin', I'm second to none, from Doug E. Fresh to LL and DJ Run.

If Hammer had said "straight out rappin'," we would have had issues. But he didn't even pretend to go there. And that's the tragedy of MC Hammer, and, similarly, Young MC, Coolio, and Tone Loc. None of them was claiming to be the greatest rapper in the world. They just wanted to turn out jams. But something unfortunate happened to all four of them: lame white people fell in love with their shit. "Bust a Move," "Gangsta's Paradise," "Wild Thing" (and "Funky Cold Medina") became huge hits. Nothing tore down your street cred back then faster than having lame white people like it. I'll get into that in a minute.

Did I love "Let's Get It Started" and "Turn This Mutha Out"? Hell, yeah. For their artistic genius? Their eloquent, complex rhymes? Not by a long shot. I loved them because of their videos. I had never seen dancing like that before. And I had definitely never seen it done so well. Earlier in 1988, New Edition dropped "If It Isn't Love." Those brothers danced their asses off. Salt-N-Pepa introduced Kid 'n Play in their video for "Shake Your Thang," and they got down. Bobby Brown was rubber-legging in "Don't Be Cruel."

When "Turn This Mutha Out" came on the radio, you might have been thinking, "This nigga's flow is so wack." But your foot was bouncing to the beat just the same. It's true. Don't deny it. You might not have danced like Hammer, ya little gangsta rapper wannabe, but in some dark recess of your mind, you wished you could. Because when you saw him dance—well, goddamn, that nigga could do it all!

In 1988, no one was hating on Hammer. Everybody knew he was an astonishing dancer, and just like with Michael five years earlier, everyone in the club was moving, or trying to move, like him. Here's where I reenter the picture, and remember: it ain't bragging if it's true. Few people could dance like me. You talk about a brother who could work up a sweat on the dance floor. Yeah, that was me. I danced with purpose. See, unlike with break dancing or moonwalking, Hammer dancing was something you could easily do with a girl. Both of you are out there doing the running man. Both of you were jumping around. Then you could move in, get all up on the booty, and freak from side to side, snake, whatever. Dancing, as it always did, showed your sexual prowess. *Yeah, see how I'm moving my hips now? I move them the same way in a horizontal position. Think about it, baby.*

Why don't I dance much anymore? Three words:

Stop. Hammer time.

I'll come back to that.

You can't be mad at Hammer. What happened wasn't his fault. He didn't know. He was only doing what any of us would have done. He kept going. If only he hadn't. If only he had stopped with just one album. We would all remember him a bit more fondly.

After all, his initial spawn was tight. Kid 'n Play kicked some pretty nice moves in *House Party*. Come on, now. You know you and your boy tried that "step back, kick, step back, kick, tap your feet twice, connect ankles, hop in a circle until you're on the opposite side of the room" move. It wasn't just me. And though New Edition split up, former members Bell, Biv, and DeVoe came out with the album *Poison*, one of the earliest, most successful meldings of R&B and hip-hop—and accompanying videos that showcased them as modern-day Bojangles. Their ex-bandmate, Bobby Brown, continued his strutting on jams like "Every Little Step You Take" and "On Our Own." For a time, people argued, with merit, that *he* was the best dancer. Even LL Cool J, who previously just prowled the stage like a panther, had his own *choreography* for "Around the Way Girl." Times had changed. And the music only encouraged even more dancing. Snap came out with "The Power," one of the greatest bust-a-move songs ever. Michel'le, a protégé of N.W.A.'s frontman, Dr. Dre, dropped the truly danceable "No More Lies." All of this flowed from Teddy Riley's New Jack sound that had dominated hip R&B for a year or so and seemingly forced every song to contain the phrase "yep yep."

Or a cameo by Martha Wash. She was everywhere, but you knew if her screaming ass was on the cut, it was gonna be the jam. Who else could make us get off our asses even as the musclebound front man, Freedom Williams (himself no Rakim), promised, *"Gonna make you sweat til you bleed"*? That was passion. Passion! Everybody dance now!

And then it all came to a crashing end.

In 1990, MC Hammer released *Please Hammer Don't Hurt 'Em.* His first album had been cool but it's not like people were salivating for his next one. So no one paid the release much attention. It had an innocuous enough title. Don't hurt them on the dance floor. We got the joke. The first single, "U Can't Touch This," was catchy. Then I saw the video. Damn. See, with BBD, Bobby Brown, Kid 'n Play, all those guys, you could mimic them. You had hopes of dancing just as well as them or better than them, even if you didn't get the Gumby haircut.

With Hammer? Shit. This brother got the fuck *down*. You didn't think he could really go any further, but damn, he really was trying to hurt niggas who copied him. The song was such the jam that when they played it at the club, I was actually scared to dance to it.

Then for some reason, after the song was no longer avant-garde at the club, lame-ass white people latched on to it. The song was everywhere. The Detroit Pistons used it for their

NBA title run. Politicians trying to be hip put the phrase in their speeches. You couldn't escape it. Now, just like Barney Rubble once hawked Fruity Pebbles wearing thick gold chains, lame-asses claimed MC Hammer.

And he ate it up. Just like I would have done. Hammer, real name Stanley Burrell, seemed like a nice guy. Cocky, but friendly. Earnest. And annoying as fuck. His legion of fans were now saying he *was* the best rapper. "U Can't Touch This" won a Grammy for best rap solo. He even had a cartoon, for God's sake. He was performing everywhere. Hammer Time was *all* the time.

The backlash was vicious. It didn't come from lame-ass white people. Oh, no. It came from brothers and sisters. Tommy Davidson did a withering spoof on *In Living Color*, portraying MC Hammer being attacked by his ridiculously baggy balloon pants. Those who denounced his flowing abilities grew even louder. The other cuts from *Please Hammer* received no play in the clubs I went to. By the end of 1990, and well before Hammer dropped the MC from his name and recorded "Too Legit to Quit" or songs for *The Addams Family* movie, he had zero cred, street or otherwise. He sank even lower, challenging Michael Jackson to a dance-off, introduced a stupid-looking dance in which he pitter-pattered his legs, and really, truly, believed his own hype. I won't even dwell on his ill-fated attempt at image reversal a few years later. Please, Hammer, Don't Rap Again. When the smoke cleared, dancing was about as cool as Urkel.

Where once even 300-plus-pound Heavy D (and his Boyz) hip-hopped around the stage, few were shaking it up now. Kris Kross dropped "Jump," House of Pain dropped "Jump Around," Naughty by Nature released "Hip Hop Hooray," all rap songs that would get people on the dance floor to shaka their own rumps. But the rappers themselves weren't dancing.

Oh, wait. There was this one move, the dance du jour for rappers like Fu-Schnickens, Leaders of the New School, Black Sheep, A Tribe Called Quest, and even Shaquille O'Neal. Listen carefully, because it's pretty complicated. With your knees slightly bent, raise your left one. Then immediately lower it, but while lowering it, raise the right one. While lowering the right one, raise the left. For added hype, for when the song is really getting good to you, like maybe the part where you're preaching about old stale urine, add a little hop. Repeat ad nauseum until the song ends.

That was the new rapper dancing. For about two minutes.

Pretty soon, MCs like Snoop, Dre, Biggie Smalls, and so on couldn't even be counted on to lift their knees—not when a simple nod would do. The only dancing in their videos is done by the scantily clad wet-dream inducer grinding against the rapper's leg. She's fine, yes, likely with more "back" than the disappointingly skinny-ass chicks in Sir Mix-A-Lot's ode to boo-tay. But would she cut her hair in some geometric pattern, sport yellow overalls, and bust out the Kid 'n Play move? We'll never know.

What I knew was that I was bored. I didn't like this style of dancing. I quit going to black clubs for a time. This was all my people, the most brilliant, melodic, flow-ful dancers ever, were going to do? Step from side to side with a dance partner who looked everywhere but at you?

I started going to house clubs. They played the music I liked.

Then I stopped.

Why did I stop dancing? Once upon a time, I was MC Hammer. I would walk into the club, lead my date to the floor, and not sit down until the lights came on. If I was in between dance partners, I would pace during songs, just to keep limber until I found my next Ginger Rogers. Hours and hours of an aerobic workout that kept my abs ripped tighter than Fitty's.

And now I have the aches and pains to prove it. All that jumping around has kicked my ass. The oldest Gen Xers were born in 1965. I entered this world the next year. You do the math. How many people my age are in the NBA, playing professional tennis, winning marathons? Not many.

I still don't leave the dance floor until my partner sits down or the lights come up. I can still do that Kid 'n Play move. But I do it in slow motion now and only for fun—in the privacy of my own home.

The difference is this: I, Mister Dance Floor, am *thankful* for the lame-ass two-step these days. I give all praise for the head nod. Why? 'Cuz my knees creak when I'm on the dance floor. My back hurts. Just thinking of the acrobatics I used to perform makes me winded.

These days, instead of Hammer Time, I'm more like the old man in the barbershop. I got stories to tell. I got things to say. And trust this: they're all true.

You shoulda seen me, my brothas and sistahs. Oh, yeah— you shoulda seen me back in the day.

POSDNUOS
(OF DE LA SOUL)

THE INTERVIEW 2004

De La Soul fired a trail for what would later be
dubbed conscious rap, an alternative to the hard-
core stylistics soon to dominate the airwaves. Debut-
ing in 1989, Posdnuos, Trugoy, and Pasemaster
Mase meshed an eclectic combo of politics, goofy
humor, and around-the-way semantics to create a
brand of soul anyone could relate to. They're still alive
and kicking more than fourteen years after their last
gold-selling album. They even earned a Grammy in
1996 for their Best Pop Collaboration work with the
Gorillaz on the song "Feel Good Inc."

Our longevity? I can say [it's] luck, but [mainly] just our
determination to be a part of [the game]. We feel that
the topics that we can touch on are topics that everyone can
understand. When I got into this I was seventeen years old.
I'm thirty-five now, but still, a thirty-five-year-old man can
talk about love, he can talk about chillin', he can talk about
partying, all the things that a thirty-five-year-old man can
do, and a seventeen-year-old boy or girl can do. So the top-

ics don't really go too much off what I think a younger person can understand. I think a lot of times it's all just put on how you physically look, so we just feel like we've still been students of this game and we not only were blessed to be fans of it from the beginning and pay attention to Herc and Flash. But to this day we pay attention to Jada, Lloyd Banks—it's all the same thing. We love the music, and we don't sit up here and just get caught up in what we did when we came out and hate on anyone else after us. We love music. We love rappers.

The biggest change is obviously the business. It's very much a business. It's very much where a lot of youth can come into this and already have their game face for the business, where before it was like having your game face for creativity. You know us and Tribe and Leaders and everything, and I think even somebody like Busta coming out of Leaders can attest to that. Your business face gotta be on right, and a lot of kids come in already making sure they're not getting jerked. A lot of groups tend to focus a lot more on that side of it all and understanding maybe what they feel it takes to maintain and to keep that business running. Their thoughts are almost the same as a record label, but no one is thinking from the creative standpoint and realizing that the art as well helped play a part in your longevity. It plays a part in people not wanting to just download your songs because they . . . feel that there's only two songs on there.

This art form is here to stay [now], whereas before a lot of times it [seemed] shaky. You really didn't know where it was going, but now it has affected every facet of this world, and I think De La Soul can truly attest to that because we've been blessed to travel not only in the States but everywhere. People rap everywhere. Everywhere kids wanna know how to rhyme and how to be a part of this industry. It's just not always focusing on the bad side of it, like, "Oh yeah, there's a lot of wack records out, but there's a lot of great records too." And I think as long as you realize it you can get back to maybe a lot of artists putting out greater albums as opposed to just good singles.

You just had a lot of artists then that were young and knuckleheads or just carefree living and realize that now, you know, they're fathers. Monie [Love] got kids. A lot of us have children and we know how it is to make sure that their lives are well secured and they as well realize that when they get to a certain age, they understand and know where they stand in this world and what they could add. You can't talk about it and not be about it. Through us being entertainers we obviously know that we can help influence people to realize that maybe it is cool to vote. And then hopefully from that standpoint they'll realize, you know what, forget it being cool, it's just the right thing to do. So either way, it's just good enough to keep drilling in their minds about hey, just as much as we can party and have fun or rhyme, we can take the time out to realize what's going on in our world and make sure that the people that are put in control to represent us, we agree with them.

Our mainstay? It may not have been triple platinum every time or this amount of sales at this point, but I mean, at the end of the day, De La Soul, when you tally up everything together, the score will damn near even out, because we have been a group, as I said, that not only has been well respected but has affected the way people do music and listen to music in the States and every other continent. And I think even your biggest platinum rappers can't really say that. So our mainstay, our determination, and our love for hip-hop has lasted. And I always say this. It wasn't all about blowing up and going pop. You can explode, but then after that bomb goes off, that bomb is no more. I also like to look at it like it was like an incense that you burn. That incense just burns slowly and slowly, and even after it's finished burning, that scent is still there, so it's like our legacy still remains. And that's how I look at De La.

THE SUIT

There's no business like show business. But these days the business always matters more. From moguls like Russell Simmons to A&Rs and program directors, is anyone in hip-hop for the love anymore? Is it all just about the bottom line?

THE WORLD IS YOURS

BY WILLIAM JELANI COBB

> People be asking me all the time,
> "Yo, Mos, what you think is getting ready to happen
>   with hip-hop?"
> I tell them, ". . . whatever is happening with us." . . .
> We *are* hip-hop—you, me, everybody . . .
> So hip-hop is going wherever we're going
>   —Mos Def, "Fear Not of Man," from *Black on Both Sides*
>   (1999)

A true fact: DJ Kay Slay has in his possession a highly classified mixtape featuring Colin Powell and Beanie Sigel freestyling over the track from Nas's "The World Is Yours." Heads from the State Department and Roc-A-Fella records was talking some ill market cross-fertilization type shit, saying this was gonna help both of them blow up in those parts of the world that we routinely blow up. In coming weeks Alan Greenspan is expected to announce the new laissez-faire plan to deregulate the medical, weapons, and food industries known as the "Can't Knock the Hustle" initiative. The Federal Reserve has hired street promotions teams to blanket Wall Street with flyers stating that the new initiative drops on July first. And we ain't even gonna speak on that Lil' Kim–Condi Rice collabo where they drop jewels over the "Bombs over Baghdad" track.

We know, or ought to know by now, that, in the words of the late Notorious One, *things done changed*. Flip on your TV, turn on the radio, open a magazine, and there's a good chance that there's a rapper floating on your medium of choice. Time was when heads were being ironic, or at least hyperbolic, in speaking of the so-called hip-hop nation, but with a consumer base of 45 million people dropping somewhere around $10 billion a year on CDs, clothing, DVDs, magazines, and concerts—and $300 billion in purchasing power—hip-hop dwarfs the financial power of entire nations in the so-called third world.

And don't think there ain't big implications for this kind of cash flow. Like Madison-Avenued, focus-grouped novelties, rappers are created in accord with the reigning flavor of the nanosecond. Right about now, most rappers exist as living product placements, their gear, their rides, their whole setup as deliberately schemed as that can of Coke downed by your favorite action hero before he splits to do battle with the special-effected forces of evil. Only the mad niche marketers of American hypercapitalism could conceive of the modern rap video—basically a commercial in which products advertise other products.

Rappers have literally gone from being maligned boulevard poets à la Grandmaster Flash and the Furious Five's "The Message" to acting as melinated sales reps for the American dream. Hip-hop has highlighted the black impulse toward verbal and musical innovation and, at the same time, turned the most problematic, despair-riddled elements of American life into purchasable entertainment. The hip-hop industry is largely responsible for the global redispersal of stereotypical visions of black sexuality, criminality, material obsession, violence, and social detachment. That a brother can now fly halfway around the world and be greeted in the Czech Republic by young men who speak no English but regard you with a high five and "What up, nigga?" is a bitterly ironic testament to the power and appeal of African American culture in the age of high capitalism.

And the art ain't exempt, either. Heads were once clear on the difference between a rapper and an MC, which was when the verbal sales rep for the music industry was understood as distinct from the microphone controller. The difference between a rapper and an MC is the difference between smooth jazz and John Coltrane, the difference between studio and unplugged. Or, to sample a line from Alice Walker, the difference between indigo and sky blue. Nelly is a rapper; KRS-One is an MC twenty-five hours a day. Lauryn Hill is, straight up and down, an MC's MC; Lil' Kim is a rapper. The Fresh Prince was an MC; Will Smith is a rapper. Nas has been an MC since he breathed his first, but the P's (both Diddy and Master) are rappers down to their DNA.

The rapper is judged by his ability to move units; the measure of the MC is the ability to move crowds. The MC gets down to his task with only the barest elements of hip-hop instrumentalization: two turntables and a microphone. On that level, the Miami basspreneur Luke, who didn't even necessarily *rhyme*, was closer to being an MC than Hammer, who did—or at least attempted to. The MC writes his own material. The MC would still be writing his own material even if he didn't have a record deal. A rapper without a record deal is a commercial without a time slot.

But, to cop a line from dead prez, this really is bigger than hip-hop. Black people have been the smiling face of American capitalism for a long time. The difference, though, between Uncle Ben and Uncle L is that neither Ben nor his girl Jemima ever endorsed GOP ballers like George Pataki (LL

Cool J, that inveterate player of the stock market, knows on which side his bread is buttered). The point is that the music is the canary in our collective mine shaft. It is "The Message" in an arena where we specialize in killing the messengers.

We know the arid facts: Rocawear's generating $300 million in sales annually, Reebok's S. Carter line's accounting for 15 percent of the company's footwear sales, Rush Communications' status as the second-largest black-owned entertainment company in the United States, and a white consumer base that accounts for 75 percent of hip-hop's sales numbers. And we could trip on the irony of this: that a generation of black artists and label executives are getting rich by selling black music to white America, and by learning from the generation of black rock musicians who died broke while their pale imitations copped platinum sales.

Not surprisingly, as a Cuban MC explained to me last year, hip-hop was created in the United States, but it no longer resides there. "American hip-hop," he all but eulogized, "is dead." Its third world siblings—at least in this man's telling—are alive and thriving. And the brother had a point. Hip-hop as we know it might not be deceased, but it's damn sure on life support. Think about how often you hear an MC who makes you consistently stop the CD to replay his last line, and you'll see my point. But attempting to fix hip-hop in this here era of global grand larceny and economic terrorism might just be as hopeless as looking for a mop on the deck of the *Titanic* or facing west at sunrise. To cut to the quick, *your music is fucked up because everything else is, too.* Hip-hop's so-deemed golden age, 1988–1992, witnessed the ascent of Public Enemy, KRS-One, Queen Latifah, De La Soul, Big Daddy Kane, N.W.A., Salt-N-Pepa, A Tribe Called Quest, and Rakim. But it don't take a conspiracy theorist to see that hip-hop's artistic integrity started to decline at the same time that the United States declared victory in the cold war and all opposition to the global reign of American capitalism collapsed. Dig, if it wasn't obvious before, we should've known which way the wind was blowing when characters like Eazy-E started showing up at Republican Party fund-raisers. Materialism has always been a theme in hip-hop, but in this millennium, artists speak not of the idle longing for gold chains and white-walled Caddies, but give straight-up lyrical balance sheets of shit they actually own. So the question is, what becomes of an art that is born of poverty when its primary voices belong to the top 1 percent of the economic brackets?

And yeah, I know, before we start speaking on the virtues of the underground, let's bear in mind that Rawkus Records, the hip-hop industry's version of Miramax, was started by James Murdoch, son of Rupert Murdoch, the owner of the Fox News network—the same people whose yellow propaganda helped fan the flames of Desert Storm: The Sequel. The same people who forbade the mention of the name Osama bin Laden on air lest the country be reminded that he—not Saddam Hussein—had bombed the World Trade Center.

In hip-hop, the commercial niche artist has drowned out an array of nonmarketed voices for the same reason that Barnes & Noble ran your local bookstore into the ground, Wal-Mart sent your neighborhood hardware store owner into early retirement, and that 20,000 seat megachurch put the storefront preacher into financial purgatory. In a phrase: *market economics*. No wonder you got Jay-Z calling hisself the "rap version of T. D. Jakes." KRS-One broke this down for all posterity on "Step into a World" when he kicked the line "I'm not the run of the mill 'cause for the mill I don't run"—meaning that market logic demands that the industry go with what sells, not with what advances the art form.

Amiri Baraka points out in the classic *Blues People* that

you can chart the precise political and social position of a people by the music that they produce at a given moment. And by that standard the blues came into existence as the musical score to the great migration and the lives of the generation that lived through it. Listen to Martha & the Vandellas' "Dancing in the Street" or Aretha's "Think" and you recognize immediately that the soul music of the 1960s was the musical accompaniment to the civil rights movement. And Parliament classics like "Chocolate City" and "Up for the Downstroke" bear witness to funk's knee-deep connection to the Black Power movement.

Critics have lamented that mainstream hip-hop has no particular set of ideals attached to it, but you dead wrong, or at least mad naive, to think that the music exists outside a cultural movement; hip-hop is, among other things, the soundtrack of globalism. Not the kind of globalism marked by the peoples of color crossroading up in the Bronx in the 1970s, but the kind that allows you to buy McDonald's in Tibet. It's been pointed out that the United States has never been attacked by a country that has McDonald's—and it ain't no surprise that the first flag planted in post-Soviet soil was that of the red-yellow-white clown-faced burger dealers. And, thanks to the struggles of the 1960s, black people—or at least some of us—have been admitted as junior shareholders in this corporation called America (you can almost hear the theme song from *The Jeffersons* playing in the background). In the bitter irony of history, Martin Luther King's assassination cleared the way for a generation of black people to go as far as our talents allow—even if, tragically enough, this means becoming the first black CEO of Enron. And only because a black pacifist was murdered was a black general given the opportunity to run a war.

Free at last.

Free for all.

Hip-hop is not the first music to confront the implications of the market. Motown had lucre as preeminent concern. The fabled "Motown sound" was Berry Gordy's formula for getting into the pockets of white America. Gordy's Hitsville, USA, studio took Henry Ford's insights into mass assembly and applied it to black music in a way that made Gordy more a captain of industry than a pioneer in music. Gordy in fact hated Marvin Gaye's single "What's Going On?" which was meant to be Gaye's artistic rebellion against the formulaic sound coming out of Hitsville, USA—but in true, ironic capitalist fashion, Gordy ordered ten more songs just like it once the song caught on. Still, hip-hop is the music produced by the first generation of black people to be (limited) shareholders in America, Inc., and necessarily brings a whole 'nother set of concerns to the foreground. The materialism of hip-hop is, on one level, a measure of the extent to which the American dream has been purchased—as is—since the civil rights movement.

There's a reason that Tony Montana, Brian De Palma's "Scarface," is the patron saint of hip-hop. Recall the tagline for that flick was "He loved the American dream—with a vengeance." And this is the reason that Colin Powell and Condoleezza Rice have replaced the black dissidents Malcolm X, Muhammad Ali, and Martin Luther King (and Paul Robeson, too, if you want to be real about it) as the most recognizable African American political icons both domestically and abroad. Add into the equation Kenneth Chenault, the black CEO of Amex; E. Stanley O'Neal, the black CEO of Merrill Lynch; and Richard Parsons, CEO of Time Warner, and you'll recognize that in the post–civil rights era, the dominant African Americans are all products of the American corporate machinery or American state authority. And they rep Product America in a way that Uncle Ben and Aunt Jemima never could because they are not meant to be ironic.

So the question is not how hip-hop came to be where it is, but really, how it could be anything but this? Why have John Wayne as the face of swaggering American capital when you can have Jay-Z?

On this score, none is better than Jay. Think of Jigga as Horatio Alger with street cred, the world's first supply-side MC. Sleep if you want to, but Jay's line "Put me anywhere on God's green earth/I'll triple my worth" is the clearest statement of the capitalist credo since Calvin Coolidge declared that "the business of America is *business*." Given his standing as the only multimedia don to rise up out of the infamous Marcy 'jects, you really *can't* knock the hustle.

Or the hustler either, as it turns out.

More than any other rhyme spitter's, the life and career of Shawn Carter—the self-professed "Che Guevera with bling on"—indicate how far this game has been played. It might be facile to observe that the drug hustle is the pristine example of free market economics and that even Jay's cross-borough nemesis Nas observed, "The rap game reminds me of the crack game" way back in the *Illmatic* era, but the observation bears repeating. Elizabeth Mendez Berry broke this down deftly in her review of *The Blueprint* in *VIBE* magazine:

> Jay-Z is convincing. When he raps, "I'm representin' for the seat where Rosa Parks sat/where Malcolm X was shot, where Martin Luther was popped" on *Blueprint*'s "The Ruler's Back," you almost believe him. When he rocks his Guevara shirt and do-rag, squint and you see a revolutionary. But open your eyes to the platinum chain around his neck: Jay-Z is a hustler. It may be that he recognizes the sex-appeal-by-association of guerrilla garb. Or perhaps in the process of polishing his game till it gleams, it has begun to blind him.

From where I'm standing, Jay-Z's *Black Album* could've been one of the ten greatest in hip-hop history had the commercial diversions and mass-market confections like "Change Clothes" and "Dirt Off Your Shoulder" not gotten in the way of his autobiography. Give the man credit, though. In an arena where artists routinely downplay the corporate interests that control their music, Jay came clean, telling his audience straight up that he'd dumbed down his lyrics to double his dollars (which presumes, ironically enough, that the album's listeners are so enthralled that he can openly insult their intelligence or that they're *so* dumb as to not notice that they've even been insulted in the first place).

And all this ultimately brings us back to that freestyle with Colin Powell. In the new millennium, hip-hop is foreign policy. Why you think Cam'ron calls them cats "The Diplomats"? One might double his dollars domestically, but in order to quadruple them, you need to follow the flag of American capital abroad. In order to sell globally, you have to have MTV globally, or Amazon.com globally, or Virgin Megastores—again, globally. Plus the industrial bling glimmering from the chests of your rapper of choice is priceless public relations for America, Inc. Dig the slogan: *America, the Beautiful: Where Even Niggas in the Projects Are Rich.*

We would do well to recall that jazz musicians were sent on CIA-sponsored world tours in the 1950s as part of the cultural effort to combat communism. The U.S. Information Agency's support of Louis Armstrong's music was meant both as a cultural statement—introducing the world to America's sole classical music—and a political one, stating implicitly that even the most exploited of Americans were able to cultivate artistic genius in the grand, gold-paved streets of the U.S. of A. That young brother from Newark who came back from Operation Iraqi Freedom tripping that both the Iraqis and the Americans were listening to Tupac

CDs was speaking volumes about hip-hop's niche in the disordered New World. For all their in-family squabbling about violent, antisocial content, the voices of Official America desperately *need* hip-hop to be global—what else are you gonna sell when you open that HMV in downtown Baghdad?

Think about it for a second and you can't help but realize that we're asking hip-hop, of all things, to be exempt from the forces that have corrupted medicine, bought off the media, produced for-profit prisons, and stolen presidential elections. When you get down to the get down, those aging white hippies smashing the windows of Starbucks during the G8 summit are doing more to re-create quality hip-hop than the last dozen anointed producers and industry-heralded MCs combined. The truth is that we already knew that no country with a McDonald's has ever attacked the United States. The real scoop is that no country with BET has either.

In the end, Colin and Jigga need to be on the same track, because they're already on the same page. Hip-hop is on life support for the same reasons that capitalism is doing victory laps around the globe. The victors have always gotten to write history—it's just that now they can produce its soundtrack, too. So when you find yourself nostalgicizing over the golden age of hip-hop, you might just want to cop that unsigned independent artist's latest self-produced CD or sample the latest offerings of the MCs from anywhere that the currency is worth one one-hundredth of the dollar. And pray like hell that you can't find them on Amazon.com.

EDITORS' ACKNOWLEDGMENTS

KENJI JASPER

To Bonz Malone for schooling me on the game from that Chinese carry-out in Park Slope. To Bob Morales for teaching me how to say no. To Ytasha, Rob, and Mark for sharing the dream. To all those who listened while I shared the nightmares. In the end we made something beautiful. I hope many come to our mirror and take a gander for themselves.

YTASHA L. WOMACK

I would like to thank my supportive parents, Dr. Yvonne G. Womack and Lloyd Womack. Thanks to a wonderful family and supportive friends. Thank you, too, to Gaylon McDowell for his endearing advice.

ROBERT JOHNSON III

This is dedicated to the people who, without them, I would not have had the tools or the sanity to finish. Patti Page and Aziz, Kenji Jasper, Greg Johnson, Khari Shiver, James Taylor, Brian Armstead, the Armstead family, Damon Gunn, Irina and Evan Wender, Neil de la Pena, Glo and Tony Santamaria, Margurite Courtney, Tianna Oliver, the Oliver family, Bob Ware, Marissa Lopez and Larry Jones, Ford Lowcock, Agnius, the SMC Photo Department, Raifyeel and Marie Mahome, Lorry Rosen and the good people at Quantum Instruments, and Alex Rodriguez. You guys rock!

Most important, we thank the outstanding writers whose fine words and extraordinary lives made this book what it is.

PERMISSIONS

ESSAYS

"The Disgruntled Fan," by Faraji Whalen, copyright © 2007 by Faraji Whalen

"The Buzz," by Mark Allwood, copyright © 2007 by Mark Allwood

"Remote Control: Romance vs. Promiscuity in Mainstream Hip-Hop," by Lisa Pegram, copyright © 2007 by Lisa Pegram

"Cashmere Thoughts," by Michael A. Gonzales, copyright © 2007 by Michael A. Gonzales

"A Christmas Story," by Ytasha L. Womack, copyright © 2007 by Ytasha L. Womack

"Coughing," by Suheir Hammad, copyright © 2007 by Suheir Hammad

"Ridin' Dirty," by Robert Johnson III, copyright © 2007 by Robert Johnson III

"The Ice," by Gregory L. Johnson, copyright © 2007 by Gregory L. Johnson

"On Solace," by Mariahdessa Ekere Tallie, copyright © 2007 by Mariahdessa Ekere Tallie

"The Tag," by Chino, copyright © 2007 by Dave Chino

PHOTO CREDITS

All photos by Robert Johnson III except:
Photograph above "The Whip" by Tianna Oliver
Photograph above "The Coffin" by Neil de la Peña

CONTRIBUTORS

A graduate of Morehouse College and Columbia University's Graduate School of Journalism, **Mark Allwood** covered news for *Vibe Online*, Hookt.com, and BET.com, and served as an editor and writer for *The Source*. His writing has also appeared in *Vibe, XXL, King, Oneworld, New York Resident*, the *Arizona Republic*, and the *Chicago Tribune*.

Born and raised in Queens, New York, **William Jelani Cobb** has been writing about hip-hop for more than a decade. He is also an assistant professor of history at Spelman College, and editor of *The Essential Harold Cruse: A Reader*. His column *Past Imperfect* appeared bimonthly on Africana.com. He fell in love with hip-hop the first time he heard the underground tape of Kool Moe Dee battling Bizzy Bee.

Imani Dawson is a freelance writer living in Harlem, New York. She has written for a variety of media outlets, including *Vibe, XXL,* and the Associated Press. An Aries fly girl, she has a soft spot for DJs and brainy hip-hoppers.

Dr. Michael Eric Dyson is the author of *Is Bill Cosby Right?; The Michael Eric Dyson Reader; Open Mike; Holler If You Hear*

Me: Searching for Tupac Shakur; Why I Love Black Women; I May Not Get There with You: The True Martin Luther King, Jr.; Race Rules: Navigating the Color Line; Between God and Gangsta Rap; Making Malcolm: The Myth and Meaning of Malcolm X; and *Reflecting Black*. He is the Avalon Foundation Professor in the Humanities at the University of Pennsylvania and lives in Philadelphia.

Michael A. Gonzales has written for *Essence, Spin, Latina,* the *New York Daily News, Teen People, The Village Voice, Ego Trip, Tower Pulse, Request, The Source,* and *XXL*. He is the coauthor of 1991's *Bring the Noise,* a pioneering study of hip-hop culture.

Palestinian-American poet and political activist **Suheir Hammad** has published two books of poems, *Born Palestinian, Born Black* and *ZaatarDiva,* as well as a memoir, *Drops of This Story*. She has appeared in both television and theatrical versions of Russell Simmons's *Def Poetry Jam* and is featured in *Listen Up!: Spoken Word Poetry* and *Bum Rush the Page: A Def Poetry Jam*.

Award-winning writer **Robert "Scoop" Jackson** is author of *Sole Provider: Thirty Years of Nike Basketball* (2003), *True to the Game* (1997), *The Last Black Mecca: Hip-Hop* (1995), and *The Darkside: Chronicling the Young Black Experience* with Nelson George. Scoop is currently the editor at large for *Slam, Hoops,* and *Inside Stuff* magazines. A founder and former editor in chief of *XXL*, he has written for *USA Today,* the *Washington Post,* the *Chicago Tribune,* and *Vibe*.

Kenji Jasper is the author of the novels *Dark* (2001), *Dakota Grand* (2002), and *Seeking Salamanca Mitchell* (2004), as well as the memoir *The House on Childress Street*. His journalism has appeared in the *Village Voice, Essence, Savoy, Vibe, XXL, Rappages,* and *Oneworld,* as well as on National Public Radio.

Gregory L. Johnson is a Cigar City, Florida, native; Harlem, New York, resident; and Renaissance man whose several hustles include freelance writing and editing, recording and performing South Coast hip-hop (as his alter ego, 'El Juba), and his main gig—researching culture, history, and environments for a major video game company. Juba's passion for the African and Latin diasporas, his inspiration for "The Ice," was nurtured not only by his Morehouse and NYU studies but by his FAMU-trained paternal grandmother, herself a Florida scholar, teacher, historian, and community activist for more than forty years. As for his passion for hip-hop, he himself nurtures that on a daily basis (true, true!).

A native of Detroit, **Robert Johnson III** is a filmmaker and activist whose photos have appeared in *Vibe, The Source, Essence,* and *King.* "DMV" is his first piece of published writing.

Bob Meadows covers pop culture for *People,* profiling music icons such as Michael Jackson, Puffy Combs, Jay-Z, Whitney Houston, and Russell Simmons. He previously worked at the *Charlotte Observer,* where he helped report a Pulitzer Prize–nominated series on Charlotte's poorest neighborhoods. The Detroit native and University of Michigan graduate has written for numerous publications, including *Essence, Emerge,* the *Detroit News,* the *Detroit Free Press,* the *Cleveland Plain Dealer,* and Salon.com.

Lisa Pegram, known onstage as Lady Pcoq, is a poet, teacher, and vocalist. Her performance poetry background includes featured appearances in theaters and nightclubs of D.C., New York, Philadelphia, Boston, and several universities on the East Coast college circuit. She received a Top Emerging Artist in Washington, D.C., award from Mayor Anthony Williams in 1999. Black Entertainment Television and *Emerge* magazine featured her as a member of the Generation 2000 collective on *Strength of a Woman*, a compilation CD honoring Dr. Betty Shabazz. Her work is also featured in E. Ethelbert Miller's anthology *Beyond the Frontier*. She is currently working to complete her first solo recording project.

The work of poet, writer, performer, and educator **Mariahdessa Ekere Tallie** has been published in several journals and anthologies, including *Beyond the Frontier, Bum Rush the Page, Role Call, Listen Up!,* and *Catch the Fire.* She is the author of a chapbook, *Permanent Rain* (Savage Goddess), and has shared her ideas about healing and writing with students in Oakland, New York City, Ramapo, Amsterdam, and London.

Faraji Whalen is a writer and financier from Washington, D.C. He has lived in Atlanta, Zambia, Guinea, and Ethiopia, and a short stint in Liberia before shit got really, really unpleasant. He has written for the *Atlanta-Journal Constitution, OneWorld,* BET.com, Hoopshype.com, and the esteemed *Morehouse Maroon Tiger.* He also cofounded *Apex* magazine, a one-issue self-absorbed vanity piece produced at the expense of Morehouse College's student fees.

Ytasha L. Womack is a filmmaker and journalist. She directed *The Engagement: My Phamily BBQ 2,* produced/wrote the award-winning film *Love Shorts: Vol. 1,* and co-produced the Billboard chart topper *Tupac: Before I Wake.* She's a contributing writer for *Upscale* magazine and guest editor for *NV* (New Vision in Business). Other works have been published in *Essence, Vibe, King,* the *Chicago Tribune,* the *Chicago Reader,* and the *Chicago Defender.* A Chicago native, she has a B.A. in mass media arts from Clark Atlanta University, and she studied media management at Columbia College in Chicago.